W9-ARB-356

The Act of Poetry

The Act of Poetry

A PRACTICAL INTRODUCTION TO THE READING OF POEMS

by Christopher Collins

NEW YORK UNIVERSITY

Random House, New York

Published in the United States by Random House, Inc., New York, and simultaneously in Canada by Random House of Canada Limited, Toronto.

Library of Congress Catalog Card Number: 78–96116

Manufactured in the United States of America.

FIRST PRINTING

Printed and bound by the Haddon Crafstmen, Inc., Scranton, Pa.

ACKNOWLEDGMENTS

I wish to thank my students for their imagination and responsiveness. I wish especially to thank my Literary Heritage and Introduction to Literature classes at New York University, 1968–69, for their openness, interest, and challenging candor.

Grateful acknowledgment is made to the following for permission to reprint previously published material:

City Lights Books: "But I Do Not Need Kindness," by Gregory Corso in *Gasoline.* Copyright © 1969 by Gregory Corso.

Doubleday & Company, Inc.: "Dolor," by Theodore Roethke, from *Words From the Wind.* Copyright 1943 by Modern Poetry Association, Inc.

Farrar, Straus & Giroux, Inc.: "The Death of the Ball Turret Gunner," by Randall Jarrell in *Complete Poems.* Copyright © 1945, 1969 by Mrs. Randall Jarrell.

Harcourt, Brace & World, Inc.: "Children of Light," by Robert Lowell from *Lord Weary's Castle.* Copyright 1944, 1946 by Robert Lowell. "A Black November Turkey," by Richard Wilbur from *Things of this World.* Copyright 1953 by The New Yorker Magazine, Inc. "The Beautiful Changes," by Richard Wilbur from *The Beautiful Changes and Other Poems.* Copyright 1947 by Richard Wilbur. "The Love Song of J. Alfred Prufrock," by T. S. Eliot from *Poems 1909–1962* is also reprinted by permission of Faber & Faber Ltd. Copyright 1936 by Harcourt, Brace & World, Inc.; Copyright © 1963, 1964 by T. S. Eliot. "Naming of Parts," and "Judging Distances" by Henry Reed from *A Map of Verona* are also reprinted by permission of Jonathan Cape Ltd. Copyright 1947 by Henry Reed. "Buffalo Bill's" and "o sweet spontaneous" by E. E. Cummings in *Poems 1923–1954.* Copyright 1923, 1951 by E. E. Cummings. "next to of course god" and "ponder darling these busted statues," by E. E. Cummings in *Poems 1923–1954.* Copyright 1926 by Horace Liveright. "who's most afraid of death," by E. E. Cummings in *Poems 1923–1954.* Copyright 1925, 1953 by E. E. Cummings.

Harvard University Press: "There's a Certain Slant of Light," "I Like to

See it Lap the Miles," "The Bustle in a House," "As Imperceptibly as Grief," "The Soul Selects Her Own Society," by Emily Dickinson in *The Poems of Emily Dickinson,* reprinted by permission of the publishers and the Trustees of Amherst College from Thomas H. Johnson, Editor, Cambridge, Mass.: The Belknap Press of Harvard University Press. Copyright 1951, 1955 by The President and Fellows of Harvard College. "Cold are the Crabs," by Edward Lear in *Teapots and Quails and Other New Nonsenses.* Copyright 1953 by the President and Fellows of Harvard College.

Holt, Rinehart and Winston, Inc.: "Mowing," "Acquainted With The Night," "Design," "The Road Not Taken," and "Birches," by Robert Frost from *Complete Poems of Robert Frost.* Copyright 1916, 1928, 1930, 1934, 1939 by Holt, Rinehart and Winston, Inc. Copyright 1936, 1944, © 1956, 1958, 1962 by Robert Frost. Copyright © 1964, 1967 by Lesley Frost Ballantine. "In White," by Robert Frost, the original version of "Design" from *The Dimensions of Robert Frost* by Reginald L. Cook. Copyright © 1958 by Reginald L. Cook. "With rue my heart is laden" and "When smoke stood up from Ludlow" by A. E. Housman from "A Shropshire Lad"—Authorized Edition—from *The Collected Poems of A. E. Housman* are also reprinted by permission of The Society of Authors. Copyright 1939, 1940, © 1959 by Holt, Rinehart and Winston, Inc. Copyright © 1967, 1968 by Robert E. Symons. "The night is freezing fast," by A. E. Housman from *The Collected Poems of A. E. Housman* is also reprinted by permission of The Society of Authors. Copyright 1922 by Holt, Rinehart and Winston, Inc. Copyright 1950 by Barclays Bank Ltd.

Houghton Mifflin Company: "The End Of The World," and "Memorial Rain," by Archibald MacLeish.

Alfred A. Knopf, Inc.: "So-and-So Reclining On Her Couch," by Wallace Stevens from *The Collected Poems of Wallace Stevens.* Copyright 1947 by Wallace Stevens. "Of Modern Poetry," by Wallace Stevens from *Collected Poems.* Copyright 1942 by Wallace Stevens. "The Course Of A Particular," by Wallace Stevens from *Opus Posthumous.* Copyright © 1957 by Elsie Stevens and Holly Stevens. "Sunday Morning," and "Disillusionment of Ten O'Clock," by Wallace Stevens from *Collected Poems.* Copyright 1923, 1951 by Wallace Stevens. "Bells for John Whiteside's Daughter," by John Crowe Ransom from *Selected Poems.* Copyright 1924, 1952 by John Crowe Ransom.

The Macmillan Company: "Among School Children," by William Butler

Yeats from *Collected Poems.* Copyright 1928 by The Macmillan Company. Copyright © 1956 by Georgie Yeats. "The Circus Animal's Desertion," and "The Wild Old Wicked Man," by William Butler Yeats in *Collected Poems.* Copyright 1940 by Georgie Yeats. Copyright © 1968 by Bertha Georgie Yeats, Michael Butler Yeats and Anne Yeats. The Yeats poems are also reprinted by permission of A. P. Watt & Son, Ltd. "During Wind and Rain," by Thomas Hardy in *Collected Poems* is also reprinted by permission of The Macmillan Company of Canada Limited. Copyright 1925 by The Macmillan Company.

New Directions Publishing Corporation: "Hugh Selwyn Mauberley" V, by Ezra Pound in *Personae.* Copyright 1926 by Ezra Pound. "A Refusal to Mourn the Death, by Fire, of a Child in London," and "Do Not Go Gentle into That Good Night," by Dylan Thomas in *Collected Poems* are also reprinted by permission of J. M. Dent & Sons, Ltd. Copyright 1952 by Dylan Thomas. "The Red Wheelbarrow," by William Carlos Williams in *Collected Earlier Poems.* Copyright 1938 by William Carlos Williams.

The University of Michigan Press: "Spider" by Richmond Latimore in *Sestina for A Far-Off Summer.* Copyright © 1962 by The University of Michigan Press.

W. W. Norton Publishing Company: "Der Panther," by Rainer Maria Rilke. Author's translation made with the permission of W. W. Norton & Co., Inc., publishers of *Translations from the Poetry of Rainer Maria Rilke* by M. D. Herter Norton. Copyright 1938, 1966 by M. D. Herter Norton.

October House, Inc.: "To My Mother," by George Barker from *Collected Poems 1930 to 1965.* Copyright © 1957, 1962, 1965 by George Barker.

Oxford University Press, Inc.: "Pied Beauty," "Hurrahing in Harvest," "The Caged Skylark," and "God's Grandeur," by Gerard Manley Hopkins from *Poems of Gerard Manley Hopkins,* Third Edition. Copyright 1948 by Oxford University Press, Inc.

"Elegy For Minor Poets," by Louis MacNeice in *Poems of Louis MacNeice* is also reprinted by permission of Faber and Faber Ltd. Copyright © 1966 by The Estate of Louis MacNeice.

Random House, Inc.: "As You Say It," by Karl Shapiro from *The Bourgeois Poet.* Copyright © 1964 by Karl Shapiro. "Buick," by Karl Shapiro in *Selected Poems.* Copyright 1942 by Karl Shapiro. "Musée des Beaux Arts," "Our Bias," and "The Unknown Citizen," by W. H. Auden in *Collected Shorter Poems 1927–1957* are also reprinted by permission of Faber and Faber Ltd. Copyright 1940, © 1968 by W. H. Auden. "The

IN GRATITUDE TO JOHN MAURUS CARR
AND CLEMENT WELLS

Contents

The Act of Poetry

[I]

The Reader as Artist

Know thyself. [*Temple of Apollo at Delphi*]

In what form do I know myself? Always, it seems, in the form of something other, something strange. The landscape I am watching is also a state of myself, of the neurons of my head. I feel the rock in my hand in terms of my own fingers.

ALAN WATTS: *The Joyous Cosmology*

WHAT YOU "GET OUT OF POETRY"

A hundred years ago it was fashionable to paste ornamental name plates in one's books: "From the Library of . . ." Along with the name there might be a picture of the family's coat of arms, or library, or some scene emblematic of a love of literature. Among the designs most popular at the time was an image of a four-masted sailing ship; a part of the inscription read: "A good book is a ship that carries us on voyages of adventure." For most people the implication was that reading literature was the safest possible mode of experience, one that provided involvement without risk, excitement without anxiety, and wisdom minus the pains usually associated with the process of becoming wise.

Poetry, in particular, was praised for its "uplifting" effects. It was supposed to "instill" within its devotees notions of ideal Goodness and Beauty. An educational institution was somewhat like a department store. Each department offered its unique merchandise to the customer in the market for self-enrichment. Out of mathematics one "got" techniques for figuring one's insurance policy and stock investments. Out of French one got methods of impressing elegant people at elegant dinners. Out of poetry one got models of refined diction and refined behavior, plus a supply of capsule profundity.

This cheery belief prevailed despite the age-old fact that a person *gets nothing out of poetry*. It adds nothing to his sum of experience (except perhaps the experience of reading a poem well). It does not engage him, body and mind, in improving his environment, nor does it, usually, leave him with a workable plan of action, an uplifting consolation, or an earnest moral.

We get nothing out of poetry—it is poetry that gets something out of us. To put it most simply, *the words of a poem make us remember, in a precise way, what we already know*. Reading the *Rime of the Ancient Mariner,* for example, we are not presented with someone else's images as in a picture gallery; we are prompted to supply our own individual images and feelings in concert with the words of the poem. (For further discussion of responses to this poem see Maud Bodkin, *Archetypal Patterns in Poetry* [London: Oxford University Press, 1963], pp. 26–60.)

> The fair breeze blew, the white foam flew,
> The furrow followed free,
> We were the first that ever burst
> Into that silent sea.

What memories do the first two lines reactivate in us? Each of us will find a different picture emerging out of his past: a motor boat purring across a glassy New England lake early on a July morning or a crisp day on the deck of a transatlantic liner; or, if we have not actually experienced the sensations of sailing, we might remember a vivid seascape and then visualize ourselves somewhere in its midst. Certainly none of us has had the experience explicitly described in the last two lines, but we have all sensed the sudden change in mood that they convey. We have all, for example, "burst" once into a "silent" room or turned a bend in an upland road and glimpsed a sudden vast panorama of hills and valleys: those then will be the memory-material that the words of the poem will get out of us. Obviously, however, if we have never known the sea nor seen it in a picture, we will have trouble reading Coleridge's poem. But this will not be an aesthetic problem; it will be a vocabulary problem.

Reading a poem is indeed like making a voyage. But it is not a vicarious, safe little tour through the outer world. It is a penetrating, sometimes perilous, trip within one's self. There is nothing new about this notion. Socrates said that it was his personal mission to know himself and to teach others to do the same. The speculative Frenchman, Montaigne, put on his personal seal the question *Que sçais-je?*—"What do I know?"—and then, in essay after essay, proceeded to attempt an answer. Poetry, like philosophy, assumes that a person has within himself all the important answers, but in an unassembled form, and that only by questioning can poetry get a person to examine his random memories and make some sense out of his experience. Some of the questions it asks of a reader are: What do you know about yourself? What have you thought and felt? What are you really like beneath the surface? Poetry will always be unpopular with those who are too weak or too frightened to approach these questions.

Every poet must continually muster the courage to ask himself those questions. His answers may be startlingly new formulations of perennial wisdom or they may appear, at least to himself, as totally fresh discoveries, realities he had never thought existed within the universe and the human condition. When one thinks one has discovered something, one often wants another person to corroborate the fact. The more strange and improbable the situation is, the more urgent is the need for confirmation. Imagine yourself walking with a friend up a deserted country road. Everything seems pleasantly ordinary and restful. Then suddenly you spot there among the bushes a little green man with antennae sprouting out of his forehead. After you catch your breath, you grab your friend and say "Do you see what I see?" Before any action can be initiated, your unearthly discovery must be confirmed by another observer. Similarly, the poet's vision is corroborated when another person can say "Yes, you've made me see something that has been there all the time—in me as it was in you—but I've just never taken the time to look at it before." What we "get out of a poem," then, is nothing that we do not possess already in some jumbled, jigsaw puzzle condition. The poem is the product of one man's attempt to put in order several jigsaw pieces of his experience. If they actually fit together, they may reveal some striking detail of a picture and may help someone else (the reader) put some order into his own jumble of experiences.

The poet, therefore, selects, arranges, and rearranges his own memories, that is, anything that has touched his consciousness —emotions, thoughts, sights, sounds, tastes, smells—and fits them together into the pattern of a poem. The reader then allows this pattern to evoke within him a set of corresponding memory-events. This process of memory-evocation is a marvelous human achievement. But poetry is capable of even greater magic: it can make a reader remember an experience that he has never had. For example:

> I never saw a Purple Cow,
> I never hope to see one;
> But I can tell you, anyhow,
> I'd rather see than be one.

This is certainly not a sublime illustration of poetic sorcery, but nevertheless Burgess' little nonsense poem proves that even though one has never seen a particular thing, one can visualize it. The poet and the reader have both seen the color "purple" and the animal "cow." If he absolutely must, the reader is quite able to put those two memory-images together into one composite image. As long as we know what the parts are, we can form any grouping of them into one picture.

Poetry operates in the realm of the *conceivable* and not merely in the realm of the *actual*. The aim of poetry is not a restatement of what our eyes see, but an exploration of that uncharted world of man's thoughts and impulses, his desires and his fears, that all-important inner world out of which flow all his actions, his arts of peace and his arts of war, his acts of love and his acts of savagery, his total history and his questionable future. To acquire precise restatements of the outside world is a simple matter. We have tape recorders and cameras for that.

The following poem is just such an exploration. It will not be simple, because to simplify complex emotional responses is usually to falsify them. It will not be *logically* convincing: we will not go away from the poem nodding our heads and saying, "Well, that was a very interesting point he made. I've always wondered what life and death were all about and now I know." And finally, although the scene is London and the time is probably during the World War II blitz, no amount of history or travel photography will be able to guide us through the imagery of this poem. For the "setting" of the poem is the *inner* geography of a man obsessed, a man struggling with the apparent meaninglessness of a child's death. As in every poem we read, we will be asked to use our store of memories to identify simple objects, in this case such images as a flower, a harness, a synagogue, a shadow, an ear of corn, and a valley. As we read this poem by Dylan Thomas, we must allow each word to work upon our memory and must not panic when the poet makes startling combinations of images, for one of his objectives is precisely to startle our memory-fragments into new combinations.

A Refusal to Mourn the Death, by Fire, of a Child in London

Never until the mankind making
Bird beast and flower
Fathering and all humbling darkness
Tells with silence the last light breaking
And the still hour
Is come of the sea tumbling in harness

And I must enter again the round
Zion of the water bead
And the synagogue of the ear of corn
Shall I let pray the shadow of a sound
Or sow my salt seed
In the least valley of sackcloth to mourn

The majesty and burning of the child's death.
I shall not murder
The mankind of her going with a grave truth
Nor blaspheme down the stations of the breath
With any further
Elegy of innocence and youth.

Deep with the first dead lies London's daughter,
Robed in the long friends,
The grains beyond age, the dark veins of her mother,
Secret by the unmourning water
Of the riding Thames.
After the first death, there is no other.

No good poem is as difficult as it may seem at first sight. If you are unfamiliar with this poem, you might begin by noting the sentence structure and sequence. The poem is four sentences, the paraphrasable content of which might run as follows:

1. Never before I, myself, die will I mourn the child's death;
2. I will not write a pompous elegy for her;
3. In death she is now one with the materials and forces out of which life is made;
4. She is therefore no longer subject to death.

In paraphrase, this rather simple line of reasoning is neither very persuasive nor very original nor very interesting, rather a piece of cool, detached afterdinner philosophizing. But observe how different Thomas' approach is! He refuses to mourn this child's death, but what a passionate refusal! Not content with a cut-and-dried refusal, he must by means of images search out his own mysterious meanings. His most straightforward phrases pertain to the child ("the majesty and burning of the child's death . . . innocence and youth . . . London's daughter"), and to his act of refusal ("Never . . . shall I let pray the shadow of a sound . . . I shall not murder . . . with a grave truth"). However, his most ambitious imagery occurs when he grapples with his feelings about death and about what happens to life after it is extinguished. The problem is one of naming a negative thing, namely "death," the absence of what we know as life. In lines 1–3 it is called the "darkness" out of which bird, beast, flower, and man emerge and into which all forms of life return. This is the darkness that lies in wait for the poet and fatefully determines his last hour of light, that is, consciousness, when the circulation of his blood, the "sea tumbling in harness," is stopped.

And I must enter again the round
Zion of the water bead
And the synagogue of the ear of corn . . .

At this point he makes his reader rearrange remembered images: "Zion"? A reader might recall that Zion was a hill in Jerusalem where the ancient Jews erected their Temple and that during the exile of the Jewish People in Babylon their prophets constantly spoke of their glorious return to their God "in Zion." But this is a "round Zion of the water bead"—a drop of water, a random condensation of the air. These two concepts, then, must be visualized or "remembered" together and made to fit into one compound image. The implication? Perhaps it is that after death our glorious "homecoming" is our dissolution into our chemical components. No personal immortality awaits us, the images imply. Instead, fresh-sprouting living things reassimilate the dead, the traces of whom mysteriously reappear, like tiny worshipers, in such things as an ear of corn.

In this poem the sensitive reader must undergo the poet's struggle to name the unnameable. The reader should note the inadequacy of the four-sentence paraphrase to reproduce this wrestling with the darkness. He should be prepared to conceive of a "sound" having a "shadow," "sackcloth" having "valleys," the "breath" having "stations" (of the cross), and the dead child's "veins" being at the same time "grains" of life-stuff, suddenly spilled out and thereby made available for the production of new life.

The reader must undergo the poem, any poem. In an important sense, the reader *is* the living, breathing poem. For all the nonhuman universe, even for the most civilized, laboratory-educated chimpanzee, a poem is just a two-dimensional thing, just a series of horizontal scratchings. However, for the human reader who knows the language and knows the art of reading poetry, these scratchings may be made to come to life within him. The poem is not simply the typography or the intricate form or the profoundly original content. It is, in the last analysis, the *process* that goes on inside the reader, the process of discovering what hidden feelings, thoughts, and associations he has within himself. As we have seen, one essential attitude must be maintained: the reader must allow the poet's words to lead him into his own—the reader's—memories. He gets nothing out of poetry. It is the poetry which draws revelations out of him. He does not read the poem as much as he himself is *read by the poem.*

Nevertheless, a certain specialized skill has always been necessary. Among nonliterate peoples, today and in the past, profound and often sophisticated works of poetry were composed and handed down orally from generation to generation. Some examples of these are the Homeric epics, the epics and ballads of the Middle Ages, the ancient sacred hymns of India, and, probably, a great deal of the poetry in the Bible. Until quite recently in man's history, poetry was performed as a spoken art and so was seldom intended to be read silently. It was the special province of the minstrel or the bard or the professional reciter. Reading—reciting—poetry was the work of a person professionally trained in that art. It took more than mere literacy to qualify as a reader of poetry: it took years of training with a master. Literacy no more qualified a person to read poetry than the ability to move one's fingers qualified him to play the harp.

Before the age of the printing press, poetry reading was the art of the expert who could reveal, through his virtuoso performance, hidden nuances in the poet's words and embody in himself all the emotions that his audience was to feel. More and more, since Gutenberg's day, this expert performer and his audience have had to be one person—the so-called "silent reader." Nevertheless, though the situation has changed, the need for expertise remains. For how silent, after all, is the silent reader? Does not poetry remain a marriage of sound and significance? The silent reader is not adding numbers in his head, but is still "hearing" the sound of the words he is reading. He may not be moving his lips as he reads, but scientists assure us that the minute muscles of his throat, his larynx, and his lungs are reproducing, at a greatly reduced level, the same physical functions as reciting aloud. Thus, whatever complex effects enunciation and rhythm have on us continue to be felt despite our outward silence.

Generally speaking, all the skill the poetic performer required is still needed by the present-day silent reader. To be an untrained reader shipwrecked on a desert island with a book of poems is as miserable a fate as that of a tone-deaf castaway whose only souvenir is a violin. Even if one performs for one's own benefit, the performance, to be satisfying, must be fairly decent. To follow this analogy further: the reader of poetry must either systematically learn the principles of his art (just as the musician learns to read musical notation), or he must pick up these principles by spending a great deal of time reading poems (just as some musicians learn to perform by ear). And, no matter how he learns the fundamentals, he must (like the musician) practice regularly, for every art is a habit: no miraculous modern device has eliminated the artist's need for repeated practice in the learning and mastering of his craft.

The good reader, therefore, may consider himself a legitimate artist. Like a great musician, a great reader is an interpreter of a creator's composition. It is out of his own unique experience that the reader "re-composes" the poem. Yet it would be unwise to forget that the poem remains forever the work of the person who wrote it. One often hears the narrow-minded view, "This poem is simply what it says. Any person of intelligence sees that it obviously means this. All other interpretations are just plain erroneous." But one also hears the mindless view that lies at the other extreme: "You read it and get one thing out of it. I read it and get something completely different. Who's to say that either of us is more correct than the other?"

This latter view, just as destructive as the former, bases itself on the undeniable fact that we each see the world with a different sensory apparatus and with a different frame of reference. When I read "purple" and you read "purple," each of us imagines a slightly different shade. Yet, if we return to Burgess' poem "The Purple Cow," my mind could never paint that animal the color of grass nor could yours paint it the color of daffodils. Even such ambiguous and suggestive words as "love" and "war" and "justice" are limited by their poetic context. Two persons reading the same poem will never be affected identically. This is undeniable. Their internal performances, like the performances of two violinists, will be characteristically their own interpretations. Nevertheless, if they are competent readers, their experiences will be recognizably similar, at least to the extent that, after their reading, they can agree as to what the essential questions posed by the poem are. Like any interpretive artist, the reader of poetry must allow his entire, unique, personality to interreact with the poem, while at the same time remaining in all particulars faithful to the poem itself. As any musician will tell you, interpretation is one thing, improvisation another.

Read the following sets of poems carefully. Throughout this book you will encounter exercises like this. In every case you should let one poem reflect against the other. In some sets a good poem will be placed in contrast with a poem of poor workmanship; an imitation will sometimes be contrasted with an original; and occasionally, two or three poems on similar themes will display contrasting treatments. In your text authors' names will not be indicated. Your job will be to apply to these poems whatever reading techniques you have studied in the preceding section. For example: in the first set the moods of the poems are similar, yet the demands each poet makes on the reader are different. As you read on, allow your associations free rein. If you do, you may notice some of your thoughts separating themselves perilously from the context: "finer than flour" may remind you of your grandmother preparing a cake; happy, secure reminiscences may well up in you, and you would thereupon find yourself quite removed from the mood of the poem "Dolor." Remember that no part of a good poem is separable from the total poem. You should let the words of the poem *read you.* You must therefore know what they mean. What is "silica" and what is a "multigraph"? The dictionary offers two very different meanings for the word "periwinkle": Which definition do you think most suited to the context? In the second set you are asked to compare two poems, one by a contemporary of Shakespeare, the other an imitation. Which is which? More important, how different are the poets' intentions? Examine the poems line by line: What difference in mood is conveyed by each difference in word or phrase?

POEMS FOR COMPARISON

[A] *Disillusionment of Ten O'Clock*

The houses are haunted
By white night-gowns
None are green,
Or purple with green rings,
Or green with yellow rings,
Or yellow with blue rings.
None of them are strange,
With socks of lace
And beaded ceintures.

People are not going
To dream of baboons and periwinkles.
Only, here and there, an old sailor,
Drunk and asleep in his boots,
Catches tigers
In red weather.

[B] *Dolor*

I have known the inexorable sadness of pencils,
Neat in their boxes, dolor of pad and paper-weight,
All the misery of manila folders and mucilage,
Desolation in immaculate public places,
Lonely reception room, lavatory, switchboard,
The unalterable pathos of basin and pitcher,
Ritual of multigraph, paper-clip, comma,
Endless duplication of lives and objects.
And I have seen dust from the walls of institutions,
Finer than flour, alive, more dangerous than silica,
Sift, almost invisible, through long afternoons of tedium,
Dropping a fine film on nails and delicate eyebrows,
Glazing the pale hair, the duplicate gray standard faces.

* * *

[A] *The Hour Glass*

Behold this little dust, here in the glass,
By atoms moved.
Could you believe that this the body was
Of one that loved;
And in his loved-one's flame burned till he died,
Enflamed by what he was denied?
Yes; and in death, as life, unblest,
If fates decide,
E'en lover's ashes find no rest.

[B] *The Hour Glass*

Consider this small dust, here in the glass,
By atoms moved.
Could you believe that this the body was
Of one that loved;
And in his mistress' flame playing like a fly,
Was turned to cinders by her eye?
Yes; and in death, as life, unblest,
To have 't expressed,
Even ashes of lovers find no rest.

THE USES OF BAD POETRY

If good poetry gets something out of a reader, a preliminary definition of bad poetry might be *that type of verse that consistently* (over a period of time and for the majority of experienced readers) *gets nothing out of a person except boredom and, perhaps, laughter.* In such poetry the line of communication between the pattern of printed words and the expectant consciousness of the reader is broken. The reader cannot take the poem seriously; there seems to be an insincerity about it. It does not appear to mean what it says—or at least the reader feels reluctant to allow its form of expression to direct his deepest, most intimate responses. For example, an excerpt from an elegy by the once popular poet acclaimed as the "Sweet Singer of Michigan," Julia Moore (1847–1920):

Little Libbie

While eating dinner, this dear little child
  Was choked on a piece of beef.
Doctors came, tried their skill awhile,
  But none could give relief.

. . .

Her friends and schoolmates will not forget
  Little Libbie that is no more;
She is waiting on the shining step,
  To welcome home friends once more.

Most readers will find it difficult to get very worked up over Little Libbie's passing. An event, in itself, may call for pity but the artistry used to inspire that emotion in others must never itself be pitiable. The trained reader of poetry will be as agonized by such verse as a fine violinist would be if compelled to render, with the appropriate fervor, such works as "Hearts and Flowers" or "Pop Goes the Weasel."

Most of the poetry ever written is wretched work; most never gets into print. A surprisingly large amount does, however, and some of it is written by otherwise excellent poets. Great poets, reclining upon their laurels, are sometimes subject to drowsiness; as Horace says, there are times when even Homer nods.

The reader, however, is seldom exposed to bad verse. Coddled by overprotective editors, the student is blanketed and nearly suffocated with excellence. Every poet he reads is presented as a creator of irreproachable artistry. Every instructor is expected automatically to praise the poem he has assigned his class—for why assign anything but the best? As for the student—his role is to agree with convincing earnestness that such and such a poem is indeed unassailably great. He has dutifully learned that education teaches one to "appreciate the finer things in life." So, he is obliged to "appreciate" poetry, or at least persuade his instructor that he does. This is one of the rules of the game.

But what does that cliché "appreciation" really mean? As it is used today it commonly means the act of approving or liking something. A rather bland reaction, at best. Yet every cliché was once alive and had its own specific character. "Appreciate" comes from the Late Latin word *appretiare,* "to set a price (on something)." When you offer something for sale to a second hand dealer he looks it over, then "appraises" it, that is, he sets a price on it based primarily upon its comparative excellence. Without making distinctions and comparisons, no true "appreciation" of any thing is possible. He would be a poor appraiser if, for example, he valued all pocket watches alike. Within every category of merchandise he must have a scale of values to fit the range from the best to the shoddiest object, and, if something is so poorly put together as to be absolutely worthless, his trained eye will spot it and reject it. Like any other appraiser, the reader of poetry must be familiar with a range of values large enough to include the writings of Shakespeare and of Milton and of Julia Moore.

Real appreciation, the act of really knowing the value of a thing, is impossible if everything is superlative. "What's good today?" you ask the man in the luncheonette. He wipes his hands on his apron and answers, "Everything's good." An hour later you find yourself back in a classroom with a textbook of poems open on your desk and for the thousandth time that shadow of a question occurs to you: "What's good today?" And from the front of the room, from the editors of your book, from the well-schooled attitudes of your classmates comes that tired, it-goes-without-saying answer: "Everything's good." If by this time you are still awake you might catch yourself murmuring under your breath, perhaps for the thousandth time, "But everything *can't* be good."

Anyone who has spent much time trying to write poetry knows that everything isn't good. In any skill, success and failure are fundamental to the process of learning. A person learning to write poetry is, or should be, faced at every line and every word with crucial decisions. Two or three possibilities arise and he must select what is comparatively best and reject the others. Decisions may be quick, they may be unconscious, but alternatives arise and choices are made, choices upon which the ultimate life of the poem depends. He may at the end choose to revise his draft into a totally new creation or abandon the idea altogether. It is upon his choices that the outcome depends, and any practitioner of a skill, be he poet or carpenter or athlete, operates in a world in which triumph and defeat are conscious everyday realities. Failure can be a great temptation. The expert carpenter who decides to save time by not sanding the back of a finely finished buffet cabinet consciously denies it the final touches of excellence. Its future owner will not fail to notice this. The baseball player who allows himself to be distracted from his performance makes his move too late and allows the ball to skip under his outstretched glove into the outfield. His failure is obvious and he is immediately credited with an error.

Even a good poet succumbs at times to this temptation to fail.

He does so, usually, when he avoids focusing on the inevitable conclusion of his poem out of fear of defining his feelings or when, like the carpenter or the athlete, he yields to impatience or distraction. Great poems, like great men, are great only after the powerful temptation to give up has been again and again overcome. Unless a reader is familiar with poetic failures, he will never comprehend the greatness of a poetic triumph. How can one judge the worth of a particular success except against the background of possible defeat?

Anthologies are the museums in which well-intentioned editors hang only the well-proven masterpieces, the triumphs of human language. In the course of a liberal education, class after class of young people is herded through the halls of these museums and obliged to gape approvingly at the works of master poets. Unfortunately, this anthology-education generally backfires despite its good intentions. Excellence has a way of looking easy when all one sees is "excellent." If one is forced to praise a work of art without really knowing *why* it is praiseworthy, one may come to the unspoken, blasphemous conclusion that excellence is something of a bore.

As is often the case with words, the key to the nature of the word "anthology" lies in its origin. In Greek, *anthologia* signified a "garland of flowers." Today we might think of it as a bouquet one buys from a florist. If we have never tried to grow things ourselves, we do not have the same admiration as does a person who has struggled with frosts and fertilizers and insects and weeds and blights and prunings for several years in order to behold the triumphal blooming of two or three perfect roses. When we put our money down, we are entitled to our dozen flowers and we expect that each will be fresh and faultless. We who see only the end product, if we only knew, would be astonished at the near-miraculous process of germination, growth, and survival against fearful odds of these twelve roses. An anthology is just such a collection of triumphs produced out of the honesty and bravery of men's lives. The anthology's neat florist wrapper gives an erroneous impression. Excellent poems are not *easily* produced. Human triumphs happen only when the stakes are high, the difficulties great, and the chances for failure numerous.

. . .

In this first chapter we have discussed the artistry of the reader: how he must let the poem "read" him and how he may learn something of the art of poetry by studying failures as well as artistic triumphs. Since art is a *habit of doing something well,* the reader as artist must be trained. He must pass through his apprenticeship. Old habits of reading may have to be abandoned and new ones learned. Just like the process of learning to play an instrument, this period of training is difficult and at first may seem unrewarding. But no art, after all, was ever learned by merely taking down notes in a lecture room. No amount of poring over rule books and sports magazines will teach a person to be an athlete. The reader, too, must practice his art.

But practice is not enough. Two other factors are essential: intelligence and an open mind.

In the course of his apprenticeship the reader will be called upon to exert his intelligence as much as his emotions. He will be asked to "take a poem apart." If his reaction is "I just love poetry and all this close reading and analysis ruins the poem for me," he will have missed the point. The reason a poem is taken apart in the classroom is not to anatomize the poem but to anatomize the reader's response to it. After the discussion ends, the poem is as whole and fresh as it was when it received its creator's last finishing stroke. The only things that may be ruined by this close analysis are the reader's hasty assumptions about the poem.

Moreover, the apprentice will be called upon to learn a great number of small points. He will learn, for example, to *scan* a line of verse by marking off every rhythmic division in it and then assign a Greek-sounding name to each of these units. If his reaction is "I thought I was here to read poetry, not just memorize all these useless academic terms," he will have again missed the point. The fundamentals of an art must come first and, in order to refer to them, we must have names for them. In grade school the art of writing decent prose paragraphs was taught by continual reference to such things as "subject" and "predicate" and "agreement" of "pronouns" with their "antecedents." None of us would now be able to spell our own names if we had never been made to learn (in fact, memorize) that dry, old academic device, the alphabet. Yet, despite their initial tediousness, all fundamentals are learned in order to be forgotten. We no longer have to concentrate on spelling our name correctly—stringing together that particular pattern of letters has become second nature to us. Talking, walking, dancing, driving a car, speaking a foreign language, playing a sport or a musical instrument—all these begin with tedious small points that, when the skill is perfected, may be safely forgotten. That is to say, we know them without being aware of them.

The reader as artist must also keep an open mind. A *little* practice at reading and a *little* grasp of fundamentals may tempt a person to assume the role of Final Arbiter of All Poetry. His designation as "appreciator," that is, appraiser of poems, is his only after many years of careful reading. Even then, he should avoid the temptation of sitting in judgment like a medieval God and sentencing every poem to its appropriate level of damnation or its sphere of bliss. We can never be absolutely sure about poems. We know a poem only through a process of self-knowledge, and we can never be absolutely sure about ourselves. A "judge of poetry," once he has worked out his criteria for poetic "goodness," ironed out all the wrinkles, and eliminated all the possible loopholes, tends to approach every poem with one set of rigid specifications. He only seems to prejudge the poem. Actually he has long ago prejudged himself; he has said: "I can respond only to this particular area of myself; I am capable only of these particular thoughts and emotions."

POEMS FOR COMPARISON

[A] *Hattie House*

Come all kind friends, wherever you may be,
  Come listen to what I say,
It's of a little girl that was pleasant to see,
  And she died while outdoors at play.

Hattie had blue eyes and light flaxen hair,
  And her little heart was light and gay,
And she said to her mother, that morning fair,
  "Mother can I go out and play?"

Her mother tied her little bonnet on,
  Not thinking it would be the last
She would ever see her dear little one,
  In this world, little Hattie House.

She left the house, this merry little girl,
  That bright and pleasant day—
She went out to play with two little girls
  That were near about her age.

She was not gone but a little while
  When they heard her playmates call—
Her friends hastened there to save the child,
  But, alas, she was dead and gone.

Those little girls will not forget
  The day little Hattie died,
For she was with them when she fell in a fit,
  While playing by their side.

She was her parents' only child,
  And her age was near six years,
And she has left them for a while—
  Left all her friends in tears.

Left this world of grief and woe,
  Dear friends, she has left behind—
She is waiting on the other shore,
  To meet them bye and bye.

One fine morning, the fifth of July,
  The summer flowers were in bloom.
Eighteen and seventy-one, little Hattie died,
  And is sleeping in her tomb.

[B] *Bells for John Whitesides' Daughter*

There was such speed in her little body,
And such lightness in her footfall,
It is no wonder that her brown study
Astonishes us all.

Her wars were bruited in our high window.
We looked among orchard trees and beyond,
Where she took arms against her shadow,
Or harried unto the pond

The lazy geese, like a snow cloud
Dripping their snow on the green grass,
Tricking and stopping, sleepy and proud,
Who cried in goose, Alas,

For the tireless heart within the little
Lady with rod that made them rise
From their noon apple dreams, and scuttle
Goose-fashion under the skies!

But now go the bells, and we are ready;
In one house we are sternly stopped
To say we are vexed with her brown study,
Lying so primly propped.

* * *

[A] *Piano*

Softly, in the dusk, a woman is singing to me;
Taking me back down the vista of years, till I see
A child sitting under the piano, in the boom of the tingling strings
And pressing the small, poised feet of a mother who smiles as she sings.

In spite of myself, the insidious mastery of song
Betrays me back, till the heart of me weeps to belong
To the old Sunday evenings at home, with winter outside
And hymns in the cozy parlour, the tinkling piano our guide.

So now it is vain for the singer to burst into clamour
With the great black piano appassionato. The glamour
Of childish days is upon me, my manhood is cast
Down in the flood of remembrance, I weep like a child for the past.

[B] *The Old Arm-Chair*

I love it, I love it! and who shall dare
To chide me for loving that old arm-chair?
I've treasured it long as a sainted prize,
I've bedewed it with tears, I've embalmed it with sighs,
'Tis bound by a thousand bands to my heart;
Not a tie will break, not a link will start.
Would you know the spell?—a mother sat there!
And a sacred thing is that old arm-chair.

In childhood's hour I lingered near
The hallowed seat with listening ear;
And gentle words that mother would give
To fit me to die and teach me to live.
She told me that shame would never betide
With truth for my creed, and God for my guide;
She taught me to lisp my earliest prayer,
As I knelt beside that old arm-chair.

I sat and watched her many a day,
When her eyes grew dim, and her locks were gray;
And I almost worshiped her when she smiled,
And turned from her Bible to bless her child.
Years rolled on, but the last one sped,—
My idol was shattered, my earth-star fled!
I learned how much the heart can bear,
When I saw her die in her old arm-chair.

'Tis past, 'tis past! but I gaze on it now,
With quivering breath and throbbing brow;
'Twas there she nursed me, 'twas there she died,
And memory flows with a lava tide.
Say it is folly, and deem me weak,
Whilst scalding drops start down my cheek;
But I love it, I love it! and cannot tear
My soul from a mother's old arm-chair.

[c] *To My Mother*

Most near, most dear, most loved and most far,
Under the window where I often found her
Sitting as huge as Asia, seismic with laughter,
Gin and chicken helpless in her Irish hand,
Irresistible as Rabelais, but most tender for
The lame dogs and hurt birds that surround her,—
She is a procession no one can follow after
But be like a little dog following a brass band.
She will not glance up at the bomber, or condescend
To drop her gin and scuttle to a cellar,
But lean on the mahogany table like a mountain
Whom only faith can move, and so I send
O all my faith, and all my love to tell her
That she will move from mourning into morning.

ADDITIONAL READINGS

from *Song of Myself*

WALT WHITMAN

– 1 –

I celebrate myself, and sing myself,
And what I assume you shall assume,
For every atom belonging to me as good belongs to you.

I loafe and invite my soul,
I lean and loafe at my ease observing a spear of summer grass.

My tongue, every atom of my blood, form'd from this soil, this air,
Born here of parents born here from parents the same, and their parents the same,
I, now thirty-seven years old in perfect health begin,
Hoping to cease not till death.

Creeds and schools in abeyance,
Retiring back a while sufficed at what they are, but never forgotten,
I harbor for good or bad, I permit to speak at every hazard,
Nature without check with original energy.

– 2 –

Houses and rooms are full of perfumes, the shelves are crowded with perfumes,
I breathe the fragrance myself and know it and like it,
The distillation would intoxicate me also, but I shall not let it.

The atmosphere is not a perfume, it has no taste of the distillation, it is odorless,
It is for my mouth forever, I am in love with it,
I will go to the bank by the wood and become undisguised and naked,
I am mad for it to be in contact with me.

The smoke of my own breath,
Echoes, ripples, buzz'd whispers, love-root, silk-thread, crotch and vine,
My respiration and inspiration, the beating of my heart, the passing of blood and air through my lungs,
The sniff of green leaves and dry leaves, and of the shore and dark-color'd sea-rocks, and of hay in the barn,
The sound of the belch'd words of my voice loos'd to the eddies of the wind,
A few light kisses, a few embraces, a reaching around of arms,
The play of shine and shade on the trees as the supple boughs wag,
The delight alone or in the rush of the streets, or along the fields and hill-sides,
The feeling of health, the full-noon trill, the song of me rising from bed and meeting the sun.

Have you reckon'd a thousand acres much? have you reckon'd the earth much?
Have you practis'd so long to learn to read?
Have you felt so proud to get at the meaning of poems?

Stop this day and night with me and you shall possess the origin of all poems,

You shall possess the good of the earth and sun, (there are millions of suns left,)
You shall no longer take things at second or third hand, nor look through the eyes of the dead, nor feed on the spectres in books,
You shall not look through my eyes either, nor take things from me,
You shall listen to all sides and filter them from your self.

There Was a Child Went Forth

WALT WHITMAN

There was a child went forth every day,
And the first object he look'd upon, that object he became,
And that object became part of him for the day or a certain part of the day,
Or for many years or stretching cycles of years.

The early lilacs became part of this child,
And grass and white and red morning-glories, and white and red clover, and the song of the phœbe-bird,
And the Third-month lambs and the sow's pink-faint litter, and the mare's foal and the cow's calf,
And the noisy brood of the barnyard or by the mire of the pond-side,
And the fish suspending themselves so curiously below there, and the beautiful curious liquid,
And the water-plants with their graceful flat heads, all became part of him.

The field-sprouts of Fourth-month and Fifth-month became part of him,
Winter-grain sprouts and those of the light-yellow corn, and the esculent roots of the garden,
And the apple-trees cover'd with blossoms and the fruit afterward, and wood-berries, and the commonest weeds by the road,
And the old drunkard staggering home from the outhouse of the tavern whence had lately risen,
And the schoolmistress that pass'd on her way to the school,
And the friendly boys that pass'd, and the quarrelsome boys,

And the tidy and fresh-cheek'd girls, and the barefoot negro boy and girl,
And all the changes of city and country wherever he went.

His own parents, he that had father'd him and she that had conceiv'd him in her womb and birth'd him,
They gave this child more of themselves than that,
They gave him afterward every day, they became part of him.

The mother at home quietly placing the dishes on the supper-table,
The mother with mild words, clean her cap and gown, a wholesome odor falling off her person and clothes as she walks by,
The father, strong, self-sufficient, manly, mean, anger'd, unjust,
The blow, the quick loud word, the tight bargain, the crafty lure,
The family usages, the language, the company, the furniture, the yearning and swelling heart,
Affection that will not be gainsay'd, the sense of what is real, the thought if after all it should prove unreal,
The doubts of day-time and the doubts of night-time, the curious whether and how,
Whether that which appears so is so, or is it all flashes and specks?
Men and women crowding fast in the streets, if they are not flashes and specks what are they?
The streets themselves and the façades of houses, and goods in the windows,
Vehicles, teams, the heavy-plank'd wharves, the huge crossing at the ferries,
The village on the highland seen from afar at sunset, the river between,
Shadows, aureola and mist, the light falling on roofs and gables of white or brown two miles off,
The schooner near by sleepily dropping down the tide, the little boat slack-tow'd astern,
The hurrying tumbling waves, quick-broken crests, slapping,
The strata of color'd clouds, the long bar of maroon-tint away solitary by itself, the spread of purity it lies motionless in,
The horizon's edge, the flying sea-crow, the fragrance of salt marsh and shore mud,
These became part of that child who went forth every day, and who now goes, and will always go forth every day.

Spider

RICHARD LATTIMORE

Bright captures, wing-shimmers, facts
of heart, sense, and fancy, as material
dreamed deep in my organs, anticipate
futures formed and radiant, when all
experience dissolves, desperate.

I eat my memories. Stomach stuff
of life is caught, shaped, and spread,
and what it was in the air,
gone from the flesh of thread
as form stays there.

Pearls and strings, rainwash, once
silent furies, now cling
quiet on heart-shapen leaves.
Spider does not sing,
only sits, sees, eats, and weaves.

The Bourgeois Poet—67

KARL SHAPIRO

As you say (not without sadness), poets don't see, they feel. And that's why people who have turned to feelers seem like poets. Why children seem poetic. Why when the sap rises in the adolescent heart the young write poetry. Why great catastrophes are stated in verse. Why lunatics are named for the moon. Yet poetry isn't feeling with the hands. A poem is not a kiss. Poems are what ideas feel like. Ideas on Sunday, thoughts on vacation.

Poets don't see, they feel. They are conductors of the senses of men, as teachers and preachers are the insulators. The poets go up and feel the insulators. Now and again they feel the wrong thing and are thrown through a wall by a million-volt shock. All insulation makes the poet anxious: clothes, strait jackets, iambic five. He pulls at the seams like a boy whose trousers are cutting him in half. Poets think along the electric currents. The words are constantly not making sense when he reads. He flunks economics, logic, history. Then he describes what it feels like to flunk economics, logic, history. After that he feels better.

People say: it is sad to see a grown man feeling his way, sad to see a man so naked, desireless of any defenses. The people walk back into their boxes and triple-lock the doors. When their children begin to read poetry the parents watch them from the corner of their eye. It's only a phase, they aver. Parents like the word "aver" though they don't use it.

Dejection: An Ode

SAMUEL TAYLOR COLERIDGE

Late, late yestreen I saw the new Moon,
With the old Moon in her arms;
And I fear, I fear, my Master dear!
We shall have a deadly storm.
[*Ballad of Sir Patrick Spence*]

– i –

Well! If the bard was weather-wise, who made
The grand old ballad of Sir Patrick Spence,
This night, so tranquil now, will not go hence
Unroused by winds, that ply a busier trade
Than those which mould yon cloud in lazy flakes,
Or the dull sobbing draft, that moans and rakes
Upon the strings of this Æolian lute,
Which better far were mute.
For lo! the new moon winter-bright!

And overspread with phantom-light,
(With swimming phantom-light o'erspread
But rimmed and circled by a silver thread)
I see the old moon in her lap, foretelling
The coming-on of rain and squally blast.
And oh! that even now the gust were swelling,
And the slant night-shower driving loud and fast!
Those sounds which oft have raised me, whilst they awed,
And sent my soul abroad,
Might now perhaps their wonted impulse give,
Might startle this dull pain, and make it move and live!

– ii –

A grief without a pang, void, dark, and drear,
A stifled, drowsy, unimpassioned grief,
Which finds no natural outlet, no relief,
In word, or sigh, or tear—
O Lady! in this wan and heartless mood,
To other thoughts by yonder throstle wooed,
All this long eve, so balmy and serene,
Have I been gazing on the western sky,
And its peculiar tint of yellow green:
And still I gaze—and with how blank an eye!
And those thin clouds above, in flakes and bars,
That give away their motion to the stars;
Those stars, that glide behind them or between,
Now sparkling, now bedimmed, but always seen;
Yon crescent moon, as fixed as if it grew
In its own cloudless, starless lake of blue;
I see them all so excellently fair,
I see, not feel, how beautiful they are!

– iii –

My genial spirits fail;
And what can these avail
To lift the smothering weight from off my breast?
It were a vain endeavor,
Though I should gaze for ever
On that green light that lingers in the west:

I may not hope from outward forms to win
The passion and the life, whose fountains are within.

– iv –

O Lady! we receive but what we give,
And in our life alone does Nature live;
Ours is her wedding garment, ours her shroud!
  And would we aught behold, of higher worth,
Than that inanimate cold world allowed
To the poor loveless ever-anxious crowd,
  Ah! from the soul itself must issue forth
A light, a glory, a fair luminous cloud
    Enveloping the earth—
And from the soul itself must there be sent
  A sweet and potent voice, of its own birth,
Of all sweet sounds the life and element!

– v –

O pure of heart! thou need'st not ask of me
What this strong music in the soul may be!
What, and wherein it doth exist,
This light, this glory, this fair luminous mist,
This beautiful and beauty-making power.
  Joy, virtuous Lady! Joy that ne'er was given,
Save to the pure, and in their purest hour,
Life, and life's effluence, cloud at once and shower,
Joy, Lady! is the spirit and the power,
Which wedding Nature to us gives in dower,
  A new earth and new heaven,
Undreamt of by the sensual and the proud—
Joy is the sweet voice, joy the luminous cloud—
    We in ourselves rejoice!
And thence flows all that charms or ear or sight,
  All melodies the echoes of that voice,
All colors a suffusion from that light.

– vi –

There was a time when, though my path was rough,
  This joy within me dallied with distress,

And all misfortunes were but as the stuff
  Whence Fancy made me dreams of happiness;
For hope grew round me, like the twining vine,
And fruits, and foliage, not my own, seemed mine.
But now afflictions bow me down to earth,
Nor care I that they rob me of my mirth;
    But oh! each visitation
Suspends what nature gave me at my birth,
  My shaping spirit of Imagination.
For not to think of what I needs must feel,
  But to be still and patient, all I can;
And haply by abstruse research to steal
  From my own nature all the natural man—
  This was my sole resource, my only plan:
Till that which suits a part infects the whole,
And now is almost grown the habit of my soul.

– vii –

Hence, viper thoughts, that coil around my mind,
    Reality's dark dream!
I turn from you, and listen to the wind,
  Which long has raved unnoticed. What a scream
Of agony by torture lengthened out
That lute sent forth! Thou Wind, that rav'st without,
  Bare crag, or mountain-tairn, or blasted tree,
Or pine-grove whither woodman ever clomb,
Or lonely house, long held the witches' home,
  Methinks were fitter instruments for thee,
Mad Lutanist! who in this month of showers,
Of dark-brown gardens, and of peeping flowers,
Mak'st devils' yule, with worse than wintry song,
The blossoms, buds, and timorous leaves among.
  Thou Actor, perfect in all tragic sounds!
Thou mighty Poet, e'en to frenzy bold!
    What tell'st thou now about?
    'Tis of the rushing of an host in rout,
  With groans, of trampled men, with smarting wounds—
At once they groan with pain, and shudder with the cold!
But hush! there is a pause of deepest silence!

And all that noise, as of a rushing crowd,
With groans, and tremulous shudderings—all is over—
It tells another tale, with sounds less deep and loud!
A tale of less affright,
And tempered with delight,
As Otway's self had framed the tender lay,—
'Tis of a little child
Upon a lonesome wild,
Not far from home, but she hath lost her way:
And now moans low in bitter grief and fear,
And now screams loud, and hopes to make her mother hear.

– viii –

'Tis midnight, but small thoughts have I of sleep;
Full seldom may my friend such vigils keep!
Visit her, gentle Sleep! with wings of healing,
And may this storm be but a mountain-birth,
May all the stars hang bright above her dwelling,
Silent as though they watched the sleeping earth!
With light heart may she rise,
Gay fancy, cheerful eyes,
Joy lift her spirit, joy attune her voice;
To her may all things live, from pole to pole,
Their life the eddying of her living soul!
O simple spirit, guided from above
Dear Lady! friend devoutest of my choice,
Thus mayest thou ever, evermore rejoice.

The Circus Animals' Desertion

William Butler Yeats

– i –

I sought a theme and sought for it in vain,
I sought it daily for six weeks or so.
Maybe at last, being but a broken man,
I must be satisfied with my heart, although
Winter and summer till old age began
My circus animals were all on show,

Those stilted boys, that burnished chariot,
Lion and woman and the Lord knows what.

– ii –

What can I but enumerate old themes?
First that sea-rider Oisin led by the nose
Through three enchanted islands, allegorical dreams,
Vain gaiety, vain battle, vain repose,
Themes of the embittered heart, or so it seems,
That might adorn old songs or courtly shows;
But what cared I that set him on to ride,
I, starved for the bosom of his faery bride?

And then a counter-truth filled out its play,
The Countess Cathleen was the name I gave it;
She, pity-crazed, had given her soul away,
But masterful Heaven had intervened to save it.
I thought my dear must her own soul destroy,
So did fanaticism and hate enslave it,
And this brought forth a dream and soon enough
This dream itself had all my thought and love.

And when the Fool and Blind Man stole the bread
Cuchulain fought the ungovernable sea;
Heart-mysteries there, and yet when all is said
It was the dream itself enchanted me:
Character isolated by a deed
To engross the present and dominate memory.
Players and painted stage took all my love,
And not those things that they were emblems of.

– iii –

Those masterful images because complete
Grew in pure mind, but out of what began?
A mound of refuse or the sweepings of a street,
Old kettles, old bottles, and a broken can,
Old iron, old bones, old rags, that raving slut
Who keeps the till. Now that my ladder's gone,
I must lie down where all the ladders start,
In the foul rag-and-bone shop of the heart.

The Poet

ALFRED LORD TENNYSON

The poet in a golden clime was born,
  With golden stars above;
Dowered with the hate of hate, the scorn of scorn,
  The love of love.

He saw through life and death, through good and ill,
  He saw through his own soul.
The marvel of the everlasting will,
  An open scroll,

Before him lay: with echoing feet he threaded
  The secretest walks of fame:
The viewless arrows of his thoughts were headed
  And winged with flame,

Like Indian reeds blown from his silver tongue,
  And of so fierce a flight,
From Calpe unto Caucasus they sung,
  Filling with light

And vagrant melodies the winds which bore
  Them earthward till they lit;
Then, like the arrow-seeds of the field flower,
  The fruitful wit

Cleaving, took root, and spring forth anew
  Where'er they fell, behold,
Like to the mother plant in semblance, grew
  A flower all gold,

And bravely furnished all abroad to fling
  The winged shafts of truth,
To throng with stately blooms the breathing spring
  Of hope and youth.

So many minds did gird their orbs with beams,
  Though one did fling the fire.

Heaven flowed upon the soul in many dreams
  Of high desire.

Thus truth was multiplied on truth, the world
  Like one great garden showed,
And through the wreaths of floating dark upcurled,
  Rare sunrise flowed.

And Freedom reared in that august sunrise
  Her beautiful bold brow,
When rites and forms before his burning eyes
  Melted like snow.

There was no blood upon her maiden robes
  Sunned by those orient skies;
But round about the circles of the globes
  Of her keen eyes

And in her raiment's hem was traced in flame
  WISDOM, a name to shake
All evil dreams of power—a sacred name.
  And when she spake,

Her words did gather thunder as they ran,
  And as the lightning to the thunder
Which follows it, riving the spirit of man,
  Making earth wonder,

So was their meaning to her words. No sword
  Of wrath her right arm whirled,
But one poor poet's scroll, and with *his* word
  She shook the world.

Only a Thought

CHARLES MACKAY

'Twas only a passing thought, my love,
  Only a passing thought,
That came o'er my mind like a ray o' the sun
  In the dimples of waters caught;

And it seemed to me, and I say to thee,
  That sorrow and shame and sin
Might disappear from our happy sphere,
  If we knew but to begin;
If we but knew how to profit
  By wisdom dearly bought:
It was only a passing thought, my love,
  Only a passing thought.

Elegy for Minor Poets

LOUIS MACNEICE

Who often found their way to pleasant meadows
Or maybe once to a peak, who saw the Promised Land,
Who took the correct three strides but tripped their hurdles,
Who had some prompter they barely could understand,
Who were too happy or sad, too soon or late,
I would praise these in company with the Great;

For if not in the same way, they fingered the same language
According to their lights. For them as for us
Chance was a coryphaeus who could be either
An angel or an *ignis fatuus.*
Let us keep our mind open, our fingers crossed;
Some who go dancing through dark bogs are lost.

Who were lost in many ways, through comfort, lack of
    knowledge,
Or between women's breasts, who thought too little, too
    much,
Who were the world's best talkers, in tone and rhythm
Superb, yet as writers lacked a sense of touch,
So either gave up or just went on and on—
Let us salute them now their chance is gone;

And give the benefit of the doubtful summer
To those who worshipped the sky but stayed indoors
Bound to a desk by conscience or by the spirit's
Hayfever. From those office and study floors

Let the sun clamber on to the notebook, shine,
And fill in what they groped for between each line.

Who were too carefree or careful, who were too many
Though always few and alone, who went the pace
But ran in circles, who were lamed by fashion,
Who lived in the wrong time or the wrong place,
Who might have caught fire had only a spark occurred,
Who knew all the words but failed to achieve the Word—

Their ghosts are gagged, their books are library flotsam,
Some of their names—not all—we learnt in school
But, life being short, we rarely read their poems,
Mere source-books now to point or except a rule,
While those opinions which rank them high are based
On a wish to be different or on lack of taste.

In spite of and because of which, we later
Suitors to their mistress (who, unlike them, stays young)
Do right to hang on the grave of each a trophy
Such as, if solvent, he would himself have hung
Above himself; these debtors preclude our scorn—
Did we not underwrite them when we were born?

[II]

The Sense of Sight: The Excitement of Things

I am learning to see. I don't know why, but everything enters me more deeply and doesn't just stop at that one place where it always used to finish. I have something inside me which I never realized.

RILKE: *The Notebooks of Malte Laurids Brigge*

If poetry is a reorganization of a person's memories, it must be able to evoke a wide range of effects. We have some very separate categories of memories. If asked to recollect an experience, one usually pictures, dimly at first, a certain place. As the visual outlines become better defined (let us say the place is a park), one remembers perhaps the sound of some friend's voice and the words he said, audible above the sound of car horns and of children playing. If they form important parts of this experience, perhaps other memories are dimly renewed: the brush of a hand, the heat or cold or wind of the day, the taste of a sandwich, the smell of burning leaves. Finally, as one gets more involved in this mental reenactment, one can even remember how one's body felt: if one were riding a bicycle, or climbing a slope, or strolling contentedly along, if one were depressed and breathing shallowly or exuberantly drinking down the air, if one's pulse were slow and calm or rapid with excitement—however we felt, this specific "body memory" may emerge and be added to this complexly remembered scene.

Each of the senses has a way of giving its identifying stamp to one part of the total memory. What we experienced through our senses we remember sensuously. In our minds we seem to *see* images, *hear* sounds, *touch* surfaces, *smell* and *taste* substances, and *feel the motions* of our body in action.

Poetry depends on our ability to recall not some whole episode of our past (like a particular afternoon in a park), but a set of remembered fragments. Reading a poem, then, becomes experiencing a fresh arrangement of old experiences, a new action composed totally of bits and pieces of past actions. In the next several chapters we will examine this new action, this act of poetry. Like any action that really matters, the act of poetry must involve us totally. Like a dream, it is an internal event in which our sense memories fill a scene with, principally, sights, sounds, and sensations of motion, together with that indispensable ingredient, emotionally charged meaning. Unlike a dream, this act of poetry is performed in an acutely conscious state by a person who chooses to cooperate with it in its representation of his own past.

IN PURSUIT OF THE CONCRETE IMAGE

Since man's most acute and discriminative sense is his sense of sight, it is natural that poetry should take artistic advantage of our power to visualize. As readers, we are called upon again and again to "see" in our mind's-eye the pictures that the words of the poem suggest.

Seldom, however, does the poet simply present us with a random set of pictures. We don't need a verbal artist to do for us what we ourselves do every day—simply by walking about with our eyelids raised. The poet, the "fashioner," *uses* his words to form images and uses the images to help himself and us see and understand something which he feels is true about us and the world. His images, then, become *composite words* that communicate an idea or feeling which no single word could embody. It is as though the poet were to say: "What I want to tell you you will never feel if I simply say 'I'm happy,' or 'I'm depressed,' or 'I'm afraid'—what I must do is give you a picture; you must go with it, submit your mind to it, and let it work up within you a set of complex feelings, which may approximate my own."

In Emily Dickinson's "There's a Certain Slant of Light" the poet refuses to say simply "I'm suffering from despair," not because she wants to complicate her statement by poetizing it, but because the word "despair" is a pitifully weak label for a powerfully complex state of mind.

There's a certain slant of light
Winter afternoons,
That oppresses like the heft
Of cathedral tunes.

Heavenly hurt it gives us;
We can find no scar,
But internal difference
Where the meanings are.

None may teach it any
'Tis the seal, despair—
An imperial affliction
Sent us of the air.

When it comes, the landscape listens,
Shadows hold their breath;
When it goes, 'tis like the distance
On the look of death.

If she could have said it more simply, she no doubt would have done so. Simple feelings demand simple presentation and, in a poem, simple imagery. "My luve is like a red, red rose," Burns declared quite directly, quite simply because his feelings were relatively uncomplicated. William Blake's "Sick Rose" (p. 99), however, embodies a much more complicated set of feelings and contains, accordingly, more complex imagery.

The poet, then, uses the world of images, the visual world common to all of us, in order to say something which he feels is true. Like individual words, images are instruments of thought and communication. Dickinson was not primarily concerned with winter afternoons or cathedrals or landscapes, but with that intense, indefinable mood, that "internal difference, where the meanings are." Yet, without those somber, solemn images her internal meanings might have remained mutely locked within her. And we, by means of those images, are also able to understand a little better a state of mind that in some degree we have all experienced.

If language is any indication, man is a very shy and evasive animal. Never at a loss to name the phenomena of his outer world, he stammers shamefacedly when forced to talk about himself. Thousands of varieties of butterflies and automobiles and postage stamps he has had the patience to classify with minute specificity, while his closest, most powerful internal realities he labels with such blanket terms as "love" and "anger" and "longing." The love he has for his grandfather is not the same love he has for his wife, or his country, or his dog, or his after-dinner cigar. With every love object one's state of mind alters, and yet the word one uses remains blandly the same. Our contemporary language, it seems, is best suited to communicate precisely about things and to assert generalities about people.

Blanket terms, abstractions, are essential to human thought. These large category words are general concepts drawn from a number of particular things. For example, if we had before us a beach ball, an orange, and a marble, we could abstract (that is, "draw away") from them the common characteristic of roundness. If we were witness to several examples of persons' acting politely to one another, we might say that those persons had a sense of courtesy. (The more abstract, or general, a word is, the more particular instances may be potentially included under its heading. Thus "animal" is a larger category than "dog" and "dog" is larger than "dachshund.") Abstractions are absolutely indispensable for some forms of thought, but man, the bashful animal, has too often used them as a means of concealing, rather than communicating, his most important thoughts and feelings. Unfortunately, the words we use to understand and convey our inner states are either colorless abstractions—"I'm bored to death," "I'm pretty satisfied with things," "I'm sorry I did it"; or they are misappropriated psychoanalytic jargon—"I've been sensing some strong ego-drives recently," "I can't overcome my inhibitions," "I've got this block against identifying with authority figures."

Especially over the past two centuries, poets have been attempting to counter this trend. By the use of the visual image they have been able to employ *things,* about which our language allows us to speak precisely, to stand for or evoke *states of mind or feeling,* about which our language is equipped to say very little.

The people who complain that poetry is too "abstract" usually misuse the term. If it were abstract, it would demand little of them. The trouble with most good poetry is that it is disconcertingly concrete, particular, immediate. We feel most comfortable when cozily swathed in generalities. Concrete images which specify particular states of mind often reveal within us more than our prudish sense of privacy can tolerate.

If we compare Dickinson's poem of despair with an early poem by Lord Byron we will see how indispensable the verbal image can be in conveying emotional intensity:

Remembrance

'Tis done!—I saw it in my dreams:
No more with Hope the future beams,
  My days of happiness are few;

Chill'd by misfortune's wintry blast,
My dawn of life is overcast,
  Love, Hope, and Joy, alike adieu!—
  Would I could add Remembrance too!

In both poems we are not briefed on the particular causes or circumstances of the despair; we are simply asked to participate with the poet in a state of deeply felt emotion. But in the first poem we are allowed to picture for ourselves the images of despair, while in the second we are merely the sounding board for a short, violent tirade of desperation. We are not asked to feel Byron's despair, but to admire his vehemence and perhaps feel a bit sorry that such an admirable personage has gotten himself so upset.

There are several kinds of images and several specialized functions that images perform:

1. They can represent things, that is, their meaning may be lodged more or less firmly within the object they denote (for example, parts of the body in an erotic poem, or objects that the poet, for mystical or philosophical reasons, glorifies simply because they exist).
2. They can be "figures of speech" that are used to invigorate the poet's language (for example, he may personify abstract concepts, like Hope or Death, by giving them human qualities or make the wind "moan" and the sea "rage").
3. They can be used as clarifying comparisons, that is, metaphors and similes (as Dickinson used the wintry details of her poem to suggest to us her state of motionless despair).
4. Finally, they can, as pure symbols, loose themselves from the everyday visual world and appear to us as visions charged with a meaning totally discovered by and totally contained within the image (for example the Tiger in Blake's visionary poem, p. 109).

For any healthy human animal there are few more satisfying experiences than the efficient use of his body and his sense apparatus. If he is a poet he may not decide to write about sex or food or breathing fresh air, but if he is alive he is at least equipped to enjoy the sensuous feel of external things. Many poets, in fact, have found that the greatest significance things have is their mystifying "thingness."

Such poets do not use objects as comparisons as in Dickinson's "certain slant of light," nor do they fragment and fuse them as in Dylan Thomas' "synagogue" and "ear of corn." Such poets merely present them. These objects may have a significance beyond their pure external thingness. They may, for instance, reveal the glory of God or the ingenuity of man. Yet even in these cases they remain very solid examples and not mere visual comparisons to something else.

To treat things as objects is no idle option for a poet. Within the past several generations Western poets have rediscovered a fact that has always been understood in Oriental cultures—things exist separate and independent from man. Our scientific civilization has been based on the proposition that things derive their meaning from their usefulness to man. A field is good farm land, a forest good timber land, a river navigable, and an animal either edible, fur-bearing, or otherwise useful. For Westerners the most important question to be asked concerning an object is "What is it *for*?" and not "What *is* it?"

In his poem, entitled "Mowing," Robert Frost asks the more difficult question, "What is it?" No *human* answer is given, and yet we sense that knowledge is somehow evoked from the reader.

Mowing

There was never a sound beside the wood but one,
And that was my long scythe whispering to the ground.
What was it it whispered? I knew not well myself;
Perhaps it was something about the heat of the sun,
Something, perhaps, about the lack of sound—
And that was why it whispered and did not speak.
It was no dream of the gift of idle hours,
Or easy gold at the hand of fay or elf:
Anything more than the truth would have seemed too weak
To the earnest love that laid the swale in rows,
Not without feeble-pointed spikes of flowers
(Pale orchises), and scared a bright green snake.
The fact is the sweetest dream that labor knows.
My long scythe whispered and left the hay to make.

The poet is here a farmer involved in exploiting nature for its economic usefulness. Yet it is not he who is doing the important speaking, but his "long scythe whispering to the ground." Things, objects—what do they say? They don't discuss the price of hay or the number of bales necessary to feed twenty head of cattle over the winter months. They don't even discuss whetstones or steel or alfalfa. "Perhaps it was something about the heat of the sun,/ Something, perhaps, about the lack of sound"—not man-talk, certainly, but thing-talk. "It was no dream," it was no poet's fanciful conception, no reconstruction of reality fashioned in a human mind, no dream but the nonhuman "truth" that seemed to have a thing's "love" for what it did.

Contemplating the pure nonhumanity of his scythe, the poet also begins to see other things as independent existences. He does not see just rows of mown hay, but is able to distinguish among them "feeble-pointed spikes of flowers." He even identifies them as "pale orchises." He sees a snake and, without recording his own surprise, records the snake's surprise, together with its brilliant color. Labor, for Frost the col*labor*ation of man and nature, has a dream, but this dream is no fanciful "gift of idle hours." It is the thing itself: fact—not as an idea, such as a verifiable statement made by a newspaper, but as a direct experience of external reality. The scythe has *acted* and, in the last line, has no further concern for the use subsequently made of its action.

Whitman wrote:

> Beginning my studies the first step pleas'd me so much,
> The mere fact consciousness, these forms, the power of motion,
> The least insect or animal, the senses, eyesight, love,
> The first step I say awed me and pleas'd me so much,
> I have hardly gone and hardly wish'd to go any farther,
> But stop and loiter all the time to sing it in ecstatic songs.

This "first step," however, is no place for the poet who is not a verbal artist. No grocery list ever by itself became a real poem. A poet's evocation of the actual world of objects must be conditioned by the poet's implicit or stated *attitude* toward that reality—and the thoughtful reader must agree that this attitude is, for want of a better word, "interesting." In reading such a poem we must respond to that elusive quality, *tone*—the implied or stated attitude of the writer to himself, his subject matter, and his audience. It does not take much literary sophistication to discover whether a writer of a love lyric is really emotionally involved in the contemplation of his beloved or if he is just giving us a list of anatomical parts. In poems that seem to use images as a direct presentation of actual objects we should always try to sense the poet's tone, his worshipful or astonished or loving or humorous or angry participation in the object of contemplation.

POEMS FOR COMPARISON

[A] *The Temple of Nature*

So still the Tadpole cleaves the watery vale,
With balanc'd fins and undulating tail;
New lungs and limbs proclaim his second birth,
Breathe the dry air, and bound upon the earth.
Allied to fish, the Lizard cleaves the flood,
With one-cell'd heart, and dark frigescent blood;
Half-reasoning Beavers long-unbreathing dart
Through Eirie's waves with perforated heart;
With gills and lungs respiring Lampreys steer,
Kiss the rude rocks, and suck till they adhere;
With gills pulmonic breathes th' enormous Whale,
And spouts aquatic columns to the gale.

[B] *Pied Beauty*

Glory be to God for dappled things—
  For skies of couple-colour as a brinded cow;
    For rose-moles all in stipple upon trout that swim;
Fresh-firecoal chestnut-falls; finches' wings;
  Landscape plotted and pieced—fold, fallow, and plough;
    And áll trádes, their gear and tackle and trim.
All things counter, original, spare, strange;
  Whatever is fickle, freckled (who knows how?)
    With swift, slow; sweet, sour; adazzle, dim;
He fathers-forth whose beauty is past change:
                Praise him.

* * *

[A] *To a Locomotive in Winter*

Thee for my recitative,
Thee in the driving storm even as now, the snow, the winter-day
declining,
Thee in the panoply, thy measur'd dual throbbing and thy
beat convulsive,
Thy black cylindric body, golden brass and silvery steel,
Thy ponderous side-bars, parallel and connecting rods,
gyrating, shuttling at thy sides,
Thy metrical, now swelling pant and roar, now tapering
in the distance,
Thy great protruding head-light fix'd in front,
Thy long, pale, floating vapor-pennants, tinged with
delicate purple,
The dense and murky clouds out-belching from thy
smoke stack,
Thy knitted frame, thy springs and valves, the
tremulous twinkle of thy wheels,
Thy train of cars behind, obedient, merrily following,
Through gale or calm, now swift, now slack, yet
steadily careering;
Type of the modern—emblem of motion and power—pulse
of the continent,
For once come serve the Muse and merge in verse, even
as here I see thee,
With storm and buffeting gusts of wind and falling snow,
By day thy warning ringing bell to sound its notes,
By night thy silent signal lamps to swing.

Fierce-throated beauty!
Roll through my chant with all thy lawless music,
thy swinging lamps at night,
Thy madly-whistled laughter, echoing, rumbling like
an earthquake, rousing all,
Law of thyself complete, thine own track firmly holding,
(No sweetness debonair of tearful harp or glib piano thine,)
Thy trills of shrieks by rocks and hills return'd,

Launch'd o'er the prairies wide, across the lakes,
To the free skies unpent and glad and strong.

[B] *I Like to See It Lap the Miles*

I like to see it lap the miles,
And lick the valleys up,
And stop to feed itself at tanks;
And then, prodigious, step

Around a pile of mountains,
And, supercilious, peer
In shanties by the sides of roads;
And then a quarry pare

To fit its sides
And crawl between
Complaining all the while
In horrid, hooting stanza;
Then chase itself down hill

And neigh like Boanerges;
Then, punctual as a star
Stop—docile and omnipotent—
At its own stable door.

[C] from *London*

Magnificent, too, is the system of drains,
Exceeding the far-spoken wonders of old:
So lengthen'd and vast in its branches and chains,
That labyrinths pass like a tale that is told:
The sewers gigantic, like multiplied veins,
Beneath the whole city their windings unfold,
Disgorging the source of plagues, scourges, and pains,
Which visit those cities to cleanliness cold.
Well did the ancient proverb lay down this important text,
That cleanliness for human weal to godliness is next.

THE TRANSFIGURED IMAGE

When an image is used simply to describe an object interesting *in itself,* the poet asks the reader to view it with him. He may do one of two things: he may stand back and let the actual details of the object speak for themselves; or he may powerfully conjure up a vision of it through the medium of his own emotions. If he chooses the latter, he will tend to slip into certain modes of feeling that are as common today as they were forty-thousand years ago. The human perception, whenever a person is deeply moved or intensely excited by some object or event, invariably undergoes a certain distortion. At high peaks of emotion we cannot maintain our rationality or our decorum: we would become something higher—or lower—than human, if we could. When excitement thus alters our view of reality, we often express ourselves in "figures of speech," expressive forms that are probably as old as language itself.

Figure of speech is a very loose term used to identify an expression that is not intended to be taken *literally*. Figures of speech may not accurately describe an object, yet they can accurately describe the impression that that object makes on its viewer. In this section we will consider only three figures: personification, apostrophe, and emblem. (Simile, metaphor, and symbol, though traditionally termed figures of speech, will be discussed separately in Chapter III.)

Perhaps the most common figure is **personification**. Anthropologists have noted among primitive peoples a tendency to endow all things with life, willfulness, and more or less human personality. Waves, trees, rocks, clouds—are all treated as, more or less, free persons. They *decide* to behave like waves or trees or rocks or clouds; they are not bound to do so and at times may act as capriciously as any human. This primitive assumption, which anthropologists call *animism,* remains just beneath the surface of our (recently civilized) consciousness. Instinctively we revert to it in moments of great stress. Narrating his own shipwreck experience in "The Open Boat," Stephen Crane wrote of waves that were "most wrongfully and barbarously abrupt and tall":

As each slaty wall of water approached, it shut all else from the view of the men in the boat, and it was not difficult to imagine that this particular wave was the final outburst of the ocean, the last effort of the grim water. There was a terrible grace in the move of the waves and they came in silence, save for the snarling of the crests.

Since personification is a perennial way we have of reacting to our world, it is not surprising that poetry has, from its very origins, made extensive use of it. Greek poets, in adaptations of their traditional myths, personified as men such natural phenomena as winds, rivers, and mountains. Hebrew poets customarily personified cities such as Jerusalem, Nineveh, and Babylon, as women. In many of its more exalted passages the Bible reveals a vision of transfigured reality. In Psalm 24 even details of architecture come humanly alive at the advent of God into His holy city:

> Lift up your heads, O ye gates; and
> be ye lifted up, ye everlasting doors; and
> the King of glory shall come in.

And later, in Isaiah 55:12, the whole landscape, participating in the joy of man, rejoices humanly:

> For ye shall go out with joy, and be
> led forth with peace: the mountains and
> the hills shall break forth before you
> into singing, and all the trees of the
> field shall clap their hands.

When man first looked beyond such everyday phenomena as trees and wind, and such man-made instruments as cities and gates, he came to recognize certain general forces or laws operating in his world. We are all familiar with the personifications he devised to embody them. Some force, he reasoned, must be responsible for making things so predictably unpredictable. What modern science calls the "random factor" or the "principle of indeterminacy" the ancients named "Fortuna" (Lady Luck) and, together with a whimsical personality, they endowed her with a magical wheel upon which each man's prosperity rose, reached its zenith, and then slowly, inevitably, declined. Some other force was at work, obviously, attracting oddly-matched persons to one another: the ancients took their abstract noun "desire" (in Greek *eros,* in Latin *cupido*) and gave it the playful, moody attributes of an adolescent boy.

Yet the source of infatuation and youthful "crushes" was, these early psychologists thought, some greater, more august power whose presence was felt as intense pleasure and whose gift was the conception of new life. To this force the Latins assigned the abstract term *venus,* "pleasure" and then, true to the human habit of personifying, they said that Venus (what moderns might call the "pleasure principle") was the mother of Cupid. When the Roman poet-philosopher Lucretius sought to convey to his readers the miraculous workings of this pleasure principle, he did not have to use lifeless categories and ponderous abstractions, but could invoke this force *as a person:*

> . . . O joy of gods and men,
> Under the wheeling seasons of the sky
> You who attend upon the cargoed seas
> As on the earth heavy with harvests (since
> Through you alone is every life begot
> And, risen, gazes at the brilliant sun).

"Venus" here is still a vaguely envisioned force, interfusing the world. But now, in the next lines, this "it" becomes very decidedly a "she," a divine woman who approaches the earth in springtime and impels all things to merge in love. Yet notice the poet's artistry: he uses this figure of speech, but does not let it run away with him. His main focus remains on this pervasive pleasure principle and not on the image of a woman.

> Before you, goddess, there before you flee
> The winds, the clouds of heaven flee your coming.
> For you Earth in her artistry puts forth—
> Delicately—flowers, for you the Sea
> Across his vast expanses laughs aloud
> And Sky, turned peaceful, glows in showered light.
> Soon as one spring-like dawn appears, soon as
> The loosed, engendering southwind surges free,
> Then birds, high-flying, are the first to cry
> Your coming, O Divine One, for your might
> Has pierced each through the heart, and next wildly

The herds leap across glad pastures and swim
The rapids: so, caught by the sweetness, each
Must follow out of longing where you lead.

When several of these idea-personifications are woven into a logical, narrative structure, the end product is called an **allegory.** If, for example, your intention were to describe the interplay of forces within a guilt-ridden man who feels himself isolated from humanity and abandoned by God, you might say:

In such instances the individual, alienated from himself, contemplates as though from a distance his two options: to die (kill himself) or to remain passively alive and thereby perhaps expiate his guilt. By leaving his decision up to chance or to some "external" determinant, he relieves himself of the responsibility for this painful choice. He becomes, in other words, a mere bystander while uncontrollable forces determine his fate.

But if you were a poet like Coleridge, you might decide to have your lonely Mariner view a spectral ship approaching his own and have two figures aboard dicing for his soul:

And its ribs are seen as bars on the face of the setting Sun.

Alas! (thought I, and my heart beat loud)
How fast she nears and nears!
Are those *her* sails that glance in the Sun,
Like restless gossameres?

The Specter-Woman and her Deathmate, and no other on board the skeleton ship.

Are those *her* ribs through which the Sun
Did peer, as through a grate?
And is that Woman all her crew?
Is that a DEATH? and are there two?
Is DEATH that woman's mate?

Like vessel, like crew!

Her lips were red, *her* looks were free,
Her locks were yellow as gold:
Her skin was as white as leprosy,
The Nightmare LIFE-IN-DEATH was she,
Who thicks man's blood with cold.

Death and Life-in-Death have diced for the ship's crew, and she (the latter) winneth the ancient Mariner.

The naked hulk alongside came,
And the twain were casting dice;
"The game is done! I've won! I've won!"
Quoth she, and whistles thrice.

No twilight within the courts of the Sun.

The Sun's rim dips; the stars rush out:
At one stride comes the dark;
With far-heard whisper, o'er the sea,
Off shot the specter bark.

Thus we see that personification and allegory, if rightly used, retain their primitive power. A comparison of the prose translation with Coleridge's transfigured vision again illustrates how prose gives us *statements to understand* and how poetry gives us *images to experience*. Here, among the images we are asked to remember and supply to the poem are those nightmare phantasies that inhabit the twilight regions of our mind.

Another vestige of our past is called **apostrophe.** Here the writer or storyteller abruptly discontinues his monologue to his audience, turns away from that audience, and addresses some third party as though it had suddenly and magically appeared. In good oral narration the effect is often startling and eerie; it is invariably dramatic.

When Lady Macbeth finishes reading her husband's letter, she immediately formulates new plans for his political advancement. A messenger enters to announce that King Duncan will spend the night at Macbeth's castle and that Macbeth himself has ridden ahead and will arrive momentarily. "Give him tending," she says. "He brings great news." The messenger exits. Lady Macbeth is alone on the stage. She muses to herself: "The raven himself is hoarse/ That croaks the fatal entrance of Duncan/ Under my battlements." Then, suddenly, she looks up and she is no longer alone: calling them into being, she *apostrophizes,* somewhere there in the theater, an invisible troop of horrors:

Come, you spirits
That tend on mortal thoughts, unsex me here;
And fill me, from the crown to the toe, top-full
With direst cruelty. Make thick my blood,
Stop th' access and passage to remorse,
That no compunctious visitings of nature
Shake my fell purpose nor keep peace between
Th' effect and it. Come to my woman's breasts,
And take my milk for gall, you murd'ring ministers;
Wherever in your sightless substances
You wait on nature's mischief.

Then in a crescendo of fury she conjures up the personified presence of night and for the first time makes her plan explicit:

> Come, thick night,
> And pall thee in the dunnest smoke of hell.
> That my keen knife see not the wound it makes,
> Nor heaven peep through the blanket of the dark
> To cry 'Hold, hold.'

At that very moment, as the imaginary knife is poised and she fears heaven's detection of her crime, her diabolical phantasy is cut short by the entrance of Macbeth. The "murd'ring ministers," apostrophized into existence by her speech, vanish and we are back again in the world of visible human actors.

Apostrophe and personification, often used together as in the preceding passage, are treasured heirlooms that have come down to us from our prehistoric past. However, like any set of heirlooms, they are misused when they are overdisplayed. Like ancestral silverware, they should be brought out only at the proper occasion; their effect is diminished if they are shown off every day. These ancestral figures of speech have in the past been used often to ornament the calm dignity of classical and neoclassical poetry. As *ornament,* the personified or apostrophized image is not the central focus of the poem, but is merely used as a gracefully indirect way to speak of something else. Robert Burns begins his love lyric:

> Flow gently, sweet Afton, among thy green braes,
> Flow gently, I'll sing thee a song in thy praise;
> My Mary's asleep by thy murmuring stream,
> Flow gently, sweet Afton, disturb not her dream.

He is speaking to the stream and says he will praise it, but, as the poem develops, it is clear that his real subject is, of course, his sleeping sweetheart. This delicate, ornamental use of personification and apostrophe is typical of eighteenth-century taste, which frowned upon a direct statement of feelings and preferred light playfulness, wit, and indirection.

Although these figures of speech have in recent centuries been used more as ornaments than as vital, organic parts of poems, they still can be charged with some of their primitive intensity, as in the passage from *Macbeth,* and with some of their original surprise, as in the last two lines of the following poem by E. E. Cummings:

Buffalo Bill's

Buffalo Bill's
defunct
          who used to
          ride a watersmooth-silver
                                                  stallion
and break onetwothreefourfive pigeonsjustlikethat
                                                                      Jesus
he was a handsome man
                                    and what i want to know is
how do you like your blueeyed boy
Mister Death

Generally, personification and apostrophe are successful if the object personified or addressed appears in a context so emotionally charged that the object seems literally to "come alive." The focus is *direct,* the image is transfigured through the emotions of the onlooker, because the thing is important in itself, like "Mister Death" in Cummings' poem and Venus in the excerpt from Lucretius. When, on the other hand, these figures are applied to an object of secondary importance in the poem, as in the Burns excerpt, they are used as *indirect* devices and must be subtly subordinated to the object of primary emotional concern. If these ornaments entirely dominate the poem, the effect can be quite ludicrous.

No poetic devices can sound sillier than misused personification and apostrophe. Direct personification, if taken to absurdly ingenious lengths, results in such concoctions as the following, "A Posset for Nature's Breakfast" by the Duchess of Newcastle (1624–74):

Life scums the cream of Beauty with Time's spoon,
And draws the claret-wine of Blushes soon;
Then boils it in a skillet clean of Youth,
And thicks it well with crumbled bread of Truth;
Sets it upon the fire of Life which does
Burn clearer much when Health her bellows blows;
Then takes the eggs of fair and bashful Eyes,
And puts them in a countenance that's wise,
Cuts in a lemon of the sharpest Wit—

Discretion as a knife is used for it—
A handful of chaste Thoughts, double-refined,
Six spoonfuls of a noble and gentle Mind,
A grain of Mirth to give't a little taste,
Then takes it off for fear the substance waste,
And puts it in a basin of good Health,
And with this meat doth Nature please herself.

For the unskilled poet one great temptation in handling apostrophe is to engage his unseen auditor in small talk. After all, invoking unseen presences is a serious matter. Robert Montgomery (1807–55) looses sight of this when he interrupts his list of Creation's wonders to remind the Deity of the importance of His position:

Yes! pause and think, within one fleeting hour
How vast a universe obeys Thy power . . .

The last figure of speech to be discussed in this chapter may, for want of a better label, be termed the **emblem.** (In dictionaries of literary terms this device corresponds to *metonymy* and *synecdoche.*) Although, like the foregoing figures, it has been traditionally put to very sober and refined uses, the emblem, too, originally embodied an intense, "transfigured" vision of reality. The psychological experience that probably lies at the source of this figure of speech is common enough. When we are presented with a sight that deeply affects us, we may *feel* the impact of the total scene, but our emotions may be too powerfully stirred for us to *see* that totality: we therefore find ourselves riveting our attention upon some single detail. For example, a shy smile or a clenched fist or an impatient drumming of a finger on a desk might become a "substitute-image" not only for an entire person but for an entire set of circumstances. The Psalmist both explained and illustrated this process when he wrote:

. . . the eyes of servants look unto the
hand of their masters . . . the eyes of a
maiden unto the hand of her mistress . . .

[*Psalm 123:2*]

And for Isaiah it is the messenger's feet, his instruments of locomotion, that are the object of attention, the substitute-image for the messenger himself:

How beautiful upon the mountains are the
feet of him that bringeth good tidings,
that publisheth peace.

[*Isaiah 52:7*]

This way of perceiving things has worked its way into our language. We use emblems when we speak of hired "hands" and the sanctity of one's "hearth." In slang a girl may be referred to as a "skirt" and a car as a "set of wheels." Sometimes the origin of an emblem is less poetical than commonsensical, as in the expression so many "head of cattle"—a large number of milling cattle are most easily counted if one just counts the heads.

Some emblems are not so much fragments that stand for totalities, but objects which have come to be *associated* with particular persons, offices, or groups; for example, the cross = Christianity, a crown = a king, the White House = the President of the United States. This sort of mental shorthand condenses complex subjects into small, hieroglyphic images. The only problem with their use in poetry is that to present-day readers almost all seem worn out journalistic clichés. Even in 1802, Wordsworth's use of associative emblems (here italicized) must have seemed a bit dry and tired:

Milton! thou shouldst be living at this hour:
England hath need of thee: she is a fen
Of stagnant waters: *altar, sword,* and *pen,*
Fireside, the heroic wealth of *hall* and *bower,*
Have forfeited their ancient English dower
Of inward happiness . . .

All segments of the population, he says, have degenerated: the clergy, the military, the press, the private citizenry, the townspeople, and the country folk. It is perhaps fortunate that he chose to get his emblems over with quickly in one line and a half.

POEMS FOR COMPARISON

[A] from *Ode upon Dr. Harvey*

Coy Nature (which remain'd, though aged grown,
A beauteous virgin still, enjoy'd by none,

Nor seen unveil'd by any one),
When Harvey's violent passion she did see,
Began to tremble and to flee,
Took sanctuary, like Daphne, in a tree:
There Daphne's lover stopt, and thought it much
The very leaves of her to touch,
But Harvey, our Apollo, stopt not so,
Into the bark and root he after her did go. . . .
What should she do? through all the moving wood
Of lives endow'd with sense she took her flight;
Harvey pursues and keeps her still in sight.
But as the deer long-hunted takes a flood
She leapt at last into the winding streams of blood;
Of man's Meander all the purple reaches made,
Till at the heart she stay'd,
Where, turning head, and at a bay,
Thus, by well-purged ears, was she o'erheard to say:
"Here sure shall I be safe," said she;
"None will be able sure to see
This my retreat, but only He
Who made both it and me.
The heart of man, what art can e'er reveal?
A wall impervious between
Divides the very parts within,
And doth the heart of man ev'n from itself conceal."
She spoke, but ere she was aware,
Harvey was with her there. . . .

William Harvey: English scientist (1578–1657) who discovered the principle of the circulation of blood.

l. 6. *Daphne:* according to the Greek myth, a girl who attracted the amorous attention of the god Apollo. In her flight from him she was transformed into a laurel tree.

l. 16. *Meander:* in ancient times, a river noted for its winding course.

[B] *O sweet spontaneous*

O sweet spontaneous
earth how often have

the
doting

fingers of
prurient philosophers pinched
and
poked

thee
, has the naughty thumb
of science prodded
thy

beauty . how
often have religions taken
thee upon their scraggy knees
squeezing and

buffeting thee that thou mightest conceive
gods
(but

true

to the incomparable
couch of death thy
rhythmic
lover

thou answerest

them only with

spring)

* * *

[A] *Song*

Go, lovely rose,
Tell her that wastes her time and me,
That now she knows,
When I resemble her to thee,
How sweet and fair she seems to be.

Tell her that's young,
And shuns to have her graces spied,
That hadst thou sprung
In deserts where no men abide,
Thou must have uncommended died.

Small is the worth
Of beauty from the light retired:
Bid her come forth,
Suffer her self to be desired,
And not blush so to be admired.

Then die, that she
The common fate of all things rare
May read in thee,
How small a part of time they share,
That are so wondrous sweet and fair.

l. 4. *resemble:* liken.

[B] *On His Mistress Drowned*

Sweet stream, that dost with equal pace
Both thyself fly, and thyself chase,
Forbear awhile to flow,
And listen to my woe.
Then go, and tell the sea that all its brine
Is fresh, compared to mine;
Inform it that the gentle dame,
Who was the life of all my flame,
In th' glory of her bud

Has pass'd the fatal flood.
Death by this only stroke triumphs above
The greatest power of love:
Alas, alas! I must give o'er,
My sighs will let me add no more.
Go on, sweet stream, and henceforth rest
No more than does my troubled breast;
And if my sad complaints have made thee stay,
These tears, these tears shall mend thy way.

ADDITIONAL READINGS

The Red Wheelbarrow

WILLIAM CARLOS WILLIAMS

So much depends
upon

a red wheel
barrow

glazed with rain
water

beside the white
chickens.

Expostulation and Reply

WILLIAM WORDSWORTH

"Why, William, on that old grey stone,
Thus for the length of half a day,
Why, William, sit you thus alone,
And dream your time away?

"Where are your books?—that light bequeathed
To Beings else forlorn and blind!

Up! up! and drink the spirit breathed
From dead men to their kind.

"You look round on your Mother Earth,
As if she for no purpose bore you;
As if you were her first-born birth,
And none had lived before you!"

One morning thus, by Esthwaite lake,
When life was sweet, I knew not why,
To me my good friend Matthew spake,
And thus I made reply:

"The eye—it cannot choose but see;
We cannot bid the ear be still;
Our bodies feel, where'er they be,
Against or with our will.

"Nor less I deem that there are Powers
Which of themselves our minds impress;
That we can feed this mind of ours
In a wise passiveness.

"Think you, 'mid all this mighty sum
Of things for ever speaking,
That nothing of itself will come,
But we must still be seeking?

"—Then ask not wherefore, here, alone,
Conversing as I may,
I sit upon this old grey stone,
And dream my time away."

Hurrahing in Harvest

GERARD MANLEY HOPKINS

Summer ends now; now, barbarous in beauty, the stooks arise
  Around; up above, what wind-walks! what lovely behaviour
  Of silk-sack clouds! has wilder, wilful-wavier
Meal-drift moulded ever and melted across skies?

I walk, I lift up, I lift up heart, eyes,
  Down all that glory in the heavens to glean our Saviour;
  And, éyes, heárt, what looks, what lips yet gave you a
Rapturous love's greeting of realer, of rounder replies?

And the azurous hung hills are his world-wielding shoulder
  Majestic—as a stallion stalwart, very-violet-sweet!—
These things, these things were here and but the beholder
  Wanting; which two when they once meet,
The heart réars wíngs bold and bolder
  And hurls for him, O half hurls earth for him off under his feet.

So-and-So Reclining on Her Couch

WALLACE STEVENS

On her side, reclining on her elbow.
This mechanism, this apparition,
Suppose we call it Projection A.

She floats in air at the level of
The eye, completely anonymous,
Born, as she was, at twenty-one,

Without lineage or language, only
The curving of her hip, as motionless gesture,
Eyes dripping blue, so much to learn.

If just above her head there hung,
Suspended in air, the slightest crown
Of Gothic prong and practick bright,

The suspension, as in solid space,
The suspending hand withdrawn, would be
An invisible gesture. Let this be called

Projection B. To get at the thing
Without gestures is to get at it as
Idea. She floats in the contention, the flux

Between the thing as idea and
The idea as thing. She is half who made her.
This is the final Projection, C.

The arrangement contains the desire of
The artist. But one confides in what has no
Concealed creator. One walks easily

The unpainted shore, accepts the world
As anything but sculpture. Good-bye,
Mrs. Pappadopoulos, and thanks.

The Course of a Particular

WALLACE STEVENS

Today the leaves cry, hanging on branches swept by wind,
Yet the nothingness of winter becomes a little less.
It is still full of icy shades and shapen snow.

The leaves cry . . . One holds off and merely hears the cry.
It is a busy cry, concerning someone else.
And though one says that one is part of everything,

There is a conflict, there is a resistance involved;
And being part is an exertion that declines:
One feels the life of that which gives life as it is.

The leaves cry. It is not a cry of divine attention,
Nor the smoke-drift of puffed-out heroes, nor human cry.
It is the cry of leaves that do not transcend themselves,

In the absence of fantasia, without meaning more
Than they are in the final finding of the air, in the thing
Itself, until, at last, the cry concerns no one at all.

The World Is Too Much with Us

WILLIAM WORDSWORTH

The world is too much with us; late and soon,
Getting and spending, we lay waste our powers:
Little we see in Nature that is ours;
We have given our hearts away, a sordid boon!
This sea that bares her bosom to the moon;

The winds that will be howling at all hours,
And are up-gathered now like sleeping flowers;
For this, for everything, we are out of tune;
It moves us not.—Great God! I'd rather be
A pagan suckled in a creed outworn;
So might I, standing on this pleasant lea,
Have glimpses that would make me less forlorn;
Have sight of Proteus rising from the sea;
Or hear old Triton blow his wreathèd horn.

Trees

JOYCE KILMER

I think that I shall never see
A poem lovely as a tree.

A tree whose hungry mouth is prest
Against the earth's sweet flowing breast;

A tree that looks at God all day,
And lifts her leafy arms to pray;

A tree that may in Summer wear
A nest of robins in her hair;

Upon whose bosom snow has lain;
Who intimately lives with rain.

Poems are made by fools like me,
But only God can make a tree.

To Autumn

JOHN KEATS

– i –

Season of mists and mellow fruitfulness,
  Close bosom-friend of the maturing sun;
Conspiring with him how to load and bless
  With fruit the vines that round the thatch-eves run;

To bend with apples the mossed cottage-trees,
  And fill all fruit with ripeness to the core;
    To swell the gourd, and plump the hazel shells
  With a sweet kernel; to set budding more,
And still more, later flowers for the bees,
Until they think warm days will never cease,
    For Summer has o'er-brimmed their clammy cells.

– ii –

Who hath not seen thee oft amid thy store?
  Sometimes whoever seeks abroad may find
  Thee sitting careless on a granary floor,
    Thy hair soft-lifted by the winnowing wind;
  Or on a half-reaped furrow sound asleep,
    Drowsed with the fume of poppies, while thy hook
      Spares the next swath and all its twinèd flowers:
  And sometimes like a gleaner thou dost keep
    Steady thy laden head across a brook;
    Or by a cider-press, with patient look,
      Thou watchest the last oozings hours by hours.

– iii –

Where are the songs of Spring? Ay, where are they?
  Think not of them, thou hast thy music too,—
While barrèd clouds bloom the soft-dying day,
  And touch the stubble-plains with rosy hue;
Then in a wailful choir the small gnats mourn
  Among the river sallows, borne aloft
    Or sinking as the light wind lives or dies;
And full-grown lambs loud bleat from hilly bourn;
  Hedge-crickets sing; and now with treble soft
  The red-breast whistles from a garden-croft;
    And gathering swallows twitter in the skies.

Old Autumn

LILY RASMUSSEN

Leave your dreary city street,
To God's country come and meet
Old Autumn.
Let him be your merry host,
Not that grey dishevelled ghost
City people call the "Fall,"
Who casts o'er the town his pall,
Pointing through the misty gloom
At dead summer in her tomb.
Leave him to his dismal ways,
Leave him in his hateful haze,
Leave the town: the sky is blue;
Come and frolic with the true
Old Autumn!

Come and meet him where he stands
There amid the harvest lands.
Let him take you by the hands—
Old Autumn!
Let him teach you joy is best,
Dreary thoughts he does detest,
Only gay songs interest
Old Autumn!
Leave your dreary city street:
To God's country come and meet,
'Midst his corn and golden wheat,
Old Autumn!

The Human Abstract

WILLIAM BLAKE

Pity would be no more
If we did not make somebody Poor;

And Mercy no more could be
If all were as happy as we.

And mutual fear brings peace,
Till the selfish loves increase;
Then Cruelty knits a snare,
And spreads his baits with care.

He sits down with holy fears,
And waters the ground with tears;
Then Humility takes its root
Underneath his foot.

Soon spreads the dismal shade
Of Mystery over his head;
And the Catterpiller and Fly
Feed on the Mystery.

And it bears the fruit of Deceit,
Ruddy and sweet to eat;
And the Raven his nest has made
In its thickest shade.

The Gods of the earth and sea
Sought thro' Nature to find this Tree;
But their search was all in vain:
There grows one in the Human Brain.

But I Do Not Need Kindness

GREGORY CORSO

I have known the strange nurses of Kindness,
I have seen them kiss the sick, attend the old,
give candy to the mad!
I have watched them, at night, dark and sad,
rolling wheelchairs by the sea!
I have known the fat pontiffs of Kindness,
the little old grey-haired lady,
the neighborhood priest,
the famous poet

the mother,
I have known them all!
I have watched them, at night, dark and sad,
pasting posters of mercy
    on the stark posts of despair.

– 2 –

I have known Almighty Kindness Herself!
I have sat beside Her pure white feet,
gaining Her confidence!
We spoke of nothing unkind,
but one night I was tormented by those strange nurses,
those fat pontiffs
The little old lady rode a spiked car over my head!
The priest cut open my stomach, put his hands in me,
and cried:—Where's your soul? Where's your soul!—
The famous poet picked me up
and threw me out of the window!
The mother abandoned me!
I ran to Kindness, broke into Her chamber,
and profaned!
with an unnamable knife I gave Her a thousand wounds,
and inflicted them with filth!
I carried Her away, on my back, like a ghoul!
down the cobble-stoned night!
Dogs howled! Cats fled! All windows closed!
I carried Her ten flights of stairs!
Dropped Her on the floor of my small room,
and kneeling beside Her, I wept, I wept.

– 3 –

But what is Kindness: I have killed Kindness,
but what is it?
You are kind because you live a kind life.
St. Francis was kind.
The landlord is kind.
A cane is kind.
Can I say people, sitting in parks, are kinder?

[III]

The Sense of Sight: The Images of Things Unseen

In looking at the objects of Nature . . . I seem rather to be seeking, as it were *asking* for, a symbolical language for something within me that already and forever exists, than observing anything new.

—Samuel Taylor Coleridge

We have seen how poets can produce images that are meaningful because the objects they describe are meaningful. On the next level we saw how certain figures of speech can enhance or transfigure an idea or image. On the third level, the level of analogy, the poet's potential to define his (and our) feelings is greatly enlarged. Up to this point we have studied his use of *single* vision. Now with analogy we come to explore the possibilities of *multiple* vision—the presentation of one image or idea as the primary object of attention and the use of a secondary image to clarify that object.

THE IMAGE AS ANALOGY

The most familiar form of analogy is the **simile**—the explicit comparison of two things by means of such expressions as "like," "as," or "resembles"; or in such comparative constructions as "whiter than snow," "sweeter than honey," and so forth. Similes are generally used only when the primary object is an abstract idea like "love," "war," or "justice"; or is too large, too dim, or too insubstantial to be easily visualized. Two examples from Wordsworth will suffice. The poet, viewing the still sleeping city of London from Westminster Bridge, was awestruck with the vast majesty of the sight:

Composed Upon Westminster Bridge

Earth has not anything to show more fair:
Dull would he be of soul who could pass by
A sight so touching in its majesty:
This City now doth, like a garment, wear
The beauty of the morning; silent, bare,
Ships, towers, domes, theatres, and temples lie
Open unto the fields, and to the sky;
All bright and glittering in the smokeless air.
Never did sun more beautifully steep
In his first splendour, valley, rock, or hill;
Ne'er saw I, never felt, a calm so deep!
The river glideth at his own sweet will:
Dear God! the very houses seem asleep;
And all that mighty heart is lying still!

This vision of London was important in itself. In the dawn light he could pick out all the important concrete details: "Ships, towers, domes, theatres, and temples . . ." Furthermore, he could use personification: the sun is alive—"Never did sun more beautifully steep/ In his first splendour, valley, rock, or hill." And the city, too, is a living thing—"all that mighty heart is lying still!" But one further touch is needed. How can he deal with what is largest and most important in his picture—the "beauty of the morning"? And how can he pin down his feelings about such a dangerously vague subject? Perhaps "The beauty of the morning covered the City"? "The City is very beautiful in the morning"? His solution was the simile:

> This City now doth, like a garment, wear
> The beauty of the morning . . .

Note how that more specific image "garment" clarifies the vague, almost imageless image "beauty of the morning" and unifies the effect of the time of day upon the city.

In another poem of similar mood, "It Is a Beauteous Evening," Wordsworth has an object to clarify which is even more indefinable —a period of time. His solution was to link the idea of time with the image of a nun:

> It is a beauteous evening, calm and free,
> The holy time is quiet as a Nun
> Breathless with adoration . . .

As a clarifying device, the simile generally works well if the poet has remembered two rules: (1) The clarifying image should be more visualizable than the object to which it is being compared. Compare the following similes with Wordsworth's versions: "This girl doth, like the beauty of the morning,/ Wear the garment . . ." and "Breathless with adoration, now the Nun/ Is quiet as a holy time . . ." Such similes do not clarify. Only if they are meant to dim or subtly transform the primary object are such reversed comparisons successful. (2) The clarifying image should be accompanied by a specifying word or phrase which isolates that aspect of the image that is similar to the primary object. The "beauty of the morning" is likened to a "garment." But what sort of garment? —a woolen sweater? a pair of overalls? The specifying word is the deliberately unspecific "wears," and so we picture the atmospheric effects of the morning loosely draped over the spread-out city. In the second example, the "holy time" is likened to a "Nun"—insofar as a nun wears black, uses no cosmetics, lives a celibate life. All of our normal associations with nuns and the religious life may indeed contribute to our understanding of this simile, yet the poet's specifying phrases isolate the main area of similarity: the time is nun-like in that both—here at least—are quiet and seem to have something breathless and adoring about them.

We all speak a brand of colloquial poetry, colorful though rarely original. Simile is one of the devices we use every day without having to worry our heads about its "rules." Yet we often follow these rules, as the following examples will show, with minute precision. "He's as slow as molasses in January": The multiple vision is of a person and molasses; the specifying detail, the thickness and slowness of the liquid under cool temperatures, effectively cancels out, or at least subordinates, all the other aspects of molasses—its dark color, its sweetness, its stickiness, and so forth. "The bus ride was awful—we were packed in like a bunch of sardines": The images of "we" and "sardines" are not brought together because both are small or dead or for sale or even necessarily odorous; their obvious common aspect is specified by the words "were packed." These very elementary examples illustrate how precise a tool even colloquial language is and how words, strung together one after the other according to the inner logic of language, become a *context* and, within that particular context, embody a particular meaning.

There exists a shorter, more direct form of analogy, the **metaphor.** Its process is roughly the same as that of the simile: two objects are compared; the primary object, a person, idea, or thing, is clarified by being placed close to some more visualizable object. The area of similarity is specified (or at least clearly implied) by the context. The important difference is that no word such as "like" or "as" or "resembles" is there to notify the reader that these two objects are to be compared. Such simile-words are instructions to the reader. They tell him, "Now you are to take the preceding object and place it beside the image that I am just about to mention." But the metaphor does not prepare the reader—it springs the analogy upon him instantaneously. It does not draw two things together side by side—it sets down one object (usually an abstract concept), then places the image of another object (usually a concrete thing) squarely upon the first object and calls upon the creative reader to make sense out of the comparison.

No laborious comparison-mechanism restrains Shakespeare when he has the embattled Macbeth declare:

Out, out, brief candle!
Life's but a walking shadow, a poor player
That struts and frets his hour upon the stage,
And then is heard no more; it is a tale
Told by an idiot, full of sound and fury,
Signifying nothing.

Or when he has the insinuating Iago warn Othello:

O, beware, my lord, of jealousy;
It is the green-eyed monster which doth mock
The meat it feeds on.

These are all **direct metaphors.** The classic form for the direct metaphor may be stated: *The primary object equals the clarifying object.* The primary object is the abstract idea, the clarifying object is the visual image, and the verb "to be" equates the first to the second. For example:

All flesh is grass.
[*Isaiah 40:16*]

The most often used form of metaphor, however, is not direct. Usually the poet prefers to conceal the clarifying object. He does this not because he wants to play games with the reader, but because he knows that to label the clarifying object is often to rob the reader of the *experience of discovering the comparison.* Look back at the poem "To My Mother" (p. 23). The dominant metaphor, "my mother is a mountain," is introduced in line 3 as a **submerged metaphor:** "Sitting as huge as Asia, *seismic with laughter.*" He does not say his mother, when she laughs, is a large land mass undergoing an earthquake. Such a direct metaphor would create an outlandish identification. He does not state the comparison, but he does let it flicker in our minds as a subtly hilarious analogy. When his one use of direct metaphor occurs later, in line 7, it has been carefully prepared for. When we come to the line, *"She is a procession* no one can follow after," we still have in the back of our minds the mountainous reverberations of line 3: She is not just a procession, she is a laughing mountain on parade. Finally, in line 11, the mountain image emerges in that most explicit of all analogies, the simile: She leans "on the mahogany table like a mountain/ Whom only faith can move . . ." Our discovery of the submerged metaphor is gradual and follows our discovery of the poem as a whole. As a technical device, the submerged metaphor forces us to participate in the poem and reminds us that a poem is primarily a human act and not a human artifact: we, as readers, enact the poem, and it is what the words produce in us, what circuits they connect within us, that is our most important concern.

In the following craftsmanlike poem you will be able to compare the ways in which the various types of images, which you have already studied, operate. For your quick reference, here are the categories so far. They are arranged as though on levels of a "mount of imagery":

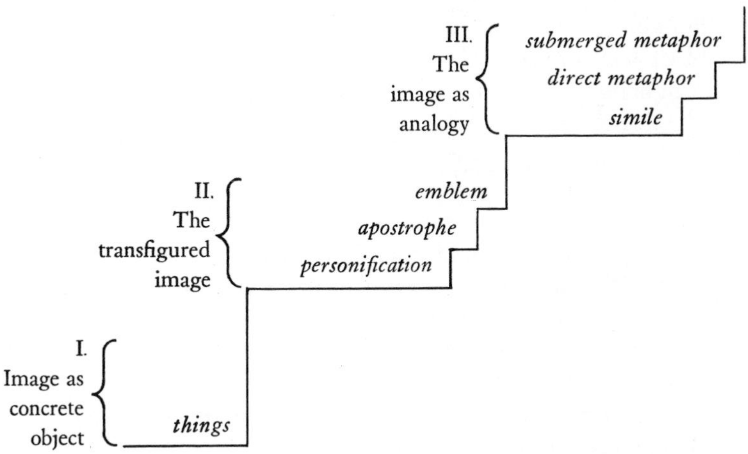

The scene depicts the climax of a heroic career. Ulysses (the name is a variant form of "Odysseus") has grown old, but not tranquil, with the passing years. His epic adventures at Troy and on his voyage home are now behind him, but he cannot content himself with nostalgia. He must act, and whatever consequences his action may bring—even if they be disastrous—are better than inaction. As you read this poem consider especially the words which are here underlined and test yourself by identifying what sort of image each of them is. Later we will discuss how effectively those images function.

Ulysses

It little profits that an idle king,
By this still hearth, among these barren crags,
Matched with an aged wife, I mete and dole
Unequal laws unto a savage race,
That hoard, and sleep, and feed, and know not me.
I cannot rest from travel; I will drink
Life to the lees. All times I have enjoyed
Greatly, have suffered greatly, both with those
That loved me, and alone; on shore, and when
Through scudding drifts the rainy Hyades
Vexed the dim sea. I am become a name;
For always roaming with a hungry heart
Much have I seen and known—cities of men
And manners, climates, councils, governments,
Myself not least, but honored of them all—
And drunk delight of battle with my peers,
Far on the ringing plains of windy Troy.
I am a part of all that I have met;
Yet all experience is an arch wherethrough
Gleams that untraveled world whose margin fades
Forever and forever when I move.
How dull it is to pause, to make an end,
To rust unburnished, not to shine in use!
As though to breathe were life! Life piled on life
Were all too little, and of one to me
Little remains; but every hour is saved
From that eternal silence, something more,
A bringer of new things; and vile it were
For some three suns to store and hoard myself,
And this gray spirit yearning in desire
To follow knowledge like a sinking star,
Beyond the utmost bound of human thought.
  This is my son, mine own Telemachus,
To whom I leave the scepter and the isle—
Well-loved of me, discerning to fulfill

This labor, by slow prudence to make mild
A rugged people, and through soft degrees
Subdue them to the useful and the good.
Most blameless is he, centered in the sphere
Of common duties, decent not to fail
In offices of tenderness, and pay
Meet adoration to my household gods,
When I am gone. He works his work, I mine.
  There lies the port; the vessel puffs her sail;
There gloom the dark, broad seas. My mariners,
Souls that have toiled, and wrought, and thought with me—
That ever with a frolic welcome took
The thunder and the sunshine, and opposed
Free hearts, free foreheads—you and I are old;
Old age hath yet his honor and his toil.
Death closes all; but something ere the end,
Some work of noble note, may yet be done,
Not unbecoming men that strove with gods.
The lights begin to twinkle from the rocks;
The long day wanes; the slow moon climbs; the deep
Moans round with many voices. Come, my friends.
'Tis not too late to seek a newer world.
Push off, and sitting well in order smite
The sounding furrows; for my purpose holds
To sail beyond the sunset, and the baths
Of all the western stars, until I die.
It may be that the gulfs will wash us down;
It may be we shall touch the Happy Isles,
And see the great Achilles, whom we knew.
Though much is taken, much abides; and though
We are not now that strength which in old days
Moved earth and heaven, that which we are, we are—
One equal temper of heroic hearts,
Made weak by time and fate, but strong in will
To strive, to seek, to find, and not to yield.

The overall form of the poem is **dramatic monologue.** Therefore, by definition it is a large apostrophe. In reading only the first section (lines 1–32), we might suppose that the speaker was thinking out loud or philosophizing at the reader. It is interesting to imagine the old hero telling us something about the meaning of human existence, but by itself this wisdom-dispensing might border on the inflated, the tediously sage. But at line 33 the scene suddenly opens up. We are not alone with the aging adventurer. A new character is made to materialize: "This is my son, mine own Telemachus . . ." With one stroke the poet (1) tells the reader he is not the only audience (in fact he is probably only an insignificant bystander who has come along at a moment that happens to be crucial for both a family and a nation); (2) provides a contrasting character (a foil) for Ulysses; and (3) introduces eleven lines of "change-of-pace," comparatively low-keyed verse, before he climaxes the poem with the hero's apostrophe to his mariners.

The structure is thus determined by apostrophe. Yet the other six image-forms are intricately interwoven within the poem. Images as concrete objects are infrequently used: Ulysses is bored to death with what he sees about him, with what he knows. The poem is about his yearning for what he does not know. Most of the literal, objective images are accordingly devoted to his dull Ithacan surroundings: He is an "idle king" matched with an "aged wife," they live hemmed in by "barren crags" and among a "savage race, / That hoard, and sleep, and feed" and cannot comprehend their restless king.

Routinized literalists are always poor judges of character. (They are also poor understanders of poetry.) From this point on, Ulysses launches into a form of poetic expression that only those bystanders who have felt deeply, and thought deeply about those feelings, can really understand.

At the second level of imagery we see, through the eyes of the speaker, the world about him leaping into life: the Hyades make the sea angry; every hour of consciousness is a "bringer of new things"; the ship seems so eager to be off that she does not even wait for a wind ("the vessel puffs her sail"); old age is a stalwart old man like Ulysses himself; the moon magically "climbs" and in response the sea "moans" eerily with "many voices," providing the place for the western stars to descend and bathe. Ulysses also uses a large number of "emblem" words: hearth = home; suns = years; scepter = kingship; souls = people; thunder = adversity; sunshine = favorable conditions; hearts = emotions; heaven = the gods;

earth = the world of man. They are not startling expressions; they are not designed to excite the imagination. They are the poet's verbal "costuming" and "stage properties." They are all classical (Latin and Greek) emblems and, therefore, appropriate idioms for this ancient adventurer.

At the third level of imagery we find the speaker striving to find images for his most urgent desire—to experience life. He uses only one simile: Knowledge is "like a sinking star." His use of metaphor is more extensive. Direct metaphor occurs twice: "I am become a name" (line 11) and "all experience is an arch" (line 19). Indirect or "submerged" metaphor occurs at least five times. His savage countrymen cannot understand him, so he first explains himself *literally:* "I cannot rest from travel" (line 6). But the literal can never embody the passion which that idea excites in him and so in the next expression he translates the literal into the metaphoric: "I will drink/ Life to the lees." The submerged image here is "wine" and the reader himself must make all the quick thought connections: life itself can be an intoxicating experience; it may seem bitter at the end (like the natural sediment at the bottom of the bottle), but those last tastes of life can still be exhilarating.

The next submerged metaphor is a variation on the first: He has "drunk delight of battle with my peers . . ." (line 16). Following line 12, which tells of Ulysses' "hungry heart," this metaphor draws a larger analogy: events are like food and drink—he consumes them, they provide him with energy, they contribute their life to his own.

Ulysses, as the next submerged metaphor clearly implies, regards himself not only as an experience-devourer, but also something of an experience-machine: "How dull it is to pause, to make an end,/ To rust unburnished, not to shine in use!" What is the submerged image in this metaphor—a sword? a plow? There is no way of telling, yet the hidden image is certainly an instrument. Who uses what? Is Ulysses an instrument used by the gods or life or his nation? Hardly. He, Ulysses, is apparently the user of himself. Pure will is urging into action a tired, aging, and presumably reluctant body. In contemporary, unheroic terms we might say that the man was "driving himself too hard."

A small, poorly-defined metaphor lies submerged in line 24: "Life piled on life." Here life (time) is implicitly compared to some spatial substance. Because this poem has a classical subject, a reader familiar with the Greek classics might detect in this phrase a subtle overtone of futility. It was the vigorous, earth-born Giants who sought in vain to ascend to and conquer the blessed abodes of the Olympian gods by piling Mount Pelion upon Mount Ossa. Mortality is a fate which mere length of life cannot alter and to be earth-born was a fate which Ulysses bitterly embraced.

The last submerged metaphor occurs in line 29: The hero says how disgraceful it is for him to "store and hoard" himself "for some three suns [years]." What is he likening himself to? Again, a thing, this time a consumable commodity. He accuses himself of the same baseness his countrymen display when they "hoard, and sleep, and feed and know not [him]."

All five submerged metaphors occur in the first section of the poem. A curious pattern is formed if we draw these metaphors up to the surface of consciousness and translate them into similes:

1. *Life is like wine:* I want to drink it down, no matter how bitter it may be at the end.
2. I love to fight; *fighting with my equals has been like drinking wine.*
3. If I am not active, *I rust like an unused instrument.*
4. If I could pile one *Life, like a mountain,* upon another life, I would still never have enough time.
5. *I am like a substance:* I must not hoard but consume myself.

A poet creates out of his total personality. He is as much responsible for his unconscious triumphs as for conscious ones. We have no way of knowing how consciously Tennyson arranged those metaphors, but their pattern is unmistakable. Just below the surface of conscious awareness lies a set of related ideas that the perceptive reader must allow to work upon himself *at that level of preconsciousness.* What do they imply if analytically wrenched out of their shadowy undersea world? Perhaps this: The hero wishes to have the strength to "consume" life; he had done so in the past and will force his aging body once again to act as servant to his will. Despite the briefness of one's single life, he must expend himself and let himself be "consumed" by life. Here in the first section of this poem we find, under the surface, a marvelous reversal, a man's desire to consume life coupled with his realization that it is actually life which is consuming him—a submerged pattern comparable to the image of the candle that gives light and heat but does so only by consuming itself.

A *pattern of metaphors* thus underlies the first section of this poem. Its implications—shadowy, inarticulate, and tinged with self-doubt—are matched by the literal statements Ulysses makes to his mariners in the last section. "There lies the port . . ./ There gloom the dark, broad seas," "The thunder and the sunshine," "It may be that the gulfs will wash us down;/ It may be we shall touch the Happy Isles," "Made weak by time and fate, but strong in will." These statements are courageous, even cheerful, yet they are full of the same conflicts that had brooded beneath the surface of the first 32 lines. Does man "consume" experience, or does each scene, each event, claim a tiny part of the participant? It was, after all, Ulysses himself who admitted "I am a part of all that I have met . . ." (line 18). A good poet, consciously or unconsciously, is able to pose more questions than he answers. By creating a pattern of metaphors he can suggest to us unseen realities which can be explored only by this subliminal means. In "close reading" we can translate them into bald assertions and analyze them as much as we like, but it is only in experiencing them within the poem that we can ever come to grips with their dark, suggestive meanings.

The **mixed metaphor** is an inconsistent pattern of metaphors. In Tennyson's poem, Ulysses used a fairly consistent metaphor—"Man consumes experience"—and gave it a surprising twist at the end. But if Ulysses had said: "I will drink life to the lees, I will attain the summit of experience; Yet I fear I am, in the process, being worn down at the grindstone of existence," he would have been dealing in a mixed metaphor, probably a very bad one.

Mixed metaphors are never bad by definition. They are only bad if they are poorly used. In prose and in speech they are almost always absurd. "Today," the valedictorian begins, "we launch our careers on the road of life, imbued with that store of wisdom and knowledge which ever shines from those hallowed halls." (Our careers are boats that somehow propel themselves up a road; we, the sailors, are totally dyed (imbued) with a cargo that is delivered constantly on lightbeams out of sainted corridors.) It is probably just as well that most of us do not pay attention to the words of a valedictory address. Clichés like these are often dead metaphors that, when mixed, become especially grotesque. For example: "We must knuckle down, put our noses to the wheel and our shoulders to the grindstone," and "Unlike my opponent I will not stoop to logrolling the pork barrel in order to feather my own nest."

In the same year (1842) that Tennyson published "Ulysses" he published another monologue, "Locksley Hall," which became one of his most admired and most ridiculed creations. In it occurs the following metaphorical oversight:

> For I dipt into the future, far as human eye could see,
> Saw the Vision of the world, and all the wonder that would be.

Two metaphors are implicit in the first line: (1) the speaker "dipt" and (2) the future unfolded spatially into the distance. But what is this "dipping" image? Is the speaker dipping, as with a ladle, into the stream of time? No. Is he flying or diving into the "Vision of the world"? No. Is he reading here and there (dipping) in the book of life? No. Every possible image we assign to "dipt" clashes unpleasantly with the second metaphor, the future as an extended vista. Our instinct tells us to shut our eyes to this sort of obscurity and to read on, but "shutting our eyes" is an instinct that the art of poetry must constantly combat. If a mixed metaphor excites us with new clashing images that enhance the context, it is successful. If, as in this example, it gives the reader a chance to yawn or think about dinner, it has failed.

Shakespeare wrote hundreds of mixed metaphors, most of them brilliantly successful. Look back at the passage from Macbeth on page 53. Life is (1) a candle, (2) a walking shadow, (3) an unskilled actor, (4) a tale told by an idiot. These metaphors are dissimilar. There is no smooth transition from one to the other. Yet the reader understands something from this chaos of imagery. There is an order here, and there are connections to be sensed between these metaphors. "Life" suffers transformation in Macbeth's fevered brain; it becomes a candle that should be quickly snuffed out because, along with illumination, this candle produces a dark companion to every man, a shadow that mimics, like some bombastic actor, even his most sincere and passionate gestures until his life becomes a meaningless charade destined to end horribly in a spasm. Each reader will make slightly different connections between images in a mixed metaphor. But it is only the successful mixed metaphor that will welcome and reward this sort of reader participation.

POEMS FOR COMPARISON

[A] *Holy Sonnet 14*

Persuade me now, O Triune God, anew:
As yet Thou counsel'st with me like a friend;
That I be right, prove I am wrong, then lend
Thy justifying grace to keep me true.
I, though enthrall'd by Satan and his crew,
Labor to rev'rence Thee, but to no end;
Reason, Thy gift, should surely me defend
But it has proven unsure and helpless, too.
Yet dearly would I side with Thee and fain,
But am conjoin'd with Thine old enemy;
Convince me to return to Thee again;
Receive me and restrict my thought, for I,
Except Thou sway my mind, will reason free
And doctrines false are sure to enamour me.

[B] *Holy Sonnet 14*

Batter my heart, three-personed God, for you
As yet but knock, breathe, shine, and seek to mend;
That I may rise and stand, o'erthrow me, and bend
Your force to break, blow, burn, and make me new.
I, like an usurped town to another due,
Labor to admit you, but oh, to no end;
Reason, your viceroy in me, me should defend,
But is captived, and proves weak or untrue.
Yet dearly I love you, and would be lovèd fain
But am betrothed unto your enemy;
Divorce me, untie or break that knot again;
Take me to you, imprison me, for I,

Except you enthrall me, never shall be free,
Nor ever chaste, except you ravish me.

* * *

[A] *In White*

A dented spider like a snow drop white
On a white Heal-all, holding up a moth
Like a white piece of lifeless satin cloth—
Saw ever curious eye so strange a sight?—
Portent in little, assorted death and blight
Like the ingredients of a witches' broth?—
The beady spider, the flower like a froth,
And the moth carried like a paper kite.

What had that flower to do with being white,
The blue prunella every child's delight.
What brought the kindred spider to that height?
(Make we no thesis of the miller's plight.)
What but design of darkness and of night?
Design, design! Do I use the word aright?

l. 2. *Heal-all:* a flower, normally blue.
l. 12. *miller's:* moth's.

[B] *Design*

I found a dimpled spider, fat and white,
On a white heal-all, holding up a moth
Like a white piece of rigid satin cloth—
Assorted characters of death and blight
Mixed ready to begin the morning right,
Like the ingredients of a witches' broth—
A snow-drop spider, a flower like froth,
And dead wings carried like a paper kite.

What had that flower to do with being white,
The wayside blue and innocent heal-all?

What brought the kindred spider to that height,
Then steered the white moth thither in the night?
What but design of darkness to appall?—
If design govern in a thing so small.

[c] *Design*

I found a dreadful spider, huge and white,
On a white heal-all, holding up a moth
Like a white piece of lovely satin cloth—
Assembled characters of death and blight
Designed by Nature to inspire fright
Like witches dancing round a hellish broth—
A huge white spider, a flower, and a moth
Hinged like a carrier-fighter poised for flight.

What had that flower to do with being white,
The wayside blue and innocent heal-all?
What brought the similar spider to that height,
Then brought the white moth thither in the night?
What but design of darkness to appall?—
If design govern in a thing so small.

THE IMAGE AS SYMBOL

Ulysses, the sturdy old adventurer, when he spoke of drinking life down to the lees, chose one particular level of imagery. At the literal level, he could have said: "I will drink my wine down to the lees" (a statement not to his purpose, for literal wine drinking he leaves to his dull-brained countrymen). If he had used a figure of speech he could have said: "My wine once smiled up at me from my cup—and now, O bitter lees at the bottom, you too will I drink down!" (a bit theatrical, to say the least). At the simile level he could have said: "Life is like wine and I want to experience it down to the bitter end" (a prosy, ponderous way of putting it). At the next level he could have used a direct metaphor: "Life is wine and

I want to experience it down to the bitter end," or a submerged metaphor: "I will drink life to the lees." If he had chosen to go one step further and use a **symbol,** his phrase might have been: "I will drink my wine down to the lees." This is identical with the first, literal statement. Only his context would suggest to us that he meant something else, that the act of drinking signified an attitude toward "life" or "experience."

A simple way to review the poetic uses of imagery might be to draw up a table of relationships:

Level of Imagery	Primary Object or Idea	Clarifying Object
1. Literal ("image as object")	x{the object *means* the object	
2. Figurative	x{personified or apostrophized	
	x{not explicitly mentioned but customarily represented by its emblem "y"}	=y
3. Analogical	x{simile: is like}	=y
	x{metaphor, direct or submerged: is equated with}	=y
4. Symbolic		y{the object *means* something other than itself

When we arrive at the symbolic heights we leave behind the double images of analogy. Simile and metaphor, as we have noted, formally yoke one image to another, or an image to an idea. They clarify by revealing similarities between two things. Of all the forms of imagery, symbols and literal statements most resemble each other in appearance: *they mean, they do not compare.* In function, a symbol is like a word. When we read the word "tree," our minds do not compare this arrangement of letters with that familiar, vertically rising, green, branching object. We understand that the word *means* the object. There, in its four letters and in its one quick syllable, it summarizes our notion of perhaps several tons of wood and foliage. As verbal animals, we contain within us—in the miniature forms of words—all the myriad objects for which we know the name. We speak a name and suddenly that person, place, or thing is mentally present. In the human mind the identification of an object with its name is so close that among primitive peoples learning a person's name gives one magical powers over the person himself. A symbol, like a name, is an image which directly *means*. Like the simple word, it is often the shortest, most immediate way to convey certain ideas. But, unlike the literal object, the symbol means something other than, or at least more than, itself.

Compare the following uses of the image "night":

When I Heard the Learn'd Astronomer

WALT WHITMAN

When I heard the learn'd astronomer,
And the proofs, the figures, were ranged in columns before me,
When I was shown the charts and diagrams, to add, divide and
    measure them,
When I sitting heard the astronomer where he lectured with much
    applause in the lecture-room,
How soon unaccountable I became tired and sick,
Till rising and gliding out I wander'd off by myself,
In the mystical moist night-air, and from time to time,
Look'd up in perfect silence at the stars.

I am he that walks with the tender and growing night,
I call to the earth and sea half-held by the night

Press close bare-bosom'd night—press close magnetic nourishing
    night!
Night of south winds—night of the large few stars!
Still nodding night—mad naked summer night.

[WHITMAN, from *"Song of Myself"*]

She walks in beauty, like the night
    Of cloudless climes and starry skies;

And all that's best of dark and bright
Meet in her aspect and her eyes:
[BYRON, from *"She Walks in Beauty"*]

Acquainted With the Night

ROBERT FROST

I have been one acquainted with the night.
I have walked out in rain—and back in rain.
I have outwalked the furthest city light.

I have looked down the saddest city lane.
I have passed by the watchman on his beat
And dropped my eyes, unwilling to explain.

I have stood still and stopped the sound of feet
When far away an interrupted cry
Came over houses from another street,

But not to call me back or say good-by;
And further still at an unearthly height,
One luminary clock against the sky

Proclaimed the time was neither wrong nor right.
I have been one acquainted with the night.

In the first example, "night" (the night sky) is treated abstractly by the astronomer. He analyzes it to such a degree that it becomes unreal to the poet who must make sensuous contact with the thing itself, the "literal" night, the concrete object. In the second example, the poet contemplates the night with such human excitement that he personifies it in the first two lines and in the next three apostrophizes it as though it were a loving partner to himself. In the third poem we have a simple analogy: the image of a certain night superimposed on the image of a beautiful girl. In the last example, "night" performs a different function. To begin to understand this image, that is, to become acquainted with this night, one must understand what all the events in the poem mean to the poetic "I." Then one must see that "night" is the one image which incorporates all the other images and events of the poem: the rain, the watchman, the cry, the dock, the "I."

What exactly does "night" mean in Frost's poem? Loneliness? Depression? The meaninglessness of existence? None of these exactly. A symbol is a complex word for which there exists no synonym. A symbolic poem in itself might be described as an intricately complex word which can never be successfully restated or defined: Its definition is itself, its meaning is the wordless revelation which it produces in the aware reader.

The above paragraph deliberately refused to reveal the meaning of the symbol "night." In essence, it said the meaning of the symbol could be stated only in a fourteen-line definition beginning "I have been one acquainted with the night"—a definition that probably seemed intentionally mystifying. But we need to remind ourselves that poetry is a way man has devised to see things straight and to say things straight. In a good poem an obscurity is generally the clearest possible way to express a very unclear reality. Symbols are often obscure and often suggest several meanings, sometimes contradictory. However, we must remember that they are among man's supreme attempts to give names to the Unnamed and to grapple with the Not-Yet-Known within himself and the universe. If symbols share some of the dimness of the Unknown, and if to one question they sometimes respond with four contradictory answers, that only testifies to the fact that they play at the frontiers of human consciousness where darkness, ambiguity, paradox, the irrational, and the miraculous make all the rules.

We have begun by emphasizing the difficulty of symbols. They *are* difficult and often impossible to fathom—but especially for the unskilled reader. To learn to be a skilled reader of symbols is to learn a second language, a language not of words, but of things. When one has mastered the fundamentals of this language, the difficulty of most symbols will be greatly diminished.

First of all, the "words" of this new language are images, that is, descriptions of things. These images, which we term "symbols," are grouped into two categories: (1) **traditional symbols,** which take their meanings from the age-old associations man makes between things and himself, and (2) **created symbols,** to which a single poet in the context of one or more poems, assigns a special, individual meaning.

Each of us has a little private language of associations. We see a picture in a magazine that reminds us of some childhood scene. We are overcome with sudden nostalgia, or revulsion, or a sense of loss. We read a description of a countryside and suddenly (if we allow ourselves to daydream) we remember a certain day, the sound of friends' voices, the warmth of the sun—all our remembered feelings. When we are with close friends, the merest mention of a person, an event, or a scene can instantaneously communicate a certain set of feelings, if these friends have shared those experiences with us. Unfortunately, however, these "insider" languages are restricted to small numbers of speakers and cannot be handed down to subsequent generations.

Yet there are many experiences common to whole civilizations, a number of them common to all mankind. They provide us with a vast store of symbols derived from man's struggles with weather, geography, other living things, and his own creations. A good reader, in the course of his education, becomes gradually more aware that a symbolic language exists as a part of the human tradition. It is his by right of membership in the human race. Of course, each traditional symbol that appears in poetry is unique because no two poetic contexts are exactly alike. However, particular symbols usually operate within a traditionally limited area of significance. When we find a poet using "fire" symbolically we suspect that the human passions *might* be involved, and we may safely rule out the idea of, for example, drowsiness. When we read about a rose, a response of tenderness and affection *might* be appropriate and not, for example, the sense of an obstacle to be overcome. What immediately follows is a short glossary of traditional symbols. Much of it will seem quite obvious to the reader. It is by no means complete and attempts to identify only the most frequently used symbols. It will be useful to the reader only if he keeps constantly in mind the following three provisos:

1. First and most important, these "definitions" locate only the general areas of human experience that these images illuminate. In an actual poetic context every symbol interacts with every other word and symbol and thereby transforms itself into a unique meaning. General areas of meaning may be roughly ascertained, nothing more.

2. Some symbols have multiple areas of meaning, many of them contradictory. In every case it is the total context that suggests the best interpretation.
3. This is a "glossary" of *images* used symbolically—not a glossary of *words*. The literal word "ice" does not have to appear in a poem in order to convey, for example, a sense of rigidity to the reader; phrases like "the frozen river" or "the crusted snow" do just as well.

A GLOSSARY OF TRADITIONAL SYMBOLS

Subject	Image	Area of Significance
Yearly Cycle	spring	birth, youth
	summer	maturity, vigor, accomplishment
	autumn	fruition, fulfillment; aging, preparation for death
	winter	death, emptiness
Daily Cycle	dawn	birth; enlightenment; deliverance from fear
	morning	youth; optimism
	afternoon	maturity, vigor, accomplishment
	sunset	death; mortal glory
	twilight	death, departure; mystery
	night	death; the unknown, frightening, desolate, erotic
Direction	up	toward spiritual, intellectual
	down	toward material, carnal
	east	toward one's origins
	south	toward sensuality; freedom from restraint; lush antiquity
	west	toward death; adventure
	north	toward wilderness; purity, moral repressiveness
Colors	white	purity, innocence; sickness, death
	black	sorrow; evil; death
	gray	mediocrity; sickliness
	red	sexual passion; anger; healthy spontaneity

Colors (cont.)	green	youth, vigor; the natural
	yellow	sickliness, weakness
	purple	royality, riches
	blue	truth
Celestial Bodies and Weather	sun	reason, enlightenment; success; elemental energy, life
	moon	mystery; the imagination
	stars	the immutable law of the universe
	comets and meteors	unnaturalness; portents of disaster
	wind	the power of Nature; inspiration
	storm clouds	the hostility of Nature
	rain	gloom; the restoration of Life (after draught)
	snow	cessation of life; transformation of the familiar, purity
	fog	uncertainty
	sky	freedom
	water	quenching of thirst; death by drowning; purification
	fire	passion, love; destructiveness; purification
	ice	rigidity; death; compulsive symmetry
	light	reason
Topography	earth	source of life; gross materiality
	ocean	the ungovernable; the Infinite, eternity; the unfathomable
	forest	natural chaos, freedom, spontaneity
	mountain	obstacle; mystical illumination
	desert	sterility, impotence
	running water	life
	river	the course of a human life
	cavern	sexual luxuriousness, lust
	cliff	crucial situation; inaccessibility
	spring (fountain)	mysterious source of energy or inspiration
Animal Life	quadrupeds	spontaneous animality
	reptiles	deceit, horror
	horse	masculinity

Animal Life (cont.)	bull	masculinity, violence
	bee	industriousness, conscientiousness, citizenship
	ant	industriousness, anonymity
	grasshopper, cricket	carefree improvidence
	bird (wild)	freedom
	bird (caged)	unjust imprisonment, violation of nature
	rat, mouse	secretiveness
	lion, tiger	predatoriness
	spider	predatoriness; calculation; artistry
Man's Environment and Tools	home, house	a family, an inhabitant; a mother's body
	city, town	rationality, order, restraint; anonymity (city only); human fulfillment
	journey, road	the course of human life
	fireplace, hearth	security
	knife	violence
	candle	illumination; the "fire of life"
	ship	any social unit, a society, a government
	theatrical stage	the human condition; man's "role playing"
	bread	nourishment for the body
	wine	nourishment for the mind
	clock	measurement of time, calculation, rationality
Vegetative Life	trees	vegetative life of Nature; the organic principle
	rose	femininity, youth, tenderness; briefness; beauty
	sunflower, heliotrope	devotion to source of life
	violet	shy delicacy
	blades of grass	human lives
	roots	source, origin
	blossom	first indication of fertility
	fruit	fruition, fulfillment
	falling leaves	human deaths
	dark woods	confusion, abandonment

Man's Body	hair	sexuality
	forehead	intelligence
	eyes	consciousness
	lips	power to speak; power to kiss
	hands, arms	strength, power to manipulate environment
	breast	compassion; consolation (female); security
	heart	love
	genitals	aggression (male); life-giving power
	spleen	melancholy, bad temper
	legs, feet	locomotion
	blood	life, mortality

As is apparent from these examples, *a symbol is an object that means what it does or what it makes man feel.* A dark forest may make a man lose his way and so has become a symbol for loss of direction and confusion. The dawn dispels the night and thereby dispels all that the symbol "night" suggests—death, the unknown, the frightening. Frost's poem "Acquainted with the Night" is not too difficult to speak about in general terms. Nothing in the poem should deter us from reading the following main images as traditional symbols: night, rain, city, light, and clock. If we do so we may arrive at this approximate meaning:

"I have known desolate moments ('night'), moments of complete gloom ('rain'), when I have lost all touch with order ('city') and reason ('light'). I could never explain this feeling to anyone; I wanted human contact but I knew I was alone. By the most exact reasoning I could manage, by the most thorough calculation ('clock'), I knew my existence was valueless. (Thus my instinct to despair was corroborated by my reason.)"

Paraphrases such as this, though often useful in literary discussions, have their obvious shortcomings. In this general reading of the symbolic course of the poem, we lose the richness of the symbols, for in prose we are forced to abstract and to specify. A single abstract word, "gloom," is made to represent the countless sensations and emotions we feel when walking in the rain—and *all* those multiple, unspecific feelings are present in Frost's image. Also omitted is the literal setting within which these symbols operate:

the man walking alone, meeting another man whose business it is to protect the sleeping town from possibly dangerous, perhaps deranged prowlers, and the cry that for a moment he thinks may be for him but which only makes him realize how cut off he actually is from others. And finally, this "translation" has no way of conveying that one miraculous event—he sees a clock, a luminary (!) clock, that, like an existentialist philosopher, proclaims that the time is neither wrong nor right.

Our Glossary included only the most universal of traditional symbols. There are countless others that are either part of the traditional folklore of nations, have meaning within particular religions, or demand some sort of specialized knowledge. For example: Dylan Thomas takes many symbols from the folklore of his native Wales; Dante, Donne, and T. S. Eliot presuppose that their readers are versed in Christian symbolism; and Shakespeare and Shelley make extensive use of various scientific (and pseudo-scientific) symbols. Such poetry is more difficult to understand at first, but the success of a symbol is not to be judged by its initial obscurity so much as by the richness, power, and resonance it produces within the reader who has worked on it long enough to grasp its implications. The following poem uses a "picture-word" taken from one of these specialized "languages"—Christian symbolism.

The poet Gerard Manley Hopkins begins quite simply with a simile, one of the oldest and most universal analogies: a caged bird as human confinement. If he had chosen to do so, he could have spoken purely symbolically and omitted the second line reference to man; we would have understood without much effort the human implications of the scene. As the poem proceeds, the parallel is neatly developed but then in line 12 a turn in the poem that many readers will find incomprehensible occurs.

The Caged Skylark

As a dare-gale skylark scanted in a dull cage
  Man's mounting spirit in his bone-house, mean house, dwells—
  That bird beyond the remembering his free fells;
This in drudgery, day-labouring-out life's age.

Though aloft on turf or perch or poor low stage,
  Both sing sometímes the sweetest, sweetest spells,
  Yet both droop deadly sómetímes in their cells
Or wring their barriers in bursts of fear or rage.

Not that the sweet-fowl, song-fowl, needs no rest—
Why, hear him, hear him babble and drop down to his nest,
  But his own nest, wild nest, no prison.

Man's spirit will be flesh-bound when found at best,
But uncumbered: meadow-down is not distressed
  For a rainbow footing it nor he for his bónes rísen.

Unless the reader is familiar with the traditional doctrine of the Resurrection of the Body—that at the end of the world the souls of all men will return to their graves to claim their bodies—he will not understand why "man's spirit will be flesh-bound when found at best." Unless he is familiar with the story of Noah, he will miss the (slight) symbolic reference to the rainbow—the sign of God's reconciliation with man. For orthodox Christians this strange, ancient image of bones rising from the earth symbolizes the healing of the split between soul and body and the reintegrating of the two elements of man into one perfect unit. In this transfigured body, the spirit (at least of the saved) would not regard the body as a cage, but as a rainbow—light, glorious, and mounting heavenward from the earth.

So far we have only mentioned the symbols that come ready-made to the poet's pen. They are the pre-existent idioms in which he may allow his thoughts and emotions to speak and reveal themselves to him and, ultimately, to us.

As in any language, however, some symbolic words grow old and lose their effectiveness, though the reality they once embodied may remain unchanged. Twentieth-century poets, especially, have recognized the need to reenergize the old symbolic languages or to reject them altogether and create symbols of their own. Wallace Stevens referred to this problem when he wrote "Of Modern Poetry" and said that a poem is the product of

. . . the mind in the act of finding
What will suffice. It has not always had
To find: the scene was set; it repeated what
Was in the script.
Then the theatre was changed
To something else. Its past was a souvenir.

Poets have always occasionally worked with **created symbols** but never has this form been practiced more systematically than in this century during which man has felt his "theatre" drastically changed and so much of his past become useless souvenirs.

A generation after Hopkins, another poet took up this theme of man's spiritual confinement. Rainer Maria Rilke (1875–1926) chose to fashion a new symbol for an old reality. As you read this poem, compare it with the poem by Hopkins.

The Panther

His sight from always pacing past the bars
Has grown so weary it sees only blurs.
To him the only things that are are bars
And beyond a thousand bars no universe.

The soft pace of that supple-massive stride
Turns in a miniature circle, like a dance
Of strength about some middle point inside
Of which, benumbed, some powerful will stands.

At times the curtains of his eyes may part,
Soundlessly.—Then will an image enter,
Pass through tense quiet limbs, search out the heart,
And die once it has reached the center.

A panther, caged or otherwise, was never a traditional symbol for man's imprisoned spirit. When used, it has customarily suggested violence and malevolence, but Rilke, by weaving it into a very particular context, has changed all that. A comparison of the two poems reveals some very striking divergences. Rather than a denizen of the heavens, Rilke chose an animal that in his natural state is a sharp-eyed roamer among earthly things; what its captivity violates is its right to see and grasp things and possibilities. The poet's treatment of his subject matter clearly indicates that this extended image of a pacing jungle cat has a human meaning. Unlike the skylark, this image was not handed down to the poet by tradition, but was shaped by him to fit his needs. Furthermore, no traditional religious symbol implies an end to this imprisonment. The consciousness, worn down by mechanical routine, loses its ability to see beyond its artificial prison; when a real external thing presents itself, the mind, conditioned by its long captivity, has no power or will to grasp it.

Traditional symbolic languages are invaluable heritages. By means of such image-languages, and through the voices of its poets, whole civilizations have discovered meaning and identity for themselves. However, when a poet feels he can no longer use traditional symbols, he must either form new ones within the context of each poem as Rilke did, or create for himself an entire complex language of symbols that he will use throughout his poetry. Certain images, colors, characters, and events will recur as symbolic motifs and will change for the reader and gather richness in each new context. T. S. Eliot and Wallace Stevens made use of this masterful, though at first baffling, type of symbol. Poets like Blake and Yeats even went so far as to create entire mythologies as frames of reference for their poetry.

POEMS FOR COMPARISON

[A] *The Smitten Fair*

A woman, pure and gentler than a rose,
Ofttimes hides stormier passions than she shows,
  For Venus' Son, whene'er his pow'r is chid,
  Strikes deepest her by whom he's most forbid
Ah, she must languish in Love's bitt'rest throes
Who was more soft-sequester'd than the rose.

[B] *The Sick Rose*

O Rose, thou art sick!
The invisible worm
That flies in the night,
In the howling storm,

Has found out thy bed
Of crimson joy,
And his dark secret love
Does thy life destroy.

* * *

[A] *Birches*

When I see birches bend to left and right
Across the lines of straighter darker trees,
I like to think some boy's been swinging them.
But swinging doesn't bend them down to stay.
As ice-storms do. Often you must have seen them
Loaded with ice a sunny winter morning
After a rain. They click upon themselves
As the breeze rises, and turn many-colored
As the stir cracks and crazes their enamel.
Soon the sun's warmth makes them shed crystal shells
Shattering and avalanching on the snow-crust—
Such heaps of broken glass to sweep away
You'd think the inner dome of heaven had fallen.
They are dragged to the withered bracken by the load,
And they seem not to break; though once they are bowed
So low for long, they never right themselves:
You may see their trunks arching in the woods
Years afterwards, trailing their leaves on the ground
Like girls on hands and knees that throw their hair
Before them over their heads to dry in the sun.

But I was going to say when Truth broke in
With all her matter-of-fact about the ice-storm
I should prefer to have some boy bend them
As he went out and in to fetch the cows—
Some boy too far from town to learn baseball,
Whose only play was what he found himself,
Summer or winter, and could play alone.
One by one he subdued his father's trees
By riding them down over and over again
Until he took the stiffness out of them,
And not one but hung limp, not one was left
For him to conquer. He learned all there was
To learn about not launching out too soon
And so not carrying the tree away
Clear to the ground. He always kept his poise
To the top branches, climbing carefully
With the same pains you use to fill a cup
Up to the brim, and even above the brim.
Then he flung outward, feet first, with a swish,
Kicking his way down through the air to the ground.
So was I once myself a swinger of birches.
And so I dream of going back to be.
It's when I'm weary of considerations,
And life is too much like a pathless wood
Where your face burns and tickles with the cobwebs
Broken across it, and one eye is weeping
From a twig's having lashed across it open.
I'd like to get away from earth awhile
And then come back to it and begin over.
May no fate willfully misunderstand me
And half grant what I wish and snatch me away
Not to return. Earth's the right place for love:
I don't know where it's likely to go better.
I'd like to go by climbing a birch tree,
And climb black branches up a snow-white trunk
Toward heaven, till the tree could bear no more,
But dipped its top and set me down again.
That would be good both going and coming back.
One could do worse than be a swinger of birches.

[B] *Birches*

When I see birches bend to left and right
Across the lines of upright darker trees,
I wonder if the summer bent them low.
But all the wholesome passions of the sun .
Cannot compare with ice storms that attack
The birches in the flowering of their youth
And load them with the indifference of heaped ice
So that, forgetful of their skyward goal,
They droop with unshorn locks to the dull earth.
Though they seem not to break, once they are bowed
So low for long, they never right themselves.
We each must walk a long and weary road
From out the rose-strewn meadows, where at dawn
We launched our journey, onward to the heights
Where each path ends in peace, each soul in solace,
And, as we walk, the drooping roadside birches
Tempt us with the indifference of their pose
Like girls who have no better thing to do
Than dawdle and enjoy a summer's day.
They tempt us to forget the day is short
And that only the night is made for rest.
They tempt us from the business of perfection
These trees who choose to yield to nature's power:
Life should be made of sterner stuff than this!
I should prefer to have some upright youth
Be put in charge of straightening bent birches,
Some youth, right-thinking and industrious,
Whose only thought was marching straight and true
(Who never turned his gaze to left or right)
And never let the deceptive loveliness
Of field and valley lure his steadfast soul.

One by one, I'd have him straighten trees;
Not one would droop or dawdle by the road
Its long unsightly top slouching to Earth.
But all at strict attention would salute

Us heavenward marchers as we passed them by.
So was I once a straightener of birches.
And so I dream of going back to be.
But autumn twilight now hems me about—
I leave my work to younger hands and hearts.
And yet I'd like to leave the road awhile
And try my hand at straightening trees again
And then resume my journey to the stars.
May no fate willfully misunderstand me
And half grant what I wish and snatch me away
Not to return. The road's the direction of life:
I've never entertained a deviant thought.
I've spent my life correcting men's mistakes:
The willing with one timely word grew straight,
The rebels I have wrenched into respect:
One could do worse than be a straightener of birches.

ADDITIONAL READINGS

A Valediction: Forbidding Mourning

JOHN DONNE

As virtuous men pass mildly away,
  And whisper to their souls to go,
Whilst some of their sad friends do say,
  "The breath goes now," and some say, "No";

So let us melt and make no noise,
  No tear-floods nor sigh-tempests move;
'Twere profanation of our joys
  To tell the laity our love.

Moving of the earth brings harms and fears;
  Men reckon what it did and meant;
But trepidation of the spheres,
  Though greater far, is innocent.

Dull sublunary lovers' love,
  Whose soul is sense, cannot admit
Absence, because it doth remove
  Those things which elemented it.

But we by a love so much refined
  That ourselves know not what it is,
Inter-assurèd of the mind,
  Care less eyes, lips, and hands to miss.

Our two souls, therefore, which are one,
  Though I must go, endure not yet
A breach, but an expansión,
  Like gold to airy thinness beat.

If they be two, they are two so
  As stiff twin compasses are two;
Thy soul, the fixed foot, makes no show
  To move, but doth if the other do.

And though it in the center sit,
  Yet when the other far doth roam,
It leans and hearkens after it,
  And grows erect as that comes home.

Such wilt thou be to me, who must,
  Like the other foot, obliquely run;
Thy firmness makes my circle just,
  And makes me end where I begun.

Dover Beach

MATTHEW ARNOLD

The sea is calm to-night.
The tide is full, the moon lies fair
Upon the straits;—on the French coast the light
Gleams and is gone; the cliffs of England stand,
Glimmering and vast, out in the tranquil bay.

Come to the window, sweet is the night-air!
Only, from the long line of spray
Where the sea meets the moon-blanched land,
Listen! you hear the grating roar
Of pebbles which the waves draw back, and fling,
At their return, up the high strand,
Begin, and cease, and then again begin,
With tremulous cadence slow, and bring
The eternal note of sadness in.

Sophocles long ago
Heard it on the Aegaean, and it brought
Into his mind the turbid ebb and flow
Of human misery; we
Find also in the sound a thought,
Hearing it by this distant northern sea.

The Sea of Faith
Was once, too, at the full, and round earth's shore
Lay like the folds of a bright girdle furled.
But now I only hear
Its melancholy, long, withdrawing roar,
Retreating, to the breath
Of the night-wind, down the vast edges drear
And naked shingles of the world.

Ah, love, let us be true
To one another! for the world, which seems
To lie before us like a land of dreams,
So various, so beautiful, so new,
Hath really neither joy, nor love, nor light,
Nor certitude, nor peace, nor help for pain;
And we are here as on a darkling plain
Swept with confused alarms of struggle and flight,
Where ignorant armies clash by night.

l. 28. *shingles:* pebble beaches.

Sonnet 73

WILLIAM SHAKESPEARE

That time of year thou mayst in me behold
When yellow leaves, or none, or few, do hang
Upon those boughs which shake against the cold,
Bare ruined choirs, where late the sweet birds sang.
In me thou see'st the twilight of such day
As after sunset fadeth in the west,
Which by and by black night doth take away,
Death's second self, that seals up all in rest.
In me thou see'st the glowing of such fire
That on the ashes of his youth doth lie,
As the death-bed whereon it must expire
Consumed with that which it was nourished by.
  This thou perceiv'st, which makes thy love more strong,
  To love that well which thou must leave ere long.

l. 4. *choirs:* part of the church where the choir sings.

The End of the World

ARCHIBALD MACLEISH

Quite unexpectedly as Vasserot
The armless ambidextrian was lighting
A match between his great and second toe
And Ralph the lion was engaged in biting
The neck of Madame Sossman while the drum
Pointed, and Teeny was about to cough
In waltz-time swinging Jocko by the thumb—
Quite unexpectedly the top blew off:

And there, there overhead, there, there, hung over
Those thousands of white faces, those dazed eyes,
There in the starless dark the poise, the hover,
There with vast wings across the canceled skies,
There in the sudden blackness the black pall
Of nothing, nothing, nothing—nothing at all.

The Death of the Ball Turret Gunner

RANDALL JARRELL

From my mother's sleep I fell into the State,
And I hunched in its belly till my wet fur froze.
Six miles from earth, loosed from its dream of life,
I woke to black flak and the nightmare fighters.
When I died they washed me out of the turret with a hose.

My Folly

LIZBETH ORLEY FIRTH

Alas, the journey's over!
  Master, no gifts I bring.
I bring no gifts but empty hands
  To thee at evening.

When lovely April blossomed,
  I too was young with Spring,
Under the heaven's gladsome blue
  I sang as young birds sing.

Spring is the time for gladness,
  And not the time for toil—
The work of Harvest comes apace;
  Naught now my joy should spoil!

I slept through all the summer,
  And when the workmen came
Into Thy vineyard singing hymns,
  My cheek it burnt with shame.

My hands they were too tender
To pluck the fruit of Life.
They could not hold the basket up
Nor wield the pruning knife.

No work was mine in Autumn,
And now the Winter's here.
My locks are white as Winter snows;
My life like Winter drear.

Alas! Dear God, have patience:
A weak soul trembling stands
And places all her hopes and fears
Within Thy loving Hands.

The Road Not Taken

ROBERT FROST

Two roads diverged in a yellow wood,
And sorry I could not travel both
And be one traveler, long I stood
And looked down one as far as I could
To where it bent in the undergrowth;

Then took the other, as just as fair,
And having perhaps the better claim,
Because it was grassy and wanted wear;
Though as for that the passing there
Had worn them really about the same,

And both that morning equally lay
In leaves no step had trodden black.
Oh, I kept the first for another day!
Yet knowing how way leads on to way,
I doubted if I should ever come back.

I shall be telling this with a sigh
Somewhere ages and ages hence:
Two roads diverged in a wood, and I—
I took the one less traveled by,
And that has made all the difference.

Do Not Go Gentle into that Good Night

DYLAN THOMAS

Do not go gentle into that good night,
Old age should burn and rave at close of day;
Rage, rage against the dying of the light.

Though wise men at their end know dark is right,
Because their words had forked no lightning they
Do not go gentle into that good night.

Good men, the last wave by, crying how bright
Their frail deeds might have danced in a green bay,
Rage, rage against the dying of the light.

Wild men who caught and sang the sun in flight,
And learn, too late, they grieved it on its way,
Do not go gentle into that good night.

Grave men, near death, who see with blinding sight
Blind eyes could blaze like meteors and be gay,
Rage, rage against the dying of the light.

And you, my father, there on the sad height,
Curse, bless, me now with your fierce tears, I pray.
Do not go gentle into that good night.
Rage, rage against the dying of the light.

The Lamb

WILLIAM BLAKE

Little Lamb, who made thee?
Dost thou know who made thee?
Gave thee life, and bid thee feed,
By the stream and o'er the mead:
Gave thee clothing of delight,
Softest clothing, wooly, bright;

Gave thee such a tender voice,
Making all the vales rejoice?
  Little Lamb, who made thee?
  Dost thou know who made thee?

  Little Lamb, I'll tell thee,
  Little Lamb, I'll tell thee:
He is callèd by thy name,
For he calls himself a Lamb.
He is meek, and he is mild;
He became a little child.
I a child, and thou a lamb,
We are callèd by his name.
  Little Lamb, God bless thee!
  Little Lamb, God bless thee!

The Tiger

WILLIAM BLAKE

Tiger! Tiger! burning bright
In the forests of the night,
What immortal hand or eye
Could frame thy fearful symmetry?

In what distant deeps or skies
Burnt the fire of thine eyes?
On what wings dare he aspire?
What the hand dare seize the fire?

And what shoulder, and what art,
Could twist the sinews of thy heart?
And when thy heart began to beat,
What dread hand? and what dread feet?

What the hammer? what the chain?
In what furnace was thy brain?
What the anvil? what dread grasp
Dare its deadly terrors clasp?

When the stars threw down their spears
And watered heaven with their tears:
Did he smile his work to see?
Did he who made the Lamb make thee?

Tiger! Tiger! burning bright,
In the forests of the night:
What immortal hand or eye,
Dare frame thy fearful symmetry?

Blood-Thirst

ANONYMOUS (EARLY TWENTIETH CENTURY)

The Tiger prowleth through the world,
  He seeketh everywhere,
For only living souls can sate
  This Hunter's hell-wracked care.

He prowleth through the peaceful bower
  And through the busy street
But prowleth, too, the little Lamb
  On sore and aching feet.

The Tiger at the heart's door waits,
  He waits his prey to win;
The Lamb waits, too, and cries aloud
  That Man may let Him in.

About the weak and wavering will
  The Tiger stealthy creeps
And at th' unguarded moment springs—
  The Lamb He also leaps.

The Lamb He also longs for blood
  'Tis a pain that sorely smarts.
He too is mad with a thirst for souls,
  For the blood of contrite hearts.

The Tiger shambles through the world,
  He has the whole world trod,
Concealed in pseudo-reasoning
  That shouts "There is no God!"

Concealed in thickets of desire
  In bowers of sin and lust,
In accents soft the Tiger lisps
  "There is no God to trust."

But through the day and through the night
  O'er desert, sky and flood,
The Lamb he prowls on aching feet
  Athirst for the taste of blood.

Ah Sun-flower!

WILLIAM BLAKE

Ah, Sun-flower, weary of time,
Who countest the steps of the sun,
Seeking after that sweet golden clime
Where the traveller's journey is done;

Where the youth pined away with desire,
And the pale virgin, shrouded in snow,
Arise from their graves, and aspire
Where my Sun-flower wishes to go.

[IV]

The Sense of Sound

The profit of rhyme is that it drops seeds of a sweeter and more luxuriant rhyme, and of uniformity that it conveys itself into its own roots in the ground out of sight.

WHITMAN: Preface to *Leaves of Grass*

We have seen how words can produce mental images, how carefully arranged word-clusters can project objects upon an internal screen, and how the mind's eye can recognize and make meaningful relationships out of these objects. But it is not only our sense of sight that participates in the act of poetry. A second sense, which we will now examine, provides another, very different, dimension to our experience of poems. One is tempted to call it the sense of hearing, but this makes the subject deceptively simple. For one thing, the "hearing" involved in poetry is a very restricted and specialized activity because, of all the sounds audible to the human ear, poetry utters only the *sounds* of *words*. He who reads aloud, furthermore, senses these sounds of words in two distinct parts of his body: his mouth and his ears. Even if he is reading silently his vocal apparatus regularly responds to the words with miniature tensions and expansions, and his mind imagines the sound of his voice pronouncing the syllables. In this chapter, therefore, we will consider the sound of poetry as a product of an intricate two-part process, the *formation* of sounds by the mouth and the *recognition* of sounds by the ear.

THE FEELING OF SOUNDS

When we speak we actually feel in our mouths the sounds we are making. An unbelievably complex set of nerves is activating an equally complex set of throat, mouth, and face muscles. We shape our vocal instrument, then force air out of our lungs up through this adjustable cavern. The result is a *phoneme,* a simple sound element. The English language has approximately forty-five different phonemes which include the so-called "long" and "short" forms of vowels and the many variations of consonant pronunciations, like the three sounds of "g" in the phrase "the *G*erman *g*un barrage."

The following is a chart of verbal sound-values. Most of the rest of this section illustrates and comments upon this chart. The meanings associated with the various sounds, or phonemes, are only the most obvious and most traditional ones. Like the Glossary of Traditional Symbols, this chart is only a preliminary guide and *not* a set of laws. As we shall soon see, the context—that final judge of interpretation—rules over the meanings of sounds as it does over the meanings of symbols. As you glance over this chart, you will note that in the first section vowels are classified, in the second, consonants. The vowels are arranged according to the length of controlled breath used in their pronunciation, from the long rounded "ō"—made with open teeth and rounded lips—to the short closed "a" and "i"—made tightly up against the teeth with a little burst of breath. The consonants, too, take much of their sound value from the shaping action of the mouth and so are also arranged according to the ease or effort involved in producing them. "W" and "y" are called semi-vowels because they are really the sounds "o͞o" and "ē" slipped quickly in before another vowel. Then from the *liquids* to the *plosives* (as in "ex-plosives") we pass a spectrum of sounds from the smoothest to the most staccato—from, for example, the soft "r" which is made without any contact between tongue, teeth, and lips, to the "t" which is produced by first compressing the air in the mouth with the tongue held tightly against the front palate, and then allowing the tongue to drop abruptly, thus letting the air spurt out under the upper teeth.

A CHART OF VERBAL SOUND VALUES

Type	Sounds	Traditional English Meaning-Associations
Long vowels (rounded)	ō as in "no"; o͞o as in "o͞oze"; diphthong ou as in "cow"	Resonance, completion, solemnity
Long vowels (straight)	ā as in "day"; ē as in "bee"; diphthongs ī as in "sigh" and oi as in "joy"	Brightness, speed, unimpeded motion
Short vowels (open)	ä as in "alms"; ô as in "raw"; o as in "hot"; o͝o as in "foot"	Depth, hollowness
Short vowels (closed)	a as in "act"; e as in "set"; u as in "up"; i as in "kick"	Sharpness, narrowness, precision
Semi-vowels	w, y	Speed; smoothness
Liquids	l, r	Smoothness; sleepiness; calm, warmth, and brightness; r, if "rolled"; often suggests harshness
Nasals	m, n	Sleepiness; inarticulate sound; hollowness
Sibilants	s, z	Whispering, hissing; sliding motion
Fricatives	h, f, v, sh, th, ch, j	Impeded motion, friction, rubbing, scraping

Plosives (voiced)	b, d, "hard" g	In general: the dull impact of two objects Specifically: b = a dull collision or explosion d = the striking of something g = the scraping of something
Plosives (unvoiced)	p, t, k, "hard" c	In general: the sharp impact of two objects Specifically: p = small sharp collision or explosion t = the striking and piercing of something k and "hard" c = the cutting and piercing of something

The subject of sound value has been argued for centuries, mainly by two extreme factions, which we might call the "Musicalists" and the "Dictionary People." The Musicalists hold that each vowel and each consonant contains in itself some musical property, some magical essence, that it distills into the words and lines of a poem. On the other extreme, the Dictionary People, most of them rigidly rational and just a little tone deaf, maintain that sound has virtually no effect on our experience of a poem and that a poem consists of word meanings alone. Fortunately, we are not obliged to take sides in this controversy. Sounds, as we shall soon see, are in themselves unspecific properties that words just happen to possess. The sentence you have just read contained fourteen "s" sounds and yet it had no special sound value. If its meaning had suggested the sound of whispering, for example, then the meaning could activate the sound, as in: "I heard in the silence the sound of her swift, whispered syllables." This sentence contains only seven "s" sounds. To convey a specific sound value, two conditions must be present: (1) a sound must occur at least twice (usually in accented syllables and often peppered throughout a whole passage), and (2) the meaning of the passage must coincide with the traditional meaning-associations of the sound and thus *activate* it.

Repeated sounds, when they work as literary devices, may appear in any of three forms. If the sound is a vowel, the device is called **assonance,** as in the following passage:

Like as the waves make towards the pebbled shore,
So do our minutes hasten to their end;
Each changing place with that which goes before . . .
[SHAKESPEARE, from *Sonnet 60*]

If it is a repetition of consonants, especially at the beginning of words, it is called **alliteration.** For example:

When to the sessions of sweet silent thought
I summon up remembrance of things past,
I sigh the lack of many a thing I sought,
And with old woes new wail my dear time's waste . . .
[SHAKESPEARE, from *Sonnet 30*]

And if it is a repetition of a whole syllable, that is, a combination of a vowel(s) and consonant(s), it is called **internal rhyme.** For example:

If the true concord of well tunëd sounds,
By unions married do offend thine ear . . .
[SHAKESPEARE, from *Sonnet 8*]

The poet's use of repeated sounds may be merely to create an affective unifying texture or it may, like a *motif* in music, help develop an idea with which it is associated. Or again it may be directly imitative of the action or sound it describes. We will now see examples of each of these functions.

Tennyson's interesting little fragment, "The Eagle," begins quite imitatively, with the sharp "c"s cutting into the granite cliff; but in the second line it initiates a short set of harmonies that have no special relation to the word-meanings.

The Eagle

He clasps the crag with crooked hands;
Close to the sun in lonely lands,
Ring'd with the azure world, he stands.

The wrinkled sea beneath him crawls;
He watches from his mountain walls
And like a thunderbolt he falls.

In this small poem we have examples of all the sound devices we have already discussed: assonance (close, lonely; sea, beneath); alliteration (the four "c"s and the one "k" within lines 1–2; lonely, lands; watches, walls); and internal rhyme (ring'd, wrinkled). The result of all these interconnections of sounds is a neatly unified sound-picture completed at line 5. As the bird suddenly detaches himself from the crag, line 6 unexpectedly detaches itself from the placid sound harmonies of the poem. (Note that, though the "th" of "thunderbolt" and the "f" of "falls" appear in such words as "the" and "from," articles and one-syllable prepositions are almost never—and pronouns only occasionally—stressed enough to contribute to a poem's sound-texture.)

Of course any single element in a poem, be it metaphor, sound, or rhyme, if used for its own sake produces such notable monstrosities as the following regrettable imitation of Poe written by a contemporary admirer of his style, Thomas Holley Chivers (1807–1858). (Note especially the sputtering "b"s of the first three lines and the word "diaphane," chosen no doubt more for its "d" than for its sense.)

Thus she stood on the arabesque borders
  Of the beautiful blossoms that blew
On the banks of the crystalline waters,
  Every morn in the diaphane dew.
The flowers, they were radiant with glory,
  And shed such perfume on the air,
That my soul, now to want them, feels sorry,
  And bleeds for my Lily Adair.

The second poetic use of sound is in creating a motif. In music such motifs can be woven virtually anywhere into the score and as musical *leitmotifs* be used throughout the piece to remind the listener of some preceding musical idea. In poetry the motif's scope is much more limited. It must occur in a single connected passage, use the same sound or type of sound, and usually contain an emphatic, strongly positioned word which specifies its meaning. The rightness we feel in reading the sonorous beginning of Tennyson's "Morte D'Arthur" is largely caused by a careful use of sound motifs:

> So all day long the noise of battle roll'd
> Among the mountains by the winter sea,
> Until King Arthur's table, man by man,
> Had fallen in Lyonness about their lord,
> King Arthur; then, because his wound was deep,
> The bold Sir Bedivere uplifted him,
> Sir Bedivere, the last of all his knights,
> And bore him to a chapel nigh the field,
> A broken chancel with a broken cross,
> That stood on a dark strait of barren land.
> On one side lay the ocean, and on one
> Lay a great water, and the moon was full.

This passage is itself a transition between events not narrated in the poem and the mystical departure of the king to the "island-valley of Avilion." The word "battle" is the key to the dominant sound motif—a set of about ten percussive "b"s that echo through the passage like the "noise of battle" in the mountains and like the bitter memories of the heart-sick king who not only had to watch, but also participate in, the destruction of his own country. This motif is interlaced with several other minor but contributory sound-textures that might be felt to bear some slight meaning. The "l"s of line 4 might seem to suit the stillness of a field of slain soldiers; the "ch"s might suggest the effort of carrying the king to the chapel. With the last two lines the orchestration changes. The calm long and open vowels dominate. The drums of battle have faded away and something resembling the sound of oboes, eerie yet strangely consoling, has taken their place.

In Shelley's dramatic poem of world revolution, *Prometheus Unbound,* the hero, chained to a rock by Jupiter, the spirit of tyranny, has as his female counterpart Human Love, whose name in the poem is Asia. As the inevitable moment for the liberation of mankind approaches, her sister, Panthea, sees a strange transformation coming over Asia. The consort of Prometheus now reveals herself as Love, the principle of Life, long ago born from the sea (as the myth of Aphrodite, goddess of love, specifies).

As you read this passage notice that the sound texture of "l"s radiates like a gentle warmth from that one central specifying word "love" (line 11). Panthea speaks:

How thou art changed! I dare not look on thee;
I feel but see thee not. I scarce endure
The radiance of thy beauty. Some good change
Is working in the elements, which suffer
Thy presence thus unveiled. The Nereids tell
That on the day when the clear hyaline
Was cloven at thy uprise, and thou didst stand
Within a veined shell, which floated on
Over the calm floor of the crystal sea,
Among the Egean isles, and by the shores
Which bear thy name; love, like the atmosphere
Of the sun's fire filling the living world,
Burst from thee, and illumined earth and heaven
And the deep ocean and the sunless caves
And all that dwells within them; till grief cast
Eclipse upon the soul from which it came:
Such art thou now; nor is it I alone,
Thy sister, thy companion, thine own chosen one,
But the whole world which seeks thy sympathy.
Hearest thou not sounds i' the air which speak the love
Of all articulate beings? Feelest thou not
The inanimate winds enamoured of thee? List!

Notice that almost every possible permutation of "l" is included in this paragraph, combined with a significant use of rich long vowel assonances. By itself this passage is perhaps too rich, too lush for most tastes, but in the context of the entire poem it forms a very effective set piece.

The third and final use of verbal sound is in the imitation of actual auditory sounds. Every language is full of imitative words, technically termed *onomatopoetic* or *echoic* words:

to whisper: *sussurrare* (Italian); *chuchoter* (French)
to howl: *aular* (Spanish); *heulen* (German)
to slap: *schiaffare* (Italian); *claquer* (French)

These words are used so commonly that their imitative function —their appeal to the ear—is almost entirely submerged in their meaning, like the word "bomb," which in its original Latin form, *bombus,* meant simply "boom!" Poets have had to use extreme ingenuity in choosing words that, though they may not *mean* the sound, may still provide the sound effects for a passage.

Walt Whitman, never quite given his due as a careful craftsman, created some remarkable sound effects in the fifteenth section of his "Song of Myself." The passage is a long sequence of human activities out of which, he says, "I weave the song of myself." The first conspicuous use of verbal sound occurs in this line:

> The carpenter dresses his plank, the tongue of his
> foreplane whistles its wild ascending lisp.

The particular action is designated in the first clause; its sound appears in the last clause. The tool seems to strike the plank at the "p" of "foreplane," slip upward through the echoic, descriptive word "whistles" and its alliterative neighbor "wild," become more loudly sibilant in "ascending," and finally run off the top of the plank with the little plosive pop at the end of "lisp."

Further on, we come to a pair of lines that have a uniquely physical impact:

> The malform'd limbs are tied to the surgeon's table,
> What is removed drops horribly in a pail . . .

As in the preceding example, the action is designated in the first clause and the sound occurs in the second. Few examples in English of American poetry better illustrate the power of verbal sound when it is fitted to a conceptual image. The revulsion we feel when reading these lines is, first of all, caused by the impersonal treatment of the subject. No person is described as acting. Limbs are tied to a table. Something is being done to something. We seem to turn away in horror as something "is removed." (Even the language keeps its clinical distance from the real event.) Then, to climax this electrifying little scene, this human debris "drops horribly in a pail." The sounds of "p"s and "b" leave very little to the auditory imagination.

Whitman also used internal rhyme to good advantage in this

section. We hear the "repeated layers" being arranged in the repeated smack-pack of this line:

> The crew of the fish-smack pack repeated layers
> of halibut in the hold . . .

And in the next example when we read the word "change," we might remember that we have been given notice of it in advance by the sound of the word "train."

> As the fare-collector goes through the train he gives
> Notice by the jingling of loose change . . .

In the matter of sound, as in the matter of symbol, the one final determinant is the meaning of the words and of the overall context. One might speak of the "smooth liquids" of the first line of the following stanza, the "energetic fricatives" of the second and the "gloomy nasals" of the third and fourth lines.

> Thus brilliantly the sly, three doves
> Would glide and gambol in the waves
> While murm'rings filled the bord'ring groves
> Like the moans from out graves.

This is, of course, something of a sound-transcript of the first stanza of Lewis Carroll's "Jabberwocky":

> 'Twas brillig, and the slithy toves
> Did gyre and gimble in the wabe:
> All mimsy were the borogoves,
> And the mome raths outgrabe.

As Humpty Dumpty explains, the meaning of a poem often exists quite independently from its sounds.

In the next illustration, notice how appropriate are the sound values of the following lines. Note the cold clang of the "c"s, the bitter taste of "wreathed" and "tedious," the alliterative "s"s and "d"s of the second stanza that gradually, by means of the soft plosive "g"s allow the sound harmonies to resolve themselves in the "w"s and "l"s of the final lines.

> Cold are the cares that call from yonder hills
> Colder the cancelled lives that groan beneath,

And colder still the brazen cups, all wreathed
  With tedious gloom, that Suffering fills.

. . .

Yet much remains—to weave a solemn strain
That lingering sadly—slowly dies away
Daily departing with departing day
A pure green glimmer o'er a distant plain
Where windy wastelands lure the exiles feet . . .
  Such such is life—

The original poem from which these sounds are copied has quite a different effect when read. It was written by the popularizer of the limerick, Edward Lear.

Cold are the crabs that crawl on yonder hills,
Colder the cucumbers that grow beneath,
And colder still the brazen chops that wreathe
  The tedious gloom of philosophic pills!

. . .

Yet much remains—to weave a solemn strain
That lingering sadly—slowly dies away,
Daily departing with departing day.
A pea-green gamut on a distant plain
When wily walruses in congress meet—
  Such such is life—

We have examined the use of various types of sound to produce unifying textures, sound motifs, and imitative effects. There is yet another important set of effects almost entirely determined by the degree of ease or effort involved in producing the verbal sounds. Before we get to this we should establish a necessary point: The printed line of poetry is quite different from the spoken line. First of all, the printed line has gaps between each word that may not exist as a breathing pause in the spoken line. For example, the following lines from Drayton are in printed form:

Since there's no help, come let us kiss and part;
Nay, I have done, you get no more of me,
And I am glad, yea glad with all my heart
That thus so cleanly I myself can free . . .

In its spoken form it might be transcribed as follows:

Sincether'snohelp comeletuskissandpart
Nay Ihavedone yougetnomoreofme
AndIamglad yeagladwithallmyheart
ThatthussocleanlyImyselfcanfree

As the syntax of a living language demands, the continuum of speech stops, there is a pause, the speaker takes a breath, and then the flow continues. Between breaths there is only continuous, varying sound. *Only syllables matter in the sound of poetry.* It is the mind of the listener that pieces out the separable words. To the mouth and to the ear there is only breathed air, vibrating into sound.

In English there are certain individual words that are difficult to articulate. If they are to be pronounced precisely, they demand that the oral apparatus shape itself for one syllable, then quickly rearrange itself for the next. A few examples might be: flintlock, spendthrift, splitpea, toothsome. Of course we know how to utter these words (just as any German knows how to say *Korkpfropf,* "cork stopper"). Nevertheless our mouth is made to work overtime on these combinations of consonants. Because the spoken line is a continuum interrupted only by occasional breathing pauses, the letters at the end of one word usually slide, or collide, into the first letters of the next word.

If consonants appear in difficult combinations, the effect (as always) is governed by the meaning of the words. It may be harsh and contorted or it may be precise, depending upon the context. In Ezra Pound's "Hugh Selwin Mauberley," the poet uses colliding consonants to express his outrage and disgust at the needless waste of life in World War I. (The slanted lines indicate the difficult sound transitions between closely-placed syllables.)

There died a myriad,
And of the best, among them,
For an old/bitch/gone in the teeth
For a botch/ed/civilization,

Charm, smiling at the good/mouth,
Quick eyes gone under earth/'s lid,

For two gross of broken statues,
For a few thousand/battered/books

Compare the above excerpt with this dreamily smooth stanza taken from Tennyson's "The Lotus-Eaters." With only a few minor exceptions, the poet has succeeded in placing vowels or liquid or nasal consonants between every sharp consonant.

They sat them down upon the yellow sand,
Between the sun and moon upon the shore;
And sweet it was to dream of Fatherland,
Of child, and wife, and slave; but evermore
Most weary seemed the sea, weary the oar,
Weary the wandering fields of barren foam.
Then some one said, "We will return no more";
And all at once they sang, "Our island home
Is far beyond the wave; we will no longer roam."

The purpose of this section has been to reemphasize the fact that we read with our total being. A poem is not just something which operates a cerebral slide-projector in our heads. It makes us shape our breath into words that we must bite down upon or spit out or luxuriously taste or release in whispers. In an age when most of the talking is done for us by our electronic talking-boxes, and when the mechanical pandemonium of our streets has left audible no man-made sound below a shout, we have come to forget how infinitely various and expressive the human voice can be. We have grown shy even of our own voices. Most of us cannot, even in privacy, recite a poem without a twinge of stage fright.

But it is only the best and most acute sort of self-consciousness that will make us aware of the poem as an action, a bodily-mental event which we, in our total and lonely persons, perform.

POEMS FOR COMPARISON

[A] *With Rue My Heart Is Laden*

With rue my heart is laden
  For golden friends I had,

For many a rose-lipt maiden
And many a lightfoot lad.

By brooks too broad for leaping
The lightfoot boys are laid;
The rose-lipt girls are sleeping
In fields where roses fade.

[B] *With Gloom My Heart Is Heaped*

With gloom my heart is heaped
For I've had many a friend
But lasses, perfume-steeped,
And quick lads have their end.

By brooks too wide for leaping
Th' athletic lads were buried;
The maids, when Death came creeping,
To separate graves were hurried.

* * *

[A] from *The Eve of St. Agnes*

Then by the bedside, where the dim, grey moon
Shed a mild and silver dusk, he lightly placed
A bench and, then half anguish'd, threw thereon
A cloth of gold, red, black (each interlac'd.)

. . .

And still she slept in azure-lidded sleep,
In blanchèd covers, smooth and lavender'd,
While he from forth the closet brought a heap
Of sugar'd apple, grapes, and plum, and gourd;
With jams more sooth than heavy curd,
And lustrous syrups made with cinnamon;
Manna and dates, in argosy transferr'd
From Egypt; and rare morsels, every one,
From far off Samarcand to hilly Lebanon.

These delicates be put with glowing hand
On silver plates and in containers bright
Of carven gold: luxurious they stand
In the remote stillness of the night,
Loading the chamber with a perfume light.

[B] from *The Eve of St. Agnes*

Then by the bed-side, where the faded moon
Made a dim, silver twilight, soft he set
A table, and, half-anguish'd, threw thereon
A cloth of woven crimson, gold, and jet:—

. . .

And still she slept an azure-lidded sleep,
In blanchèd linen, smooth and lavender'd,
While he from forth the closet brought a heap
Of candied apple, quince, and plum, and gourd
With jellies soother than the creamy curd,
And lucent syrops, tinct with cinnamon;
Manna and dates, in argosy transferr'd
From Fez; and spiced dainties, every one,
From silken Samarcand to cedar'd Lebanon.

These delicates he heaped with glowing hand
On golden dishes and in baskets bright
Of wreathèd silver: sumptuous they stand
In the retired quiet of the night,
Filling the chilly room with perfume light.—

THE MEASURED RECURRENCE OF SOUNDS

By **rhyme** we generally mean **end rhyme**—the recurrence of a similar sound at the end of two or more lines. Since rhymed endings for English words are, in normal conversation, fairly infrequent, whenever they do occur they capture the attention immediately. Only the extraordinary catches the reader's attention. Such classical languages as Greek and Latin, with their special sets of verb and noun endings, were overstocked in easy end rhymes and so their poets almost never used rhyming in their poetry.

With rhyme, the sound value, that is, the ease or effort of sound production or the imitative nature of the words, is less important than the timing of the recurrence. If end rhyme is used, someone listening to poetry has no difficulty in sensing the length of a line: it is the length of syllable-sounds extending between one sound and its recurrence. If the timing is regular and all lines are rhymed, there is a sense of completeness about the poem, of ideas carefully cut, measured, and fitted within a container of sound. Landor's four-line poem "On His Seventy-Fifth Birthday" illustrates how sound can measure out a tight container for ideas:

I strove with none; for none was worth my strife,
  Nature I loved, and next to Nature, Art;
I warmed both hands before the fire of life,
  It sinks, and I am ready to depart.

This type of rhyme was refined during the early Italian Renaissance and was used as the organizing principle for that unit of verse that we still call by its Italian name, **stanza** (room), so named because it is a container of sound, used to house the ideas and sentiments of the poet. Most traditional verse forms were designed during the Renaissance. The most durable of them, the sonnet (which we will study in a later chapter) is a one-stanza construction. John Donne referred to the containing function of this type of rhymed verse when he wrote that

. . . if no piece of chronicle we prove,
We'll build in sonnets pretty rooms . . .

Rhyme is thus a style of poetic architecture that the ear "sees" and "measures." When every line rhymes with some other line, the stanza is totally closed and self-contained. In the following example the architecture is a bit more loosely designed:

Out upon it! I have loved
  Three whole days together;
And am like to love thee more,
  If it prove fair weather.

Unlike lines 2 and 4, the end syllables of lines 1 and 3 are not linked in rhyme and seem to move off, like adjacent galleries from the main "stanza-room."

This conflict between freedom and confinement—between unrhymed and rhymed lines—can be used to great advantage by the conscious craftsman. One excellent example is Edward FitzGerald's translation from the Persian, "The Rubáiyát of Omar Khayyám." Here the stanza form is modeled upon the symbolic architecture of the universe, a "battered Caravanserai" [inn]/whose Portals are alternate Night and Day . . ." Life in this "inn" is a beautiful confinement, a prisoning room which only pleasure can make endurable. Note how the first two lines of each stanza rhyme tightly, the third "free" line seems to rebel, and the last line slips the final bolt into place:

– 21 –

Ah, my Belovéd, fill the Cup that clears
Today of past Regrets and future Fears:
  Tomorrow!—Why, Tomorrow I may be
Myself with Yesterday's Sev'n thousand Years.

– 48 –

A Moment's Halt—a momentary taste
Of Being from the Well amid the Waste—
  And Lo!—the phantom Caravan has reached
The Nothing it set out from—Oh, make haste!

– 71 –

The Moving Finger writes, and, having writ,
Moves on; nor all your Piety nor Wit
  Shall lure it back to cancel half a Line,
Nor all your Tears wash out a Word of it.

– 72 –

And that inverted Bowl they call the Sky,
Whereunder crawling cooped we live and die,
  Lift not your hands to *It* for help—for It
As impotently moves as you or I.

Again and again throughout the poem, FitzGerald uses the unrhymed third line to suggest a flicker of hope and the recurrent fourth line to emphasize the fate of mortal man, trapped in a lovely garden where a wise man stifles within himself every hope for freedom and immortality.

As a general rule, the more a single rhyme is repeated in a stanza the more "closed" the "room" is and the more oppressive the effect can be. (But, as in all things, the context to a large degree determines the meaning of a rhyme pattern.) A parody of this doleful, tolling, repetitive rhyme occurs at the end of the last stanza of Lewis Carroll's "White Knight's Song."

> And now, if e'er by chance I put
>   My fingers into glue,
> Or madly squeeze a right-hand foot
>   Into a left-hand shoe,
> Or if I drop upon my toe
>   A very heavy weight,
> I weep, for it reminds me so
> Of that old man I used to know—
> Whose look was mild, whose speech was slow,
> Whose face was very like a crow,
> With eyes, like cinders, all aglow,
> Who seemed distracted with his woe.
> Who rocked his body to and fro,
> And muttered mumblingly and low,
> As if his mouth were full of dough,
> Who snorted like a buffalo—
> That summer evening long ago
>   A-sitting on a gate.

The effect of these lines is far from tearful nostalgia. As the White Knight persists in his rhymes we first undergo boredom, then irritation, and finally resign ourselves to the absurdity of the situation. After eleven straight "ō" rhymes, the forgetful gentleman remembers to close the stanza with the correct rhyme and links the last line's "gate" with the sixth line's "weight." He may be infuriatingly dull, but he never forgets a rhyme.

We have mentioned as special effects produced by rhyme: a sense of room-like containment, freedom within restraints, and oppressive closeness. Another important effect of rhyme—perhaps its original function—is that of inducing a trance-like mood. On his voyage home from the siege of Troy, Ulysses and his men make a stop at the land of the Lotus-Eaters. As soon as his men taste this narcotic plant, they lose all desire for home. Tennyson described this dream-like state in lush lines and repetitive rhymes:

There is sweet music here that softer falls
Than petals from blown roses on the grass,
Or night-dews on still waters between walls
Of shadowy granite, in a gleaming pass;
Music that gentlier on the spirit lies,
Than tired eyelids upon tired eyes;
Music that brings sweet sleep down from the blissful skies.
Here are cool mosses deep,
And through the moss the ivies creep,
And in the stream the long-leaved flowers weep,
And from the craggy ledge the poppy hangs in sleep.

The last three lines come, one after the other, like drowsy afterthoughts, long-drawn sighs, each two syllables longer than the preceding one and each punctuated with the same rhyming syllable.

The most important element of a rhyming word is, of course, its meaning. We are quite familiar with rhymes that have complementary meanings, for example: light, bright, white; smash, clash, dash, crash, and so forth. In 1711, Alexander Pope, at the angry age of twenty-three, launched his career with "An Essay On Criticism" in which he satirized, among other things, this tired, resourceless use of rhyming sounds with conventional "rhyming" meanings:

. . . ten low words oft creep in one dull line:
While they ring round the same unvaried chimes,
With sure returns of still expected rhymes;
Where'er you find "the cooling western breeze,"
In the next line, it "whispers through the trees";
If crystal streams "with pleasing murmurs creep,"
The reader's threatened (not in vain) with "sleep" . . .

The essence of wit is surprise and the wittiest poetry written by Pope and his contemporaries was based on the skillful use of the unexpected. Part of the acid sharpness of Pope's verse was due to his frequent use of line endings which rhymed in sound but clashed in meaning as in the first lines of his "Essay On Man":

> . . . leave all meaner things
> To low ambition and the pride of kings.

"Meaner things" are not usually associated with "the pride of kings," but Pope paradoxically declares that they should be. In his "Satirical Elegy on the Death of a Late Famous General," Jonathan Swift sharpened his bite with an unexpected rhyme:

> His Grace! impossible! what, dead!
> Of old age too, and in his bed!

Several generations later, Lord Byron, a great admirer of eighteenth-century wit, pushed rhyme to its most comic extremes in his rambling satire *Don Juan* (pronounced Don Jōō′-an). Here is the education which his doting mother meticulously planned for the hero:

– 38 –

Sagest of women, even of widows, she
  Resolved that Juan should be quite a paragon,
And worthy of the noblest pedigree
  (His sire was a Castile, his dam from Aragon).
Then for accomplishments of chivalry,
  In case our lord the king should go to war again,
He learned the arts of riding, fencing, gunnery,
And how to scale a fortress—or a nunnery.

– 39 –

But that which Donna Inez most desired,
  And saw into herself each day before all
The learned tutors whom for him she hired,
  Was that his breeding should be strictly moral:
Much into all his studies she inquired,
  And so they were submitted first to her, all,
Arts, sciences, no branch was made a mystery
To Juan's eyes, excepting natural history.

– 40 –

The languages, especially the dead,
  The sciences, and most of all the abstruse,

The arts, at least all such as could be said
  To be the most remote from common use,
In all these he was much and deeply read;
  But not a page of anything that's loose,
Or hints continuation of the species,
Was ever suffered, lest he should grow vicious.

– 41 –

His classic studies made a little puzzle,
  Because of filthy loves of gods and goddesses,
Who in the earlier ages raised a bustle,
  But never put on pantaloons or bodices;
His reverend tutors had at times a tussle,
  And for their *Aeneids, Iliads,* and *Odysseys,*
Were forced to make an odd sort of apology,
For Donna Inez dreaded the mythology.

The sheer audacity of Byron's wit was in part made possible by the witlessness of conventional "trees, breeze—creep, sleep" rhyming in which the ear, accustomed to that old drone, lets the mind drift off to a low level of consciousness. If the mind expects a pleasant doze during a reading of *Don Juan,* it is tickled awake by such unusual three-syllable rhymes as "paragon"—"Aragon"—"war again," and is snapped bolt upright by rhymes of clashing meanings, such as "gunnery" and "nunnery" and by such juxtapositions as "gods and goddesses" who went without "pantaloons or bodices."

In a sense, Byron's poem is a satire on rhyme, not rhyme as a (mere) literary device, but rhyme as a symptom of a culture that feared the unexpected and sought refuge in the status quo of customary ideas, customary emotions, and customary solutions to terrifyingly new problems. If end rhymes invariably square off the "rooms," that is the stanzas of poems, then the architecture of English poetry will have to be quite restricted. Few languages are, in fact, less endowed with exact rhymes. If a poet needs to use "love" in a rhyme he has only five word-ideas to link with it and he must bravely choose between "dove," "above," "shove," "glove," and "of." The same number of tired rhymes exist for "life" and only one word, "breath," properly rhymes with "death." English poetry, it would seem, finds itself boxed into a very sleepy little room.

In the following two excerpts try to guess the rhyme that the poet used. Remember to resist all temptations to be interesting or imaginative:

Something to love, some tree or flow'r
Something to nurse in my lonely ——,
Some dog to follow, where'er I roam,
Some bird to warble my welcome ——,
Some tame gazelle, or some gentle ——:
Something to love, oh, something to love!

At midnight, in the month of June,
I stand beneath the mystic ——.
An opiate vapour, dewy, dim,
Exhales from out her golden ——,
And, softly dropping, drop by drop,
Upon the quiet mountain ——,
Steals drowsily and musically
Into the universal ——.
The rosemary nods upon the grave;
The lily lolls upon the ——;
Wrapping the fog about its breast,
The ruin moulders into —— . . .

The first poem was written by Thomas Haynes Bayly (1797–1839), the second by Edgar Allan Poe (1809–49), and the rhymes were: for the first poem—bow'r, home, dove; for the second (entitled with ironical aptness "The Sleeper")—moon, rim, top, valley, wave, rest.

Now try another exercise in rhyme-guessing:

The bustle in a house
The morning after death
Is solemnest of industries
Enacted upon ——

The sweeping up the heart,
And putting love away
We shall not want to use again
Until ——

We are immediately stymied. The only exact rhyme for "death" is "breath." We could rhyme that line only by rewriting it something like: "Enacted without breath," but that still does not make very good sense. The last rhyme is easier: "Until the Judgment Day" would do quite well, that is, would put the final touches to a very trite little poem. Fortunately the poet, Emily Dickinson, had something else in mind. In the fourth line her choice was "earth," which only remotely rhymes with "death." This sort of rhyme is called **slant rhyme.** It does not rhyme exactly with the preceding sound; it reproduces it but with that little element of dissonance which makes the reader take notice. Slant rhyme was also her solution to the last line. Readers, especially during the mid-nineteenth century, would expect some exact rhyme like "day" to round off such a neat little moralizing stanza. But the poet's choice for the final rhyme was "eternity," an unexpected sound which draws attention to an unexpected idea. "Until" generally implies an event, but "eternity" suggests a condition or state of timelessness. In Dickinson's surprising connection of the two notions we must imagine eternity as a timeless event, a moment that occurs outside of time.

Such use of slant rhymes immeasurably increases a poet's choice of rhymed line endings and, as in Dickinson's case, recovers for the language of poetry that indispensable element of surprise. In the last half century most good poetry, if rhymed at all, has relied heavily on the use of slant rhymes. For further examples see Thomas' "Refusal to Mourn . . ." (p. 7), and Ransom's "Bells for John Whitesides' Daughter" (p. 20).

POEMS FOR COMPARISON

[A] *The Woodspurge*

The wind flapped loose, the wind was still,
Shaken out dead from tree and dale:
I had walked on at the wind's will,—
I sat now in the windless vale.

Between my knees my forehead was,—
My lips, drawn in, uttered no Woe!

My hair was over in the grass,
My naked ears heard the day go.

My eyes, wide open, had the sight
Of some ten weeds to fix upon;
Among those few, out of the light,
The woodspurge flowered, three cups in one.

From perfect grief there need not come
Wisdom or even memory:
Of my life's learning here's the sum,—
The woodspurge has a cup of three.

[B] *The Woodspurge*

The wind flapped loose, the wind was still,
Shaken out dead from tree and hill:
I had walked on at the wind's will,—
I sat now, for the wind was still.

Between my knees my forehead was,—
My lips, drawn in, said not Alas!
My hair was over in the grass,
My naked ears heard the day pass.

My eyes, wide open, had the run
Of some ten weeds to fix upon;
Among those few, out of the sun,
The woodspurge flowered, three cups in one.

From perfect grief there need not be
Wisdom or even memory:
One thing then learnt remains to me,—
The woodspurge has a cup of three.

* * *

[A] *As Imperceptibly as Grief*

As imperceptibly as grief
The summer lapsed away,—
Too imperceptible, at last,
To prompt the least dismay.
A quietness distilled,
As twilight star-bestrewn,
Or Nature, spending with herself
Sequestered afternoon.
The dusk drew earlier in,
The morning foreign shone,—
A courteous, yet harrowing grace,
As guest who'd restless grown.
And thus, without a wing,
Or service of a hull,
Our summer made her light escape
Into the beautiful.

[B] *As Imperceptibly as Grief*

As imperceptibly as grief
The summer lapsed away,—
Too imperceptible, at last,
To seem like perfidy.
A quietness distilled,
As twilight long begun,
Or Nature, spending with herself
Sequestered afternoon.
The dusk drew earlier in,
The morning foreign shone,—
A courteous, yet harrowing grace,
As guest that would be gone.
And thus, without a wing,
Or service of a keel,
Our summer made her light escape
Into the beautiful.

ADDITIONAL READINGS

Sunday Morning

WALLACE STEVENS

– i –

Complacencies of the peignoir, and late
Coffee and oranges in a sunny chair,
And the green freedom of a cockatoo
Upon a rug mingle to dissipate
The holy hush of ancient sacrifice.
She dreams a little, and she feels the dark
Encroachment of that old catastrophe,
As a calm darkens among water-lights.
The pungent oranges and bright, green wings
Seem things in some procession of the dead,
Winding across wide water, without sound.
The day is like wide water, without sound,
Stilled for the passing of her dreaming feet
Over the seas, to silent Palestine,
Dominion of the blood and sepulcher.

– ii –

Why should she give her bounty to the dead?
What is divinity if it can come
Only in silent shadows and in dreams?
Shall she not find in comforts of the sun,
In pungent fruit and bright, green wings, or else
In any balm or beauty of the earth,
Things to be cherished like the thought of heaven?
Divinity must live within herself:
Passions of rain, or moods in falling snow;
Grievings in loneliness, or unsubdued
Elations when the forest blooms; gusty
Emotions on wet roads on autumn nights;
All pleasures and all pains, remembering

The bough of summer and the winter branch.
These are the measures destined for her soul.

– iii –

Jove in the clouds had his inhuman birth.
No mother suckled him, no sweet land gave
Large-mannered motions to his mythy mind.
He moved among us, as a muttering king,
Magnificent, would move among his hinds,
Until our blood, commingling, virginal,
With heaven, brought such requital to desire
The very hinds discerned it, in a star.
Shall our blood fail? Or shall it come to be
The blood of paradise? And shall the earth
Seem all of paradise that we shall know?
The sky will be much friendlier then than now,
A part of labor and a part of pain,
And next in glory to enduring love,
Not this dividing and indifferent blue.

– iv –

She says, "I am content when wakened birds,
Before they fly, test the reality
Of misty fields, by their sweet questionings;
But when the birds are gone, and their warm fields
Return no more, where, then, is paradise?"
There is not any haunt of prophecy,
Nor any old chimera of the grave,
Neither the golden underground, nor isle
Melodious, where spirits gat them home,
Nor visionary south, nor cloudy palm
Remote on heaven's hill, that has endured
As April's green endures; or will endure
Like her remembrance of awakened birds,
Or her desire for June and evening, tipped
By the consummation of the swallow's wings.

– v –

She says, "But in contentment I still feel
The need of some imperishable bliss."

Death is the mother of beauty; hence from her,
Alone, shall come fulfilment to our dreams
And our desires. Although she strews the leaves
Of sure obliteration on our paths,
The path sick sorrow took, the many paths
Where triumph rang its brassy phrase, or love
Whispered a little out of tenderness,
She makes the willow shiver in the sun
For maidens who were wont to sit and gaze
Upon the grass, relinquished to their feet.
She causes boys to pile new plums and pears
On disregarded plate. The maidens taste
And stray impassioned in the littering leaves.

– vi –

Is there no change of death in paradise?
Does ripe fruit never fall? Or do the boughs
Hang always heavy in that perfect sky,
Unchanging, yet so like our perishing earth,
With rivers like our own that seek for seas
They never find, the same receding shores
That never touch with inarticulate pang?
Why set the pear upon those river-banks
Or spice the shores with odors of the plum?
Alas, that they should wear our colors there,
The silken weavings of our afternoons,
And pick the strings of our insipid lutes!
Death is the mother of beauty, mystical,
Within whose burning bosom we devise
Our earthly mothers waiting, sleeplessly.

– vii –

Supple and turbulent, a ring of men
Shall chant in orgy on a summer morn
Their boisterous devotion to the sun,
Not as a god, but as a god might be,
Naked among them, like a savage source.
Their chant shall be a chant of paradise,
Out of their blood, returning to the sky;
And in their chant shall enter, voice by voice,

The windy lake wherein their lord delights,
The trees, like serafin, and echoing hills,
That choir among themselves long afterward.
They shall know well the heavenly fellowship
Of men that perish and of summer morn.
And whence they came and whither they shall go
The dew upon their feet shall manifest.

– viii –

She hears, upon that water without sound,
A voice that cries, "The tomb in Palestine
Is not the porch of spirits lingering.
It is the grave of Jesus, where he lay."
We live in an old chaos of the sun,
Or old dependency of day and night,
Or island solitude, unsponsored, free,
Of that wide water, inescapable.
Deer walk upon our mountains, and the quail
Whistle about us their spontaneous cries;
Sweet berries ripen in the wilderness;
And, in the isolation of the sky,
At evening, casual flocks of pigeons make
Ambiguous undulations as they sink,
Downward to darkness, on extended wings.

A Black November Turkey

RICHARD WILBUR

Nine white chickens come
With haunchy walk and heads
Jabbing among the chips, the chaff, the stones
And the cornhusk-shreds,

And bit by bit infringe
A pond of dusty light,
Spectral in shadow until they bobbingly one
By one ignite.

Neither pale nor bright,
The turkey-cock parades
Through radiant squalors, darkly auspicious as
The ace of spades,

Himself his own cortège
And puffed with the pomp of death,
Rehearsing over and over with strangled râle
His latest breath.

The vast black body floats
Above the crossing knees
As a cloud over thrashed branches, a calm ship
Over choppy seas,

Shuddering its fan and feathers
In fine soft clashes
With the cold sound that the wind makes, fondling
Paper-ashes.

The pale-blue bony head
Set on its shepherd's-crook
Like a saint's death-mask, turns a vague, superb
And timeless look

Upon these clocking hens
And the cocks that one by one,
Dawn after mortal dawn, with vulgar joy
Acclaim the sun.

The Express

STEPHEN SPENDER

After the first powerful plain manifesto
The black statement of pistons, without more fuss
But gliding like a queen, she leaves the station.
Without bowing and with restrained unconcern
She passes the houses which humbly crowd outside,
The gasworks and at last the heavy page

Of death, printed by gravestones in the cemetery.
Beyond the town there lies the open country
Where, gathering speed, she acquires mystery,
The luminous self-possession of ships on ocean.
It is now she begins to sing—at first quite low
Then loud, and at last with a jazzy madness—
The song of her whistle screaming at curves,
Of deafening tunnels, brakes, innumerable bolts.
And always light, aerial, underneath
Goes the elate meter of her wheels.
Steaming through metal landscape on her lines
She plunges new eras of wild happiness
Where speed throws up strange shapes, broad curves
And parallels clean like the steel of guns.
At last, further than Edinburgh or Rome,
Beyond the crest of the world, she reaches night
Where only a low streamline brightness
Of phosphorus on the tossing hills is white.
Ah, like a comet through flames she moves entranced
Wrapt in her music no bird song, no, nor bough
Breaking with honey buds, shall ever equal.

Rondel

CHARLES ALGERNON SWINBURNE

Kissing her hair I sat against her feet,
Wove and unwove it, wound and found it sweet;
Made fast therewith her hands, drew down her eyes,
Deep as deep flowers and dreamy like dim skies;
With her own tresses bound and found her fair,
  Kissing her hair.

Sleep were no sweeter than her face to me,
Sleep of cold sea-bloom under the cold sea;
What pain could get between my face and hers?
What new sweet thing would love not relish worse?
Unless, perhaps, white death had kissed me there,
  Kissing her hair?

The Garden of Proserpine

CHARLES ALGERNON SWINBURNE

Here, where the world is quiet;
  Here, where all trouble seems
Dead winds' and spent waves' riot
  In doubtful dreams of dreams;
I watch the green field growing
For reaping folk and sowing,
For harvest-time and mowing,
  A sleepy world of streams.

I am tired of tears and laughter,
  And men that laugh and weep;
Of what may come hereafter
  For men that sow to reap;
I am weary of days and hours,
Blown buds of barren flowers,
Desires and dreams and powers
  And everything but sleep.

Here life has death for neighbor,
  And far from eye or ear
Wan waves and wet winds labor,
  Weak ships and spirits steer;
They drive adrift, and whither
They wot not who make thither;
But no such winds blow hither,
  And no such things grow here.

No growth of moor or coppice,
  No heather-flower or vine,
But bloomless buds of poppies,
  Green grapes of Proserpine,
Pale beds of blowing rushes
Where no leaf blooms or blushes
Save this whereout she crushes
  For dead men deadly wine.

Pale, without name or number,
  In fruitless fields of corn,
They bow themselves and slumber
  All night till light is born;
And like a soul belated,
In hell and heaven unmated,
By cloud and mist abated
  Comes out of darkness morn.

Though one were strong as seven,
  He too with death shall dwell,
Nor wake with wings in heaven,
  Nor weep for pains in hell;
Though one were fair as roses,
His beauty clouds and closes;
And well though love reposes,
  In the end it is not well.

Pale, beyond porch and portal,
  Crowned with calm leaves, she stands
Who gathers all things mortal
  With cold immortal hands;
Her languid lips are sweeter
Than love's who fears to greet her
To men that mix and meet her
  From many times and lands.

She waits for each and other,
  She waits for all men born;
Forgets the earth her mother,
  The life of fruits and corn;
And spring and seed and swallow
Take wing for her and follow
Where summer song rings hollow
  And flowers are put to scorn.

There go the loves that wither,
  The old loves with wearier wings;
And all dead years draw thither,
  And all disastrous things;
Dead dreams of days forsaken,

Blind buds that snows have shaken,
Wild leaves that winds have taken,
  Red strays of ruined springs.

We are not sure of sorrow,
  And joy was never sure;
To-day will die to-morrow;
  Time stoops to no man's lure;
And love, grown faint and fretful,
With lips but half regretful
Sighs, and with eyes forgetful
  Weeps that no loves endure.

From too much love of living,
  From hope and fear set free,
We thank with brief thanksgiving
Whatever gods may be
That no life lives for ever;
That dead men rise up never;
That even the weariest river
  Winds somewhere safe to sea.

Then star nor sun shall waken,
  Nor any change of light;
Nor sound of waters shaken,
  Nor any sound or sight;
Nor wintry leaves nor vernal,
Nor days nor things diurnal;
Only the sleep eternal
  In an eternal night.

The Bridge of Sighs

THOMAS HOOD

"Drowned! Drowned!" [*Hamlet*]

One more unfortunate,
  Weary of breath,
Rashly importunate,
  Gone to her death!

Take her up tenderly,
  Lift her with care!
Fashioned so slenderly—
  Young, and so fair!

Look at her garments
Clinging like cerements,
  Whilst the wave constantly
Drips from her clothing;
  Take her up instantly,
Loving, not loathing!

Touch her not scornfully!
Think of her mournfully,
  Gently and humanly—
Not of the stains of her;
All that remains of her
  Now is pure womanly.

Make no deep scrutiny
Into her mutiny,
  Rash and undutiful;
Past all dishonor,
Death has left on her
  Only the beautiful.

Still, for all slips of hers—
  One of Eve's family—
Wipe those poor lips of hers,
  Oozing so clammily.

Loop up her tresses
  Escaped from the comb—
Her fair auburn tresses—
Whilst wonderment guesses
  Where was her home?

Who was her father?
  Who was her mother?
Had she a sister?
  Had she a brother?
Or was there a dearer one
Still, and a nearer one
  Yet, than all other?

Alas! for the rarity
Of Christian charity
  Under the sun!
Oh! it was pitiful!
Near a whole city full,
  Home she had none.

Sisterly, brotherly,
Fatherly, motherly
  Feelings had changed—
Love, by harsh evidence,
Thrown from its eminence;
Even God's providence
  Seeming estranged.

Where the lamps quiver
So far in the river,
  With many a light
From window and casement,
From garret to basement,
She stood, with amazement,
  Houseless by night.

The bleak wind of March
  Made her tremble and shiver;
But not the dark arch,
  Or the black flowing river;

Mad from life's history,
Glad to death's mystery,
  Swift to be hurled—
Anywhere, anywhere
  Out of the world!

In she plunged boldly—
No matter how coldly
  The rough river ran—
Over the brink of it!
Picture it, think of it!
  Dissolute man!
Lave in it, drink of it,
  Then, if you can!

Take her up tenderly—
  Lift her with care!
Fashioned so slenderly—
  Young, and so fair!
Ere her limbs, frigidly,
Stiffen too rigidly,
  Decently, kindly,
Smooth and compose them;
And her eyes, close them.
  Staring so blindly!
Dreadfully staring
  Through muddy impurity,
As when with the daring
Last look of despairing
  Fixed on futurity.

Perishing gloomily,
Spurred by contumely,
Cold inhumanity,
Burning insanity,
  Into her rest!
Cross her hands humbly,
As if praying dumbly,
  Over her breast!

Owning her weakness,
  Her evil behavior,
And leaving, with meekness,
  Her sins to her Saviour!

Soliloquy of the Spanish Cloister

ROBERT BROWNING

– i –

Gr-r-r—there go, my heart's abhorrence!
  Water your damned flowerpots, do!
If hate killed men, Brother Lawrence,
  God's blood, would not mine kill you!
What? your myrtle bush wants trimming?
  Oh, that rose has prior claims—
Needs its leaden vase filled brimming?
  Hell dry you up with its flames!

– ii –

At the meal we sit together:
  Salve tibi! I must hear
Wise talk of the kind of weather,
  Sort of season, time of year:
Not a plenteous cork-crop; scarcely
  Dare we hope oak-galls, I doubt;
What's the Latin name for "parsley"?
  What's the Greek name for Swine's Snout?

– iii –

Whew! We'll have our platter burnished,
  Laid with care on our own shelf!
With a fire-new spoon we're furnished,
  And a goblet for ourself,
Rinsed like something sacrificial
  Ere 'tis fit to touch our chaps—
Marked with L. for our initial!
  (He-he! There his lily snaps!)

– iv –

Saint, forsooth! While brown Dolores
  Squats outside the Convent bank
With Sanchicha, telling stories,
  Steeping tresses in the tank,
Blue-black, lustrous, thick like horsehairs,
  —Can't I see his dead eye glow,
Bright as't were a Barbary corsair's?
  (That is, if he'd let it show!)

– v –

When he finishes refection,
  Knife and fork he never lays
Crosswise, to my recollection,
  As do I, in Jesu's praise.
I the Trinity illustrate,
  Drinking watered orange-pulp—
In three sips the Arian frustrate;
  While he drains his at one gulp.

– vi –

Oh, those melons? If he's able
  We're to have a feast! so nice!
One goes to the Abbot's table,
  All of us get each a slice.
How go on your flowers? None double?
  Not one fruit-sort can you spy?
Strange!—And I, too, at such trouble,
  Keep them close-nipped on the sly!

– vii –

There's a great text in Galatians,
  Once you trip on it, entails
Twenty-nine distinct damnations,
  One sure, if another fails:
If I trip him just a-dying,
  Sure of heaven as sure can be,
Spin him round and send him flying
  Off to hell, a Manichee?

– viii –

Or, my scrofulous French novel
  On gray paper with blunt type!
Simply glance at it, you grovel
  Hand and foot in Belial's gripe;
If I double down its pages
  At the woeful sixteenth print,
When he gathers his greengages,
  Ope a sieve and slip it in't?

– ix –

Or, there's Satan!—one might venture
  Pledge one's soul to him, yet leave
Such a flaw in the indenture
  As he'd miss till, past retrieve,
Blasted lay that rose-acacia
  We're so proud of! *Hy, Zy, Hine.*
'St, there's Vespers! *Plena gratiâ,*
  Ave, Virgo! Gr-r-r—you swine!

The Unknown Citizen (To JS/07/M/378 This Marble Monument Is Erected by the State)

W. H. Auden

He was found by the Bureau of Statistics to be
One against whom there was no official complaint,
And all the reports on his conduct agree
That, in the modern sense of an old-fashioned word, he was a saint,
For in everything he did he served the Greater Community.
Except for the War till the day he retired
He worked in a factory and never got fired,
But satisfied his employers, Fudge Motors Inc.
Yet he wasn't a scab or odd in his views,
For his Union reports that he paid his dues,
(Our report on his Union shows it was sound)
And our Social Psychology workers found
That he was popular with his mates and liked a drink.

The Press are convinced that he bought a paper every day
And that his reactions to advertisements were normal in every way.
Policies taken out in his name prove that he was fully insured,
And his Health-card shows he was once in hospital but left it cured.
Both Producers Research and High-Grade Living declare
He was fully sensible to the advantages of the Instalment Plan
And had everything necessary to the Modern Man,
A phonograph, a radio, a car and a frigidaire.
Our researchers into Public Opinion are content
That he held the proper opinions for the time of year;
When there was peace, he was for peace; when there was war, he went.
He was married and added five children to the population,
Which our Eugenist says was the right number for a parent of his generation,
And our teachers report that he never interfered with their education.
Was he free? Was he happy? The question is absurd:
Had anything been wrong, we should certainly have heard.

[V]

The Sense of Motion

True ease in writing comes from art, not chance,
As those move easiest who have learn'd to dance.
POPE: *An Essay on Criticism*

O body swayed to music, O brightening glance,
How can we know the dancer from the dance?
YEATS: *Among School Children*

Of the five traditional senses—sight, sound, touch, taste, and smell—only the first two have an immediate effect on our reading of a poem. The last three, if they affect the reader at all, do so only through the medium of word meanings. Psychologists point out, however, that we have many other separate senses: for example, our sense of hot and cold, our senses of pressure and of pain and of hunger, our sense of motion, and our sense of balance. Poetry appeals directly to the last two of these basic body-senses, and in the next two chapters we will examine why and how the act of poetry is dependent upon them.

THE DANCE OF WORDS

Man once believed that there was such a thing as inert, "dead" matter; that, if his microscope were powerful enough, he could see those final, indivisible particles called atoms, propelled about their business by immaterial forces called energies. Today our instruments are powerful enough to spy upon the atom, but what they have discovered has totally transformed our traditional idea of matter. We now know that atoms are composed of even tinier particles and that these whirling particles, which form the foundation of the universe, do not behave like matter as we know it, but like pure energy itself. This revolutionary discovery has prompted some scientists to say that matter is only energy moving in an infinite variety of speeds.

Like the universe, the microcosm (or little universe) of man also contains within it a vast variety of rhythms. Imagine a large clock shop in which a huge assortment of alarm clocks, watches, wall clocks, and grandfather clocks are all set at different speeds and chime at different intervals, some every half-minute, some every second, some every three hours. Imagine this concert of clanging, harmonizing, syncopating movements, and you will have some small idea of the rhythms that are going on at this very moment within your body. At widely different intervals you are breathing, your heart is pumping, your food is being digested and sent along the alimentary canal, your brain is emitting 100 to 1,000 microvolts, and your general metabolism is somewhere in its up and down twenty-four hour cycle. These internal movements are all closely connected with your perception of the outside world. A sudden change in your surroundings can immediately alter every one of these rhythmic actions.

We could not exist without these internal movements. But at the same time we could not survive long without our power to move ourselves in the external world. If we saw or heard an object, we would be helpless to do anything about it without our ability to move our bodies toward or away from it. Consider the many motions of the body that occur when we walk: our body weight shifts to our left foot and our right leg strides forward, the front muscles contracting and the back muscles automatically relaxing; the waist swivels; the right arm swings back as the right heel touches the floor; the head moves in opposition to the twist of the torso so as to remain facing the direction of the feet; and then the left foot is lifted and the whole process is reversed.

Man has known for many thousands of years that he can artificially stimulate internal and external movements in the body. The

Greeks believed that pitch and rhythm could work directly on the chemistry of the body and could calm, energize, put to sleep, or induce irrational acts of violence. Plato himself warned against the popularity of certain rhythms that were being imported from Asia Minor; they had, he said, a vicious effect upon all who listened. In the mid 1960s a clergyman from California gained some press notoriety by "unmasking" the Beatles as Communist agitators who used insidious "rock" rhythms to inflame young people to acts of lawlessness. Groups like the Beatles, he said, were intent upon sapping the moral strength of the non-Communist world by creating hysteria, inciting to violence, and generally mocking the dignity of their elders.

He was probably right, to a very limited degree: the rhythms of contemporary popular music create in audiences reactions uniquely different from those created by an evening of Viennese waltzes. Rhythms can leap the gap from instrument to audience. Rhythms, once released from a musical instrument, can play upon the internal rhythms of that vaster instrument, the human body/mind. To give a very simple example, tests have shown that if a repeated beat is faster than the normal breathing rate, a listener's breathing speeds up and becomes more shallow, the diaphragm muscles tighten, less oxygen enters the blood-stream, and he may show reactions of fear or excitement. Poetic rhythms, of course, work upon us less directly, but they still operate upon the same principle. "Heard melodies are sweet," Keats wrote, "but those unheard/Are sweeter." They may not appeal directly to the "sensual ear," as he said, but the haunting rhythms of his own poems prove how powerfully they can work despite their outward silence. One not very subtle example will demonstrate how a poetic rhythm can come off the page and begin pulsing within the reader:

How They Brought the Good News from Ghent to Aix

(16—)

– I –

I sprang to the stirrup, and Joris, and he;
I galloped, Dirck galloped, we galloped all three;

"Good speed!" cried the watch, as the gate-bolts undrew;
"Speed!" echoed the wall to us galloping through;
Behind shut the postern, the lights sank to rest,
And into the midnight we galloped abreast.

– 2 –

Not a word to each other; we kept the great pace
Neck by neck, stride by stride, never changing our place;
I turned in my saddle and made its girths tight,
Then shortened each stirrup, and set the pique right,
Rebuckled the cheek-strap, chained slacker the bit,
Nor galloped less steadily Roland a whit.

– 3 –

'Twas moonset at starting; but while we drew near
Lokeren, the cocks crew and twilight dawned clear;
At Boom, a great yellow star came out to see;
At Düffeld, 'twas morning as plain as could be;
And from Mecheln church-steeple we heard the half-chime,
So, Joris broke silence with, "Yet there is time!"

In this excerpt from Browning's spirited poem we quickly sense the dominant rhythm:

Ĭ spráng tŏ thĕ stírrŭp, ănd Jórĭs, ănd hé;

It is a rhythm which literally gallops away with the words of the poem, a rhythm so insistent that it constantly overrides the normal word accents of the lines. For example, in line 2 we would normally accent the proper noun "Dirck," and yet this name, though it is important and is carefully pronounced, is less important than the throbbing, galloping accent pattern of the line:

Ĭ gállopĕd, Dĭrck gállopĕd, wĕ gállopĕd ăll thrée;

Read as prose we would give accents to such words as "Speed!" (line 4), "sand" (line 5), the first "Neck" and "stride" (line 8), "chained" (line 11), "crew" and "dawned" (line 14); and we might not have heavily stressed such words as "yéllŏw" (line 15) and "chŭrch-stéeplĕ" (line 17). We simply do not speak English like that.

It is strange for one to pronounce English this way.

But, like the galloping horsemen, we can't slow down and speak Browning's lines with calm, rhetorical decorum. Once the pattern is created in the first line, it is repeated again and again throughout the poem. We sometimes call this sort of poetic line a *verse* because in Latin *versus* means a return or, in this case, a repeat of a rhythmical pattern. The line proceeds until a certain pattern of accents has been completed, then turns back to the left-hand margin and repeats that pattern. Prose (Latin *prorsus* = straight ahead) generally has no set rhythmical pattern and moves straight ahead from left to right and stops only when it reaches the right-hand limit of the page.

When we speak of accented syllables in a verse pattern we generally mean those syllables in a line which, because of their importance, we emphasize by raising the pitch and volume of our voice and by slightly lengthening the time we take in pronouncing them. Read this line aloud and listen to what your voice does to the words:

And into the midnight we galloped abreast.

First of all we know that almost all English words of more than one syllable have their accents firmly set—"into," "midnight," "galloped," "abreast"—this is the way we speak them, this is the way the dictionary marks them. Secondly we know that we usually do not emphasize conjunctions, articles, and pronouns. The accents which our voice thus gives the line are:

And I N to the M I D night we G A L loped a B R E A S T.

Rhythms may be divided according to their speed. *Fast rhythms* have a proportionately low number of accented syllables. *Moderate rhythms* have a fifty-fifty distribution of slowly-pronounced, accented syllables and quickly-skimmed-over unaccented syllables. *Slow rhythms,* obviously, have a preponderance of accents.

A fast rhythm, for example, rolls through these lines:

Like the leaves of the forest when Summer is green,
That host with their banners at sunset were seen:
Like the leaves of the forest when Autumn hath blown,

> That host on the morrow lay withered and strown.
>
> [Byron, from *The Destruction of Sennacherib*]

Note that in each line only four syllables are accented and usually two unstressed syllables lie between each accent.

In the next two lines the ratio is almost precisely even. Slight, or *hovering,* accent is marked (ˊ).

> Avenge, O Lord, thy slaughtered saints, whose bones
> Lie scattered on the Alpine mountains cold . . .
>
> [Milton, from *On the Late Massacre in Piemont*]

Accents back-to-back slow the next passage so that it must be read with a dark, ominous, stalking rhythm:

> On a starred night Prince Lucifer uprose.
> Tired of his dark dominion swung the fiend
> Above the rolling ball in cloud part screened,
> Where sinners hugged their spectre of repose.
> Poor prey to his hot fit of pride were those.
>
> [Meredith, from *Lucifer in Starlight*]

Note how lines 1, 3, and 5, with their predominance of back-to-back stressed syllables, are considerably slower to read than lines 2 and 4.

Spoken prose may be read at any speed the speaker wishes. If the subject matter is of no special urgency, he may accent syllables only in the most important words, for example, in the main nouns and verbs of each sentence. But if he thinks his audience must comprehend every word, he must slow down and stress each word, é-vén é-vér-ý sýl-lá-blé. However, most English poetry—at least from Chaucer to the early twentieth century—has used a built-in speed regulator called **meter.** Similar to a metronome, it provides a background beat with which the rhythms of the poem coincide or clash.

All over the earth people celebrate the primal realities of existence —birth, sex, community, death—with singing and dancing. In order to understand the origin and the nature of the term "poetic meter" we might for a moment imagine a sunny clearing rimmed with rocks and trees. The time could be now or twenty-thousand years ago, the place could be New York, Kenya, Mexico, or an Aegean island. A group of men and women assemble. Someone begins a song. Someone else claps in time with the voice of the singer. Soon others are singing, clapping, and moving their bodies in the rhythm of the song. The clapping is the speed regulator, the meter, of the folksong-dance.

In ancient Greece poets took this traditional type of singing dance and with great conscious art used it as a vehicle for lyric and dramatic poetry. When we talk about poetry, we still use the terms that come from these artists' adaptation of dance and poetry. We speak of a *foot* as the basic metrical unit, a set of syllables typically made up of a stressed syllable and one or two unstressed ones.

For example:

Ă vénge,|Ŏ Lórd|thy̆ sláugh|tĕred sáints,|whŏse bónes . . .

If a poet had written this line for a Greek tragedy, the obvious meter (which the words follow with precise regularity) would indicate how the singing dancers—the chorus—would move their feet. Each poetic foot would choreograph the action of each dancer's foot, the unstressed syllable being chanted as one foot was raised, the stressed syllable chanted when it struck the ground.

In English there are five main meters. In poems they serve as the background clapping, the basic beat to which the words of the poem dance. There are two fast feet which, of course, have a predominance of unaccented syllables:

1. The anapest (anapestic): ◡◡/ as in "rĭcŏchét"
2. The dactyl (dactylic): /◡◡ as in "rúnăwăy"

The moderate feet, having a fifty-fifty ratio of slow, emphatic stresses and quick, unstressed syllables are:

3. The iamb (iambic): ◡/ as in "ădvánce"
4. The trochee (trochaic): /◡ as in "báckwărd"

And finally the very slow foot that contains no unaccented syllable:

5. The spondee (spondaic): // as in "stóck-stíll"

Another valuable set of terms we also get from the Greeks are the names for line lengths:

monometer: one metrical unit (foot) per line;
dimeter: two metrical units (feet) per line;
trimeter: three metrical units (feet) per line;
tetrameter: four metrical units (feet) per line;
pentameter: five metrical units (feet) per line;
hexameter: six metrical units (feet) per line;
heptameter: seven metrical units (feet) per line.

For example, a line like Tennyson's:

He clasps the crag with crooked hands;

may be measured, or *scanned,* as follows:

Hĕ cláps|thĕ crág|wĭth cróok|ĕd hánds;

and may be termed *iambic tetrameter* because it contains four metrical units, each of them an iamb.

Two points should be remembered about meter. First of all, when we speak of the meter of a poem, we mean the overall meter. The clapping of hands does not constrain the inspired dancer from leaping up and clicking his heels, nor does the steady beat of an iambic tetrameter prevent a poet from playing infinite variations upon that basic meter. We must carefully distinguish between the meter of a line (the metronome sounding in the background) and the *rhythm* of the line, the actual dance-steps in which the words engage themselves and the reader. Secondly we must not demand scientific exactitude when we scan the rhythm of a line. Only a robot could accent his syllables with exactly the same stress and lower his voice to pronounce the unstressed syllables at a precisely regular pitch and speed. The scanning marks ˘ and / are useful, but only very rough indications of the rising and falling "dance" of words in a line.

As in all elements of poetry, a poet's choice of meter is determined by his subject matter and the general effect he is seeking. We will now examine the advantages and disadvantages of the five principal English meters in handling a specific subject, the passing of

King Arthur. If transposed into the fast meters, anapestic and dactylic, Tennyson's lines might sound like this:

Anapestic pentameter:

Through the day roll'd the noise of the furious battle of knights
'Mongst the echoing mountains and there by the cold winter sea,
Till the table of Arthur the King, every knight, every squire,
Had at last fallen dead in fair Lyonness, there by their lord.

Dactylic pentameter:

All through the day roll'd the noise of the furious battle
There 'mongst the mountains and there by the cold winter ocean,
Till the whole table of Arthur, each knight and each squire,
Lay in the field of fair Lyonness, fallen about him.

These rambling meters might be appropriate to the first line, but the sadly meditative tone of the rest of the passage, with its scene of the silent dead and the grief-stricken king, requires a less boisterous meter.

Trochaic pentameter is clearly an improvement:

All day long the noise of battle echo'd
'Mongst the mountains by the winter ocean,
Till King Arthur's table, every soldier,
Fell in Lyonness about their leader.

Yet, to ears accustomed to the sound of English rhythms, there seems to be something very contrived about this trochaic pentameter that reminds one of a melody out of a music box. And *spondaic meter,* freakishly sustained, paralyzes the line and makes this passage sound like a translation from the ancient Egyptian:

All day loud roll'd war's noise through hills by cold seas
Till Arthur's knights, each man, lay dead, slain there.

Tennyson's choice of meter was *iambic pentameter,* the most variable of English meters. In the next section we will focus on this type of line and on the rhythmic expressiveness that it makes possible.

POEMS FOR COMPARISON

[A] *The Last Word*

Creep into thy narrow bed,
Creep, and let no more be said!
Vain thy onset! all stands fast.
Thou thyself must break at last.

Let the long contention cease!
Geese are swans, and swans are geese.
Let them have it how they will!
Thou art tired; best be still.

They out-talked thee, hissed thee, tore thee?
Better men fared thus before thee;
Fired their ringing shot and passed,
Hotly charged—and sank at last.

Charge once more, then, and be dumb!
Let the victors, when they come,
When the forts of folly fall,
Find thy body by the wall!

[B] *The Last Word*

Thy narrow retreat beckons onward
  The hour for discussion is past
Thy conflict with fate was a failure.
  'T is thou who must break at the last.

Now let long contentions be ended!
  The geese they are swans, swans are geese.
However they will, let them have it!
  In thy weariness, best hold thy peace.

They out-talked thee, they hissed thee, they tore thee?
  Far better man fared thus before;

Let fly their loud shot and then vanished,
  Charged hotly—and then charged no more.

Then charge once again, and be silent!
  When the fortress of folly shall fall,
Then the victors that stand on the ruins
  Shall find thee fall'n dead by the wall!

* * *

[A] *La Belle Dame Sans Merci*

O what can ail thee, knight-at-arms,
  Alone and palely loitering?
The sedge has withered from the lake
  And all the birds have ceased to sing!

O what can ail thee, knight-at-arms,
  So haggard and so woe-begone?
The squirrel's granary is full,
  And all the harvest work's been done.

I see a lily on thy brow
  With anguish moist and fever dew,
And on thy cheeks a fading rose
  Appears to wither quickly, too.

I met a lady in the meads
  Full beautiful—a faery's child,
Her hair was long, her foot was light,
  And lovely shone her eyes, though wild.

I made a garland for her head,
  And bracelets too, and fragrant zone;
She look'd at me as she did love,
  And sweetly did she make a moan.

I set her on my pacing steed
  And nothing else saw all day long,
For sidelong would she bend, and sing
  What seem'd to be a faery's song.

She found me roots of relish sweet,
  And honey wild, and manna dew,
And sure in language strange she said—
  "I promise I will love thee true!"

She took me to her elfin grot,
  And there she wept and sighed full sore,
And there I shut her wild, wild eyes
  With kisses till she wept no more.

And there she lulléd me asleep
  And there I dreamed—ah, woe betide!
The latest dream I ever dreamed
  Upon the wintry mountainside.

I saw pale kings, and princes too,
  Pale warriors, death-pale were they all;
They cried—"La Belle Dame sans Merci
  Hath taken thee, Sir Knight, in thrall!"

I saw their starved lips in the gloam,
  With horrid warning gapéd wide,
And I awoke and found me here,
  Upon the wintry mountainside.

And this is why I sojourn here,
  Alone and palely loitering,
Although the sedge has left the lake,
  And all the birds have ceased to sing.

[B] *La Belle Dame Sans Merci*

O what can ail thee, knight-at-arms,
  Alone and palely loitering?
The sedge has withered from the lake,
  And no birds sing.

O what can ail thee, knight-at-arms,
  So haggard and so woe-begone?
The squirrel's granary is full,
  And the harvest's done.

I see a lily on thy brow
  With anguish moist and fever dew,
And on thy cheeks a fading rose
  Fast withereth too.

I met a lady in the meads,
  Full beautiful—a faery's child,
Her hair was long, her foot was light,
  And her eyes were wild.

I made a garland for her head,
  And bracelets too, and fragrant zone;
She looked at me as she did love,
  And made sweet moan.

I set her on my pacing steed
  And nothing else saw all day long,
For sidelong would she bend, and sing
  A faery's song.

She found me roots of relish sweet,
  And honey wild, and manna dew,
And sure in language strange she said—
  "I love thee true!"

She took me to her elfin grot,
  And there she wept and sighed full sore,
And there I shut her wild, wild eyes
  With kisses four.

And there she lulléd me asleep,
  And there I dreamed—ah, woe betide!
The latest dream I ever dreamed
  On the cold hill side.

I saw pale kings, and princes too,
  Pale warriors, death-pale were they all;
They cried—"La Belle Dame sans Merci
  Thee hath in thrall!"

I saw their starved lips in the gloam,
  With horrid warning gapéd wide,

And I awoke and found me here,
  On the cold hill's side.

And this is why I sojourn here,
  Alone and palely loitering,
Though the sedge is withered from the lake,
  And no birds sing.

THE IAMBIC PENTAMETER LINE

It seems, whenever people speak or write in English, always one recurrent beat predominates. Iambic meter, out of all the ancient meters, seems most suited to the accent patterns of our words and sentences. In fact, such very unpoetic prose as is contained in this initial paragraph is written in a string of iambs and maintains an almost perfect regularity of beat.

But you were not likely to have spotted it. Prose is not metered like traditional English poetry. When you read the preceding paragraph, your voice did not go up and down with every syllable:

> It seems, whenever people speak or write
> in English, always one recurrent beat
> predominates.

Unless your reading was painfully slow, you gave what is termed a rhetorical stress to only the most important words. You probably read it something like this:

> It seems, whenever people speak or write
> in English, always one recurrent beat
> predominates.

The iambic pentameter line, perhaps better than any other English line, has succeeded in harmonizing meter (the regular beat in the background) and rhetorical stress (the stress we use in emphasizing important words in a sentence). This particular harmony we call the *rhythm* of the line.

The first four lines of Shakespeare's "Sonnet 73," if printed as prose, might possibly be read with the following rhetorical stresses:

> That time of year thou may'st in me
> behold when yellow leaves, or none, or few,
> do hang upon those boughs which shake
> against the cold, bare ruined choirs, where
> late the sweet birds sang.

This sounds something like the long-range weather forecast after the eleven o'clock news. If, on the other hand, we apply the precise rules of the iambic metronome to it, the result is even more disastrous:

> That time|of year|thou may 'st|in me|behold
> When yel|low leaves,|or none,|or few,|do hang
> Upon|those boughs|which shake|against|the cold,
> Bare ru|ined choirs,|where late|the sweet|birds sang.

The living rhythm of these lines is a delicate compromise between the two extremes, a marriage in which the claims of both parties are accommodated within the possibilities of the iambic pentameter. Earlier poets often felt constrained to perfect metrical regularity, but Shakespeare and his contemporaries were realizing that this line could manage a much greater freedom. This freedom takes the form of **foot substitution:**

> That time|of year|thou may'st|in me|behold
> When yel|low leaves,|or none,|or few,|do hang
> Upon|those boughs|which shake|against|the cold,
> Bare ru|ined choirs,|where late|the sweet|birds sang.

Lines 1 and 3 may each be read so as to contain a spondaic foot, and line 4 clearly contains two spondees, substituting for the iambs in the first and fifth foot.

As a general rule, the iambic line can accommodate any variation of the two-syllable foot, the spondee (//), the trochee (/⏑), and the less frequent pyrrhic foot (⏑⏑). Any such variations can be substituted, provided that there remain enough iambic feet in the poem to allow us to sense these substitutions as variations from a norm.

But what is accomplished by these substitutions? Is this freedom accidental or for the pure sake of freedom? Like every other poetic technique rightly used, foot substitution sharpens the precision of the poet's statement. In its harmonies, which over a long passage can become very intricate, it appeals to those harmonies of motion which consciously and unconsciously we sense within us. Because the rhythms of poetry are human rhythms—no pistons, no valves, no carburetors are at work in the act of poetry—they engage us, they involve us, until the words that create these rhythms, as we read them, become as close to us as our bones and blood, become so intimately *us* that they become actually *our* thoughts, *our* memories, *our* emotions.

Before we see how poets have used this very expressive line, we should consider what particular foot variations really do. Take, for instance, a set of scanning notations:

/ ˘	˘ /	/ /	˘ /	˘ /
1	2	3	4	5

The first iamb has been reversed and appears here as a trochee. Followed by a regular iamb, this foot substitution allows for two straight unaccented syllables (which is, in effect, a dactyl). As we have noted in the first section of this chapter, a preponderance of unaccented syllables tends to make us read the words more quickly. The third foot is a spondee, in itself a very slow foot, but here, placed after an iamb, it virtually paralyzes the line. The rhythm of the line is therefore quick at the start, very slow in the middle, then regular toward the end. One line of poetry that fits this rhythm is the first line of Hamlet's first act soliloquy:

> O, that this too, too solid flesh would melt . . .

How neatly this rhythm fits Hamlet's personality: quick and impulsive at the offset, then immobilized by inner conflict, and finally submitting himself to a fatal chain of events. It is unlikely that Shakespeare had thought of this consciously, yet that remarkable sympathy he had for the character of Hamlet allowed him to reproduce for his hero again and again this type of vacillating rhythm.

Rhythmic variation, like the use of sound-textures, is graceful and pleasing in itself, yet its most striking use is probably in its coincidence with the rhythms of emotion. The following passage is taken from one of Milton's last works, *Samson Agonistes.* This play, classical in form and Biblical in subject matter, was at the same time a very passionately personal statement. Samson was betrayed to the enemy by a woman; Milton, an active supporter of Parliament, married a woman whose family supported the Royalist side in the English Civil War (1642–52) and who after a short time deserted him. Samson fought for Israel; Milton spent most of his life supporting the cause of freedom and what he felt to be the true religion. Samson was blinded; Milton since 1652 was totally blind. Samson was imprisoned by the Philistines; in 1660, when the Royalists came back to power, Milton was sentenced to house-arrest, a confinement which lasted until his death in 1674. The parallels are striking and in the speeches of the Biblical hero we hear clearly the majestic passion of the old, blind revolutionary.

The setting, in the words of the poet, is this: "Samson, made captive, blind, and now in the prison at Gaza, there to labour as in a common workhouse, on a festival day, in the general cessation from labour, comes forth into the open air, to a place nigh, somewhat retired, there to sit a while and bemoan his condition." He thinks about the glories of his past and then breaks out in bitterness:

> Whý wăs|my̆ bréed|ĭng órd|ĕred ănd|prĕscríbed
> Ás ŏf|ă pér|sŏn sé|părătĕ|tŏ Gód,
> Dĕsígned|fŏr gréat|ĕxplóits,|ĭf Ĭ|mŭst díe
> Bĕtráyed,|căptíved,|ănd bóth|my̆ éyes|pŭt óut . . .

Not only do we find initial trochees speeding up the first two lines, but the fourth foot of the first three lines seems to be a pyrrhic. The effect of this rhythm is one of unusual speed.

The following lines continue this impetuous rhythm and slow down only to taste the bitter savor of the spondees, "heáven-gíft|ĕd" (pronounced "heav'n-gifted") and "bónd-sláve." ("Israel," in this passage, is pronounced with two syllables—"Ís-ry̆el"; "Philistian" is in three syllables—"Phĭl-ís-tyăn.") Why was he born, Samson goes on, if he must be imprisoned, blinded,

> Made of my enemies the scorn and gaze.
> To grind in brazen fetters under task

With this heaven-gifted strength? O glorious strength,
Put to the labour of a beast, debased
Lower than the bond-slave! Promise was that I
Should Israel from Philistian yoke deliver; . . .

The second-to-last line ended firmly, confidently, on "I," but the last line ends with one extra syllable, "deliver." This irregular ending for an iambic line is called a "feminine ending" and, according to traditional versification, is supposed to suggest weakness or passivity. How skillfully Milton inserts this little hesitation at the end of a passage of tumultuous anger!

Part of Samson's tragedy is that he remains acutely aware of the irony of his fate:

Promise was that I
Should Israel from Philistian yoke deliver; . . .

Then the great, pathetic lines:

Ask for|this great|deliv'|rer now,|and find|him
Eyeless|in Ga|za, at|the mill|with slaves,
Himself|in bonds|under|Philis|tian yoke.

Note how the first of those lines steps forth boldly with a trochee, only to end with another soft feminine ending; how the second line almost breaks in the third foot with its pyrrhic and its comma; and how the ironic contrast of Samson's promise and his actual fate is emphasized by the trochee "under." He was supposed to deliver "Israel from Philistian yoke" but instead he, the "great deliv'rer," finds himself under that very yoke. That small, masterful touch—the reversed rhythm of the trochee—fits perfectly this reversal of the hero's role.

The iambic pentameter line was a full-voiced instrument for which some of the greatest artists in our literature composed some of their greatest works. Not only is its two-syllable iambic base open to a great many expressive variations, but its length accomplishes a very special thing for English poetry. The Old English had had a formal break in the middle as in this excerpt from Beowulf:

Thén from the moór—from the míst-crágs
Gréndel cáme—Gód's wrath he cárried.

And most folk ballads were based on a tetrameter line which very often divides after the second foot. It was the pentameter which successfully unified the rhythm of the English poetic line by inserting an extra middle foot, the third foot, to provide a smooth continuity between the beginning and the end of the line.

The break, or breath pause, within the line is called a **caesura,** the Latin word for a "cutting." The five feet of the pentameter line almost always prevent this caesura from falling directly and monotonously in the middle of the line, and so this natural pause must slip itself in elsewhere in the line. Although it sometimes occurs several times and sometimes not at all, as a rule the caesura occurs only once in a line: between phrases or clauses or at the strongest punctuation stop—in general, whenever the sense of the poetic passage seems normally to demand a pause. In the third book of his epic *Paradise Lost,* Milton makes a brief personal reference to himself and his blindness. In this passage we see how the caesura (||) may shift back and forth along the line:

. . .||Thus with the year
Seasons return;||but not to me returns
Day,||or the sweet approach of even or morn,
Or sight of vernal bloom,||or summer's rose,
Or flocks, or herds,||or human face divine;
But cloud instead||and ever-during dark
Surrounds me,||from the cheerful ways of men
Cut off,||and, for the book of knowledge fair,
Presented||with a universal blank
Of nature's works,||to me expunged and rased,
And wisdom at one entrance||quite shut out.

These natural pauses free the line from a mechanical obedience to a five-beat-STOP, five-beat-STOP rhythm that would soon put any reader to sleep.

Reading an iambic pentameter line, or any type of line, we always pause, if only for an instant, when we have completed the final foot. If there is no punctuation, we make only a minimal pause and then go directly on to the next line (as in the first, sixth, seventh, and ninth lines in the above excerpt). This rhythmic device, called **enjambment,** tends to accelerate the verses. **End-stopped lines** are those that end in some sort of punctuation. (Like musical *rests,* punctuation marks generally indicate to a reader approximately how long he should pause at the end of lines. The comma, for example, calls for a small pause; the semi-colon and the colon call for progressively longer ones; and the period demands an emphatic full-stop.) Whether it is enjambed or end-stopped, there is always a certain sense of completion at the end of a line, especially a line of iambic pentameter. This regularity is reassuringly predictable. The caesura adds that essential element of unpredictability, freshness, and freedom to the line. It enables the poet to create a great variety of rhythmic units. We might be surprised if we opened a volume entitled *Milton's Complete Poetical Works* and came upon a set of lines like this:

Thus with the year
seasons return;
but not to me returns
day,
or the sweet approach of even or morn,
or sight of vernal bloom
or summer's rose,
or flocks, or herds,
or human face divine;
but cloud instead
and ever-during dark
surrounds me,
from the cheerful ways of men
cut off,
and, for the book of knowledge fair,
presented
with a universal blank
of Nature's works,
to me expunged and rased,
and wisdom at one entrance
quite shut out.

We would be astonished at this profusion of different line lengths and rhythms, that is, if we did not already know how really free this type of line could be within its formal boundaries.

By the end of the Victorian Period (roughly the mid- and late-nineteenth century), it seemed that all the possibilities of this line had already been realized. The rhythms it could produce were revered as the rhythms of Shakespeare and Milton, but, melodious and expressive as they still were, they could no longer surprise the reader. And unless a line can shake a reader from the humdrum and from the little conventional rhythms of his thought, it can never really engage him. The history of poetry is full of artistic forms, which from generation to generation grow old and must be reactivated with an injection of surprise.

One innovation has been to enlarge the range of foot substitutions to include three-syllable feet. The basic rhythm of Frost's "Birches" is iambic pentameter:

> When I|see bir|ches bend|to left|and right
> Across|the rows||of straight|er dark|er trees . . .

But when he comes to describe the graceful outlines of bowed trees, his metrical units get longer and seem to sweep along, like the birches, careless of the upright rigidity of the iambic line:

> They are dragged|to the with|ered brack|en by|the load,
> And they|seem not|to break;||though once|they are bowed
> So low|for long,||they ne|ver right|themselves:
> You may|see their|trunks ar|ching in|the woods
> Years af|terwards,||trailing|their leaves|on the ground
> Like girls|on hands|and knees||that throw|their hair
> Before|them o|ver their heads||to dry|in the sun.

Unlike Frost, who made use of a great variety of foot substitutions, many modern poets have eliminated the foot altogether and have maintained that this measurement of unaccented and accented syllables is no longer relevant to the English language as it is spoken today. Rhythmic patterns are necessary, they say, but it is only the emphatic accents in the line that really matter, that really register in the reader's mind and give the line its unifying sense of rhythmic order. In the following poem Archibald MacLeish contrasts conventional iambic pentameter with strong, irregular **accentual rhythm,** which in this case might be called *accentual pentameter*. Two voices are heard: the voice of the French ambassador (with comments by the poet) delivering a eulogy over the graves of the American soldiers who died in World War I and the voice of the poet, whose brother was one of those who died.

Memorial Rain

for Kenneth MacLeish, 1894–1918

Ambassador Puser the ambassador
Reminds himself in French, felicitous tongue,
What these (young men no longer) lie here for
In rows that once, and somewhere else, were young . . .

All night in Brussels the wind had tugged at my door:
I had heard the wind at my door and the trees strung
Taut, and to me who had never been before
In that country it was a strange wind, blowing
Steadily, stiffening the walls, the floor,
The roof of my room. I had not slept for knowing
He too, dead, was a stranger in that land
And felt beneath the earth in the wind's flowing
A tightening of roots and would not understand,
Remembering lake winds in Illinois,
That strange wind. I had felt his bones in the sand
Listening.

. . . Reflects that these enjoy
Their country's gratitude, that deep repose,
That peace no pain can break, no hurt destroy,
That rest, that sleep . . .

At Ghent the wind rose.
There was a smell of rain and a heavy drag
Of wind in the hedges but not as the wind blows
Over fresh water when the waves lag
Foaming and the willows huddle and it will rain:
I felt him waiting.

. . . Indicates the flag
Which (may he say) enisles in Flanders plain

This little field these happy, happy dead
Have made America . . .

In the ripe grain
The wind coiled glistening, darted, fled,
Dragging its heavy body: at Waereghem
The wind coiled in the grass above his head:
Waiting—listening . . .

. . . Dedicates to them
This earth their bones have hallowed, this last gift
A grateful country . . .

Under the dry grass stem
The words are blurred, are thickened, the words sift
Confused by the rasp of the wind, by the thin grating
Of ants under the grass, the minute shift
And tumble of dusty sand separating
From dusty sand. The roots of the grass strain,
Tighten, the earth is rigid, waits—he is waiting—

And suddenly, and all at once, the rain!
The living scatter, they run into houses, the wind
Is trampled under the rain, shakes free, is again
Trampled. The rain gathers, running in thinned
Spurts of water that ravel in the dry sand,
Seeping in the sand under the grass roots, seeping
Between cracked boards to the bones of a clenched hand:
The earth relaxes, loosens, he is sleeping,
He rests, he is quiet, he sleeps in a strange land.

Beautifully sonorous language comes easily to the ambassador. But his glib eloquence, conveyed in fine iambic pentameter, is again and again interrupted by the poet's internal monologue—lines too full of personal grief to fit themselves into graceful iambs:

That peace|no pain|can break,||no hurt|destroy,
That rest,|that sleep . . .

At Ghent the wind rose.
There was a smell of rain and a heavy drag

Of wínd in the hédges but nót as the wínd blóws
Óver frésh wáter when the wáves lág . . .

The expectation these last three and a half lines create is not that of the ambassador's flowing iambic pentameter. It is only that of a pentameter rhythm, each set of five beats falling in time with the irregular impact of its words.

An entire section has been devoted to the iambic pentameter line (and its variations) because a familiarity with its special effects can add a great deal to a reader's success in reading most of the best poetry written in the English language. This is not to say that much fine poetry has not been written using other organizing principles, but a reader who has learned to move with the physical/mental rhythms of one type of poetry has become a little more sensitive to his own rhythms and will be more responsive to other, less traditional rhythms when he encounters them in poems.

POEMS FOR COMPARISON

[A] from *Anthony and Cleopatra*

The barge she sat in was a burnish'd throne.
It burned upon the water with its poop
Of beaten gold and with its purple sails.
So perfumed was it that the very winds
Were love-sick with the fragrance of those sails.
To fluted music silver oars kept stroke
And made the am'rous water which they beat
To follow even faster at the stern.
The queen herself did beggar all account;
She lay 'neath curtains made of cloth-of-gold,
O'er picturing that Venus where we see
The fancy out-work bare reality.
On either side of her stood pretty boys,
A pair of dimpled, smiling Cupids who
Did move a pair of divers-colour'd fans,
Whose wind did seem to glow the tender cheeks
Which they did cool and what they undid did.

[B] from *Anthony and Cleopatra*

The barge she sat in, like a burnish'd throne,
Burn'd on the water. The poop was beaten gold;
Purple the sails, and so perfumed that
The winds were love-sick with them; the oars were silver,
Which to the tune of flutes kept stroke, and made
The water which they beat to follow faster,
As amorous of their strokes. For her own person,
It beggar'd all description. She did lie
In her pavilion, cloth-of-gold, of tissue,
O'erpicturing that Venus where we see
The fancy out-work nature. On each side her
Stood pretty dimpled boys, like smiling Cupids,
With divers-colour'd fans, whose wind did seem
To glow the delicate cheeks which they did cool,
And what they undid did. . . .

* * *

[A] *Richard Cory*

There once lived a man, Richard Cory
Who walked in an aura of glory;
    Though he smiled in his pride,
    It was only to hide
His addiction to fidget and worry.

But alas for the close of our story:
Though an aimless young man was Dick Cory,
    When he aimed at his head,
    Well, his aim it was dead . . .
The results of such antics were gory.

[B] *Richard Cory*

Whenever Richard Cory went down town,
We people on the pavement looked at him:

He was a gentleman from sole to crown,
Clean favored, and imperially slim.

And he was always quietly arrayed,
And he was always human when he talked;
But still he fluttered pulses when he said,
'Good-morning,' and he glittered when he walked.

And he was rich—yes, richer than a king—
And admirably schooled in every grace:
In fine, we thought that he was everything
To make us wish that we were in his place.

So on we worked, and waited for the light,
And went without the meat, and cursed the bread;
And Richard Cory, one calm summer night,
Went home and put a bullet through his head.

[c] *Richard Cory*

Into the mixmaster
        of blood detonated
                by ivyleague nagasakis

Cory (I told you so
        —baNG / yr ded((!
                what will

they say?
    —"so admirably schooled"—
                while we

went without meat
        & cursedabluestreak
                at the bread

Cory with yr
        newengland angst
                who needsya.

ADDITIONAL READINGS

A Song for St. Cecilia's Day

John Dryden

– i –

From harmony, from heav'nly harmony
This universal frame began:
When Nature underneath a heap
Of jarring atoms lay,
And could not heave her head,
The tuneful voice was heard from high:
"Arise, ye more than dead."
Then cold, and hot, and moist, and dry.
In order to their stations leap,
And Music's pow'r obey.
From harmony, from heav'nly harmony
This universal frame began;
From harmony to harmony
Through all the compass of the notes it ran,
The diapason closing full in Man.

– ii –

What passion cannot Music raise and quell!
When Jubal struck the chorded shell,
His list'ning brethren stood around,
And, wond'ring, on their faces fell
To worship that celestial sound:
Less than a god they thought there could not dwell
Within the hollow of that shell,
That spoke so sweetly and so well.
What passion cannot Music raise and quell!

– iii –

The Trumpet's loud clangor
Excites us to arms,
With shrill notes of anger,

And mortal alarms.
The double double double beat
Of the thund'ring Drum
Cries: "Hark! the foes come;
Charge, charge, 'tis too late to retreat."

– iv –

The soft complaining Flute
In dying notes discovers
The woes of hopeless lovers,
Whose dirge is whispered by the warbling Lute.

– v –

Sharp Violins proclaim
Their jealous pangs, and desperation,
Fury, frantic indignation,
Depth of pains, and height of passion,
For the fair, disdainful dame.

– vi –

But O! what art can teach,
What human voice can reach,
The sacred Organ's praise?
Notes inspiring holy love,
Notes that wing their heav'nly ways
To mend the choirs above.

– vii –

Orpheus could lead the savage race;
And trees unrooted left their place,
Sequacious of the lyre;
But right Cecilia raised the wonder high'r:
When to her Organ vocal breath was giv'n,
An angel heard, and straight appeared,
Mistaking earth for heaven.

GRAND CHORUS

As from the pow'r of sacred lays
The spheres began to move,

And sung the great Creator's praise
To all the blest above;
So, when the last and dreadful hour
This crumbling pageant shall devour,
The Trumpet shall be heard on high,
The dead shall live, the living die,
And Music shall untune the sky.

Buick

KARL SHAPIRO

As a sloop with a sweep of immaculate wings on her delicate spine
And a keel as steel as a root that holds in the sea as she leans,
Leaning and laughing, my warm hearted beauty, you ride, you ride,
You tack on the curves with parabola speed and a kiss of goodbye,
Like a thoroughbred sloop, my new high-spirited spirit, my kiss.

As my foot suggests that you leap in the air with your hips of a girl,
My finger that praises your wheel and announces your voices of song,
Flouncing your skirts, you blueness of joy, you flirt of politeness,
You leap, you intelligence, essence of wheelness with silvery nose,
And your platinum clocks of excitement stir like the hairs of a fern.

But now with your eyes that enter the future of roads you forget;
Where you turned on the stinging lathes of Detroit and Lansing at night
And shrieked at the torch in your secret parts and the amorous tests,
But now with your eyes that enter the future of roads you forget;
You are all instinct with your phosphorous glow and your streaking hair.

And now when we stop it is not as the bird from the shell that I leave
Or the leathery pilot who steps from his bird with a sneer of delight,
And not as the ignorant beast do you squat and watch me depart,
But with exquisite breathing you smile, with satisfaction of love,

And I touch you again as you tick in the silence and settle in sleep.

Slow, Slow, Fresh Fount

BEN JONSON

Slow, slow, fresh fount, keep time with my salt tears;
Yet slower, yet, O faintly, gentle springs!
List to the heavy part the music bears,
Woe weeps out her division, when she sings.
Droop herbs and flowers;
Fall grief in showers;
Our beauties are not ours. O, I could still,
Like melting snow upon some craggy hill,
Drop, drop, drop, drop,
Since nature's pride is now a withered daffodil.

An Ode for Him

ROBERT HERRICK

Ah, Ben!
Say how or when
Shall we, thy guests,
Meet at those lyric feasts
Made at the Sun,
The Dog, the Triple Tun,
Where we such clusters had
As made us nobly wild, not mad;
And yet each verse of thine
Outdid the meat, outdid the frolic wine.

My Ben!
Or come again,
Or send to us
Thy wit's great overplus;
But teach us yet

Wisely to husband it,
Lest we that talent spend,
And having once brought to an end
That precious stock, the store
Of such a wit the world should have no more.

Carmen Bellicosum

GUY HUMPHREYS MCMASTER

In their ragged regimentals,
Stood the old Continentals,
Yielding not,
While the grenadiers were lunging,
And like hail fell the plunging
Cannon-shot;
When the files
Of the isles,
From the smoky night-encampment, bore the banner of the rampant
Unicorn;
And grummer, grummer, grummer, rolled the roll of the drummer,
Through the morn!

Then with eyes to the front all,
And with guns horizontal,
Stood our sires;
And the balls whistled deadly,
And in streams flashing redly
Blazed the fires
As the roar
On the shore,
Swept the strong battle-breakers o'er the green-sodded acres
Of the plain;
And louder, louder, louder, cracked the black gunpowder,
Cracking amain!

Now like smiths at their forges
Worked the red St. George's
Cannoneers;

And the villainous saltpetre
Rung a fierce, discordant metre
  Round their ears:
    As the swift
    Storm-drift
With hot sweeping anger, came the horse-guards' clangor
    On our flanks.
Then higher, higher, higher, burned the old-fashioned fire
    Through the ranks!

Then the bare-headed colonel
Galloped through the white infernal
  Powder-cloud;
And his broadsword was swinging,
And his brazen throat was ringing
  Trumpet-loud.
    Then the blue
    Bullets flew,
And the trooper-jackets redden at the touch of the leaden
    Rifle-breath;
And rounder, rounder, rounder, roared the iron six-pounder,
    Hurling death!

The Voice from out the Grave

BRIARRE SEELY

Near the White House there's a graveyard
    Where soldiers peaceful lie
Where a grateful nation drops its tears
    And mothers softly cry.

The other day I went there
    Among the monuments
Of those brave men who died
    In America's defense,

When all at once I heard a voice
    From one well-tended grave.

It was the Unknown Soldier,
The spokesman of the brave.

"The thing I want to know," he said,
"Is are my buddies glad
They saved the world for freedom:
Now what thanks have they had?

Is selling apples in the street
The only thanks they've got?
Is a Purple Heart the only gift
They get for getting shot?

And what about the amputees
What do they think of war?
And what about the mothers
Who'll see their sons no more?

I hope at least the profiteers
Are satisfied at last,
The munitions manufacturers
With all that they've amassed.

I am the Unknown Soldier
And maybe I died in vain.
Maybe my supreme sacrifice
Just wasn't worth the pain.
. . . But if I were alive and had the chance
I'd do it all over again."

"They"

SIEGFRIED SASSOON

The Bishop tells us: "When the boys come back
They will not be the same; for they'll have fought
In a just cause: they lead the last attack
On Anti-Christ; their comrade's blood has bought
New right to breed an honorable race.
They have challenged Death and dared him face to face."

"We're none of us the same!" the boys reply.
"For George lost both his legs; and Bill's stone blind;
Poor Jim's shot through the lungs and like to die;
And Bert's gone syphilitic: you'll not find
A chap who's served that hasn't found *some* change."
And the bishop said: "The ways of God are strange!"

from *King Richard the Second*

WILLIAM SHAKESPEARE

For God's sake, let us sit upon the ground,
And tell sad stories of the death of kings:
How some have been deposed; some slain in war;
Some haunted by the ghosts they have deposed;
Some poisoned by their wives; some sleeping killed;
All murdered:—for within the hollow crown
That rounds the mortal temples of a king
Keeps Death his court; and there the antick sits,
Scoffing his state, and grinning at his pomp;
Allowing him a breath, a little scene,
To monarchize, be feared, and kill with looks;
Infusing him with self and vain conceit—
As if this flesh, which walls about our life,
Were brass impregnable; and humored thus,
Comes at the last, and with a little pin
Bores through his castle-wall, and—farewell king!

from *Science Revealed*

GEORGE EVELEIGH

If, then, the State will but assistance lend
To give security to Companies,
The Public Companies with monied wings
Will fly like eagles to the scent of prey,
And every nook and corner of the world

Will find its Companies of men at work;
And, for the aid each Company receives,
Each Company could well afford to pay,
Out of its surplus revenues, the State;
If out of three but two a surplus have,
Two-thirds of each will reimburse the State,
And hold one-third a bonus to account,
Which gives the State two-thirds for profit too,
And two to reimburse the one that's lost.
Thus, if a Government agrees to give,
Whenever Public Companies are formed,
To each a dividend—say, six per cent
Per annum for a certain fixèd time,
And for security inspects accounts—
Then, of the profits which each yieldeth more
Than the same dividend of six per cent,
Two-thirds the Government itself shall claim,
The other third remaining to afford
The Company an extra dividend.

[VI]

The Sense of Balance

The rhyme and uniformity of perfect poems show the free growth of metrical laws, and bud from them as unerringly and loosely as lilacs and roses on a bush, and take shapes as compact as the shapes of chestnuts and oranges, and melons and pears. . . .

WHITMAN: Preface to *Leaves of Grass*

We have examined in "The Sense of Sound" the smallest units of language, syllables, and the sound-effects and sound patterns they produce. Then, in the next chapter, we went on to the smallest rhythmic units, feet, and examined how poets arrange them into lines. Now, to enlarge our scope, we consider groups of lines, stanza forms, and the many varied routes upon which poems move toward their objectives.

Sustained motion, at least in the human world, demands direction. And direction demands that we balance ourselves and coordinate our movements toward a particular objective. The poet, like any purposeful human worker, knows, with varying degrees of precision, where he is going. Sometimes the poem is his way of deliberately traveling from a set of details to his final goal of a single conclusion or a single powerful image. Often the poem is itself a process, a working out of a solution, a journey toward an unforeseen revelation. As Theodore Roethke said: "I learn by going where I have to go."

In any case, a good poem not only pulses within the rhythmic structure of each line, but is coordinated to move toward some conclusion, some culminating experience, or unifying vision that is usually reached in or near the final line. Its structure is, therefore, a *balanced structure*. But before we note examples of poetic balance, we should agree that there exist all sorts of balance. The drum major at the football stadium moves always at stately right angles, keeping a clockwork rhythm and a measured stride. The halfback breaks through the line, dodging the line backers, swerving, changing direction, following his blockers, until finally, out in the open, he diagonally outdistances the last safetyman. He too presents an example of balanced motion. His course might appear erratic but every irregular swerve was dictated by a perfect awareness of the immediate situation and accomplished by means of a perfect sense of balance. A poem, the goal of which cannot be achieved by a simple, direct route, requires an especially fine balance.

THE LARGER MOVEMENTS OF LINES

Earlier (in Chapter IV) we briefly noted how end rhyme can give a stanza a sense of room-like unity. But, because it also helps unify the movement of the lines, it can also provide a measured progression for the entire stanza. A regular pattern, whether end-rhymed or not, is one feature that distinguishes poetry from prose. Prose, as was mentioned before, has a straight-ahead ("prorsus") movement, but poetry tends to turn back on itself ("versus") and to move in repeated patterns. The following passage may be read as a "straight-ahead" movement of verbal images:

The Thames nocturne of blue and gold changed to a harmony in gray; a barge with ocher-colored hay dropped from the wharf: and chill and cold the yellow fog came creeping down the bridges, till the houses' walls seemed changed to shadows, and St. Paul's loomed like a bubble o'er the town.

Then suddenly arose the clang of waking life; the streets were stirred with country wagons; and a bird flew to the glistening roofs and sang. But one pale woman all alone, the daylight kissing her wan hair, loitered beneath the gas lamps' flare, with lips of flame and heart of stone.

This passage is ostensibly prose. Phrases follow phrases in a logical but unpatterned way with perhaps only the last prepositional phrase suggesting a balanced rhythm. Yet, in its original form, the words are very deliberately fitted into rhyming lines, each of which contain eight syllables and four (basically) iambic feet.

Impression du Matin

OSCAR WILDE

The Thames nocturne of blue and gold
  Changed to a harmony in gray;
  A barge with ocher-colored hay
Dropped from the wharf: and chill and cold

The yellow fog came creeping down
  The bridges, till the houses' walls
  Seemed changed to shadows, and St. Paul's
Loomed like a bubble o'er the town.

Then suddenly arose the clang
  Of waking life; the streets were stirred
  With country wagons; and a bird
Flew to the glistening roofs and sang.

But one pale woman all alone,
  The daylight kissing her wan hair,
  Loitered beneath the gas lamps' flare,
With lips of flame and heart of stone.

Set up in this form, the words move to a new pattern. Each rhymed line, like a stride, has its own direction:

First a stride (A) outward:

A′ ⟶

Then another (B) with a dissimilar rhyme:

A′ ⟶

B′ ⟶

Then a third (B″), which matches the second:

The stanza might teeter if the fourth line did not resolve the imbalance:

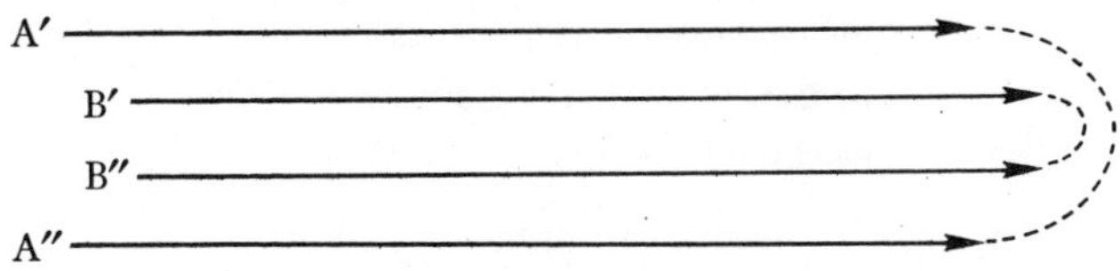

Thus each stanza is a small, balanced movement that is at the same time part of a larger progression, the poem itself, in which details of sound and color alternate and a delicate balance is achieved between inanimate things (stanzas 1 and 2) and the animate world of man (stanzas 3 and 4). The goal of the poem is reached in the last line where this impressionistic word-painting collides with a grim human reality which no amount of cosmetic or verbal paint can disguise.

Rhyme, as we have seen, helps balance the motions of lines within a poem. One of the strictest forms of poetic balance is provided by the **rhymed couplet.** For example:

> Whate'er the Passion, knowledge, fame, or pelf,
> Not one will change his neighbour with himself.
> The learned is happy nature to explore.
> The fool is happy that he knows no more,
> The rich is happy in the plenty given,
> The poor contents him with the care of Heaven.
> See the blind beggar dance, the cripple sing,
> The sot a hero, lunatic a king;
> The starving chemist in his golden views
> Supremely blest, the poet in his Muse.

In this excerpt from Pope's *Essay On Man,* each pair of lines is rhymed and within each of these couplets the poet either links his thoughts, contrasts them, or develops them toward a single conclusion. Such poetry (rhymed iambic pentameter couplets, sometimes called *heroic couplets*) is associated with precisely measured thought and terse wit, two qualities very highly esteemed in the eighteenth century.

Another stanzaic movement, one line longer than a couplet, is a **tercet.** With its three, usually single-rhymed lines, and its unbalanced number, it is often used in light verse, as in Herrick's famous little poem "Upon Julia's Clothes."

Whenas in silks my Julia goes,
Then, then, methinks, how sweetly flows
That liquefaction of her clothes.

Next, when I cast mine eyes, and see
That brave vibration, each way free,
O, how that glittering taketh me!

This form was also used by Tennyson in "The Eagle" (p. 116), where it helps suggest the unbalancing of the bird that clutches the crag and then plunges downward toward the sea.

Throughout the history of Western poetry, the most durable rhymed unit seems to be the four-line stanza, called the **quatrain.** It may be rhymed *a a a a* (as in Rossetti's dirge-like "Woodspurge," p. 134), *a a b a* (as in FitzGerald's "Rubáiyát," p. 128), *a a b b*—paired couplets—(as in Arnold's "Last Word," p. 162), or *a b b a* (as in Wilde's "Impression"). Tennyson chose this last type of quatrain as the stanza form for *In Memoriam,* a long elegy upon the death of a friend. He could have been referring to this highly controlled pattern when he wrote:

I sometimes hold it half a sin
  To put in words the grief I feel;
  For words, like Nature, half reveal
And half conceal the Soul within.

But, for the unquiet heart and brain,
  A use in measured language lies;
  The sad mechanic exercise,
Like dull narcotics, numbing pain.

In words, like weeds, I'll wrap me o'er,
  Like coarsest clothes against the cold:
  But that large grief which these enfold
Is given in outline and no more.

This type of quatrain befits a carefully "measured language," a "sad mechanic exercise" which at times achieves a stately eloquence.

The two most popular quatrains, however, are variations on the **ballad stanza.** In its traditional form, this folk song stanza has only the second and fourth lines rhyming (*a b c b*), for example the "Ballad of Sir Patrick Spens":

> The king sits in Dumferling toune,
> Drinking the blude-reid wine:
> "O whar will I get guid sailor,
> To sail this schip of mine?"
>
> Up and spak an eldern knicht,
> Sat at the kings richt kne:
> "Sir Patrick Spens is the best sailor
> That sails upon the se."

The usual variation on this stanza is one of interlocking rhymes (*a b a b*), as in Donne's "The Ecstasy":

> Where, like a pillow on a bed,
> A pregnant bank swelled up to rest
> The violet's reclining head,
> Sat we two, one another's best.
>
> Our hands were firmly cemented
> With a fast balm, which thence did spring;
> Our eye-beams twisted, and did thread
> Our eyes upon one double string . . .

Poets sometimes choose longer stanzas with intricately coordinated movements such as the **quintet** (5 lines), the **sestet** (6 lines), the **septet** (7 lines), and the **octave** (8 lines). Most of these, however, can be considered combinations of the primary three movements: the couplet, the tercet, and the quatrain. The one traditional form which does not use rhyme, the iambic pentameter "blank verse" (as in the plays of Shakespeare and the epics of Milton), depends for its balance upon the reader's sense of line length and of caesural pauses within the lines.

There is another type of balanced progression that is not based on recurrent rhyme or patterned rhythm, but relies on a recurrent motif. This may be very subtly accomplished: a color, an idea, an allusion might reappear at more or less regular intervals. If this motif is made explicit in a recurrent word or phrase, it is called a **refrain.** This device, one of the most ancient of all structural devices, is traditionally used with rhymed stanzas. It tends to return the poem again and again to a single central image or idea. The lines of the poem progress to a certain extent, but constantly return to some unchangeable fact. In the following poem there is change. What does not change is change itself, time, that fact which is constantly at work joining people, separating them, and finally obliterating even their "carved names."

During Wind and Rain

THOMAS HARDY

They sing their dearest songs—
He, she, all of them—yea,
Treble and tenor and bass,
  And one to play;
With the candles mooning each face. . . .
  Ah, no; the years O!
How the sick leaves reel down in throngs!

They clear the creeping moss—
Elders and juniors—aye,
Making the pathways neat
  And the garden gay;
And they build a shady seat. . . .
  Ah, no; the years, the years;
See, the white storm-birds wing across!

They are blithely breakfasting all—
Men and maidens—yea,
Under the summer tree,
  With a glimpse of the bay,
While pet fowl come to the knee. . . .
  Ah, no; the years O!
And the rotten rose is ript from the wall.

They change to a high new house,
He, she, all of them—aye,
Clocks and carpets and chairs
  On the lawn all day,
And brightest things that are theirs. . . .
  Ah, no; the years, the years;
Down their carved names the rain-drop ploughs.

This poem might be diagrammed as follows:

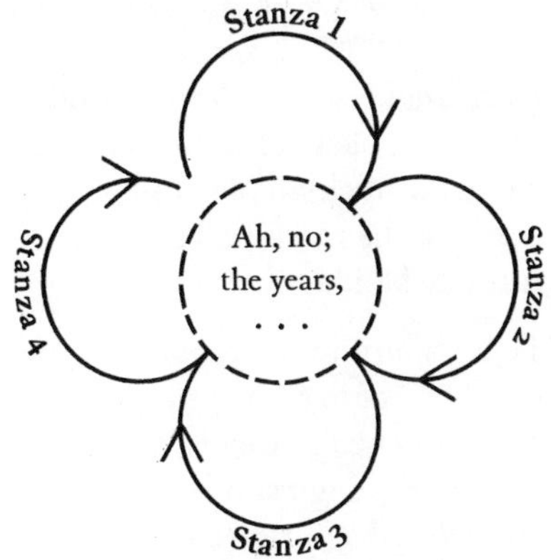

No matter what form of balanced movement the poet chooses, he is able to establish in the reader a "rhythm of expectation" early in the poem. In the last chapter we learned to move in time with the poem; now we must learn to *move in the direction the poem is going*. For, like a rider sitting behind a motorcyclist, the reader must be ready to lean in the direction of each curve. In a way, the poet has control of the reader and can maneuver his rhythms, emotions, and thoughts by means of the poem. The poet knows this and, for special effects, can abruptly alter the direction of his poem, lengthen it, or cut it suddenly short. He can even jar the reader off balance by an unexpected effect which completely violates this rhythm of expectation.

We have already noted this sort of calculated surprise. In rhyme, *expressive variation* is often achieved by slant rhyme, and in rhythm by foot substitution. In the stanzaic structure of a poem it can take many forms. One way is to present the reader with a familiar structure, for example the ballad stanza, and then, after the fourth line, which balances the stanza, add one more line. In A. E. Housman's "When Smoke Stood up from Ludlow," the poet completes that familiar, balanced stanza and then appends an ominous fifth line, as though to say: "You thought at first it was all a gay little poem about wholesome, uncomplicated country life—but take another look. Things are not what they seem."

When Smoke Stood up from Ludlow

When smoke stood up from Ludlow,
  And mist blew off from Teme,
And blithe afield to ploughing
  Against the morning beam
  I strode beside my team,

The blackbird in the coppice
  Looked out to see me stride,
And hearkened as I whistled
  The trampling team beside,
  And fluted and replied:

"Lie down, lie down, young yeoman;
  What use to rise and rise?
Rise man a thousand mornings
  Yet down at last he lies,
  And then the man is wise."

I heard the tune he sang me,
  And spied his yellow bill;
I picked a stone and aimed it
  And threw it with a will:
  Then the bird was still.

Then my soul within me
  Took up the blackbird's strain,
And still beside the horses
  Along the dewy lane
  It sang the song again:

"Lie down, lie down, young yeoman;
  The sun moves always west;
The road one treads to labour
  Will lead one home to rest,
  And that will be the best."

Another trick the poet can use is to unexpectedly shorten a line at the end of a stanza. James Russell Lowell purposefully brings us up short:

Sixty-Eighth Birthday

As life runs on, the road grows strange
With faces new, and near the end
The milestones into headstones change,
'Neath every one a friend.

The poetic craftsman not only knows how to manipulate his verse structures, he also knows that some structures in themselves convey a certain meaning or attitude. The reader normally associates, for example, folk legends, simple passions, melodrama, and mystery with the ballad stanza (Keats' "La Belle Dame Sans Merci" and Coleridge's "The Rime of the Ancient Mariner"). He associates precise, confident rationality with rhymed iambic pentameter couplets (Pope's "Essays"). He associates sudden, absurd juxtapositions with the limerick stanza. It was a mistake for William Cox Bennett to choose this form for an elegy:

Baby's Shoes

Oh those little, those little blue shoes!
Those shoes that no little feet use.
    Oh the price were high
    That those shoes would buy,
Those little blue unused shoes!

For they hold the small shape of feet
That no more their mother's eyes meet,

That by God's good will,
Years since, grew still,
And ceased from their totter so sweet.

And oh, since that baby slept,
So hushed, how the mother has kept,
With a tearful pleasure,
That little dear treasure,
And o'er them thought and wept!

For they mind her for evermore
Of a patter along the floor;
And blue eyes she sees
Look up from her knees
With the look that in life they wore.

As they lie before her there,
There babbles from chair to chair
A little sweet face
That's a gleam in the place,
With its little gold curls of hair.

Then oh, wonder not that her heart
From all else would rather part
Than those tiny blue shoes
That no little feet use,
And whose sight makes such fond tears start!

Conscious misuse of a specialized form is, of course, another matter. The reader should be prepared for this sort of aesthetic humor. The poet may be casting ridicule on a verse form that he believes has outlasted its usefulness. Lewis Carroll ridiculed the nineteenth-century vogue for strangely obscure medieval refrains when he wrote:

As It Fell upon a Day

As I was sitting on the hearth
(And O, but a hog is fat!)
A man came hurrying up the path,
(And what care I for that?)

When he came the house unto,
His breath both quick and short he drew.

When he came before the door,
His face grew paler than before.

When he turned the handle round,
The man fell fainting to the ground.

When he crossed the lofty hall,
Once and again I heard him fall.

When he came up to the turret stair,
He shrieked and tore his raven hair.

When he came my chamber in,
(And O, but a hog is fat!)
I ran him through with a golden pin,
(And what care I for that?)

This would be an example of **travesty.** If a poet intended to deflate the seriousness of a particular poet's style, he might use that style to embody a very trivial set of thoughts and feelings. The following excerpt applies the pin of **parody** to the balloon of those commonplace verbalizers who relied on the heroic couplet to conceal their want of imagination:

The feathered tribes on pinions swim the air;
Not so the Mackerel:—and still less the Bear.

Finally, a poet might jumble his form and content in order to point up the stupidity or silliness of that content. Resorting to **high burlesque,** he may take a comic subject and embellish it with the lofty rhythms, language, and traditional trappings of epic, elegy, or tragedy. The result is often called **mock-** (pseudo) **epic, mock-elegy,** and so forth. The most famous English literary burlesque is Pope's *Rape of the Lock*. It is not the loftiness of epic language which Pope finds humorous, but the little world of humorless, self-important men and women.

Close by those meads, for ever crowned with
flowers,
Where Thames with pride surveys his rising towers,

There stands a structure of majestic frame,
Which from the neighbouring Hampton takes its
name.
Here Britain's statesmen oft the fall foredoom
Of foreign Tyrants and of Nymphs at home;
Here thou, great ANNA! whom three realms obey,
Dost sometimes counsel take—and sometimes Tea.

There beneath the august ceremony of epic language, there within the royal palace of Hampton Court, Queen Anne, "by the Grace of God, Queen of Great Britain, France, and Ireland," listens to her gossipy ministers and majestically sips tea.

POEMS FOR COMPARISON

[A] *A Slumber Did My Spirit Seal*

A slumber did my spirit seal;
I had no human fears:
She seemed a thing that could not feel
The touch of earthly years.

No motion has she now, no force;
She neither hears nor sees;
Rolled round in earth's diurnal course,
With rocks, and stones, and trees.

[B] *The Night Is Freezing Fast*

The night is freezing fast,
To-morrow comes December;
And winterfalls of old
Are with me from the past;
And chiefly I remember
How Dick would hate the cold.

Fall, winter, fall; for he
Prompt hand and headpiece clever,

Has woven a winter robe,
And made of earth and sea
His overcoat for ever,
And wears the turning globe.

* * *

[A] *Feste's Song* from *Twelfth Night*

When that I was and a little tiny boy,
With hey, ho, the wind and the rain,
A foolish thing was but a toy,
For the rain it raineth every day.

But when I came to man's estate,
With hey, ho, the wind and the rain,
'Gainst knaves and thieves men shut their gate,
For the rain it raineth every day.

But when I came, alas! to wive,
With hey, ho, the wind and the rain,
By swaggering could I never thrive,
For the rain it raineth every day.

But when I came unto my beds,
With hey, ho, the wind and the rain,
With toss-pots still had drunken heads,
For the rain it raineth every day.

A great while ago the world begun,
With hey, ho, the wind and the rain,
But that's all one, our play is done,
And we'll strive to please you every day.

[B] *The Tide Rises, the Tide Falls*

The tide rises, the tide falls,
The twilight darkens, the curlew calls;
Along the sea-sands damp and brown

The traveller hastens toward the town,
  And the tide rises, the tide falls.

Darkness settles on roofs and walls,
But the sea, the sea in the darkness calls;
The little waves, with their soft, white hands,
Efface the footprints in the sands,
  And the tide rises, the tide falls.

The morning breaks; the steeds in their stalls
Stamp and neigh, as the hostler calls;
The day returns, but nevermore
Returns the traveller to the shore,
  And the tide rises, the tide falls.

[c] *Excelsior*

The shades of night were falling fast,
As through an Alpine village passed
A youth, who bore, 'mid snow and ice,
A banner with the strange device,
    Excelsior!

His brow was sad; his eye beneath,
Flashed like a falchion from its sheath,
And like a silver clarion rung
The accents of that unknown tongue,
    Excelsior!

In happy homes he saw the light
Of household fires gleam warm and bright;
Above, the spectral glaciers shone,
And from his lips escaped a groan,
    Excelsior!

"Try not the Pass!" the old man said;
"Dark lowers the tempest overhead,
The roaring torrent is deep and wide!"
And loud that clarion voice replied,
    Excelsior!

"O stay," the maiden said, "and rest
Thy weary head upon this breast!"
A tear stood in his bright blue eye,
But still he answered, with a sigh,
    Excelsior!

"Beware the pine tree's withered branch!
Beware the awful avalanche!"
This was the peasant's last Good-night;
A voice replied, far up the height,
    Excelsior!

At break of day, as heavenward
The pious monks of Saint Bernard
Uttered the oft-repeated prayer,
A voice cried through the startled air,
    Excelsior!

A traveller, by the faithful hound,
Half-buried in the snow was found,
Still grasping in his hand of ice
That banner with the strange device,
    Excelsior!

There in the twilight cold and gray,
Lifeless, but beautiful, he lay,
And from the sky, serene and far,
A voice fell, like a falling star,
    Excelsior!

THE SONNET

The sonnet provides an unusual study in balanced motion. No other poetic form has succeeded so well in coordinating so many moving parts within the structure of one stanza. If one can generalize about such an adaptable form, one can describe a sonnet as a fourteen-line, one-stanza poem, consisting of two quatrains, followed by a strong formal break, then a concluding sestet which, though it may be variously arranged, usually ends with an emphatic image or statement.

The sonnet is seldom in narrative order. It is, typically, a dance of ideas, a record of the mind's journey in quest of reasons—reasons why the world is sad, why love is deceptive, why love is sweet, why the past is irretrievable. Often this reasoning about feelings, this verbal clarification, leads to an imperative: if such-and-such is true, then let me from now on act accordingly. Thus, the typical sonnet often contains elements modeled after the formulas of logic. It may start with false premises, use fallacious arguments, and lead to untenable conclusions. Its logic may be absolutely wrong, but its effect as poetry may be absolutely right. In the last analysis, a sonnet employs logical form as a literary convention, that is, as a way of communicating, not necessarily as an end in itself.

A theme dear to sixteenth-century sonneteers was the immortality of those whom poets celebrate in verse. Probably at best merely a lavish two-way compliment, it was, nevertheless, generally presented as a carefully reasoned argument. In the first quatrain of Spenser's "Sonnet 75," the poet is seen writing his beloved's name on the moist sand of a beach. His beloved argues that, like her name, which is being washed away by the waves, she is only a transient mortal. Examine this poem. With what sort of logic does the poet round off this dialogue on life and death?

> One day I wrote her name upon the strand,
> But came the waves and washed it away:
> Agayne I wrote it with a second hand,
> But came the tyde, and made my paynes his pray.
> "Vayne man," sayd she, "that doest in vaine assay,
> A mortall thing so to immortalize,
> For I my selve shall lyke to this decay,
> And eek my name bee wypéd out lykewize."
> "Not so," quod I, "let baser things devize
> To dy in dust, but you shall live by fame:
> My verse your vertues rare shall eternize,
> And in the hevens wryte your glorious name.
> Where whenas death shall all the world subdew,
> Our love shall live, and later life renew."

"Not so," the poet declares and then makes his extravagant promise: "You shall live by fame." Finally he arrives at the conclusion: "where whenas death shall all the world subdew" (note the cumbrous, legalistic transition), "our love shall live, and later life renew" (an assertion based on an implied link between literary "fame" and actual personal survival). Not very convincing, we might say, and a miserable piece of foggy reasoning, and yet this is a lovely little poem. We read it as an expression of a man's feeling for a woman, a man who could, of course, have promised her something more reasonably within his reach—a tangible gift or a marriage proposal. But, as we all know, at certain delicate moments unreason is the most reasonable policy.

As a strictly organized form of poetry, the sonnet exists, like every poetic form, in order to be violated. One can be supremely shocking only in supremely conventional company. Similarly, the poet can create the most expressive variations when he works within the strictest artistic conventions. For example, the typical Shakespearean sonnet, the particular form adopted and popularized by Shakespeare, is an octave composed of two quatrains rhyming *a b a b, c d c d* (the eighth line is usually strongly end-stopped) and a sestet (beginning with a transitional word, like "but," "yet," "thus," "then," and so forth) composed of a quatrain rhyming *e f e f* and a final rhyming couplet, *g g*. Examine the following two sonnets of Shakespeare. Note the cause and effect development of "Sonnet 29" and the analytical precision of "Sonnet 129." Also notice in one of them a structural variation which Shakespeare uses for a special effect.

Sonnet 29

When in disgrace with fortune and men's eyes
I all alone beweep my outcast state,
And trouble deaf heaven with my bootless cries,
And look upon myself, and curse my fate,
Wishing me like to one more rich in hope,
Featured like him, like him with friends possessed,
Desiring this man's art, and that man's scope,
With what I most enjoy contented least;
Yet in these thoughts myself almost despising,
Haply I think on thee,—and then my state,
Like to the lark at break of day arising

From sullen earth, sings hymns at heaven's gate;
  For thy sweet love remembered such wealth brings
  That then I scorn to change my state with kings.

Sonnet 129

The expense of spirit in a waste of shame
Is lust in action; and till action, lust
Is perjured, murderous, bloody, full of blame,
Savage, extreme, rude, cruel, not to trust;
Enjoyed no sooner but despisèd straight;
Past reason hunted; and no sooner had,
Past reason hated, as a swallowed bait,
On purpose laid to make the taker mad;
Mad in pursuit, and in possession so;
Had, having, and in quest to have, extreme;
A bliss in proof,—and proved, a very woe;
Before, a joy proposed; behind, a dream.
  All this the world well knows; yet none knows well
  To shun the heaven that leads men to this hell.

"Sonnet 129" rushes on from the second quatrain of the octave to the first quatrain of the sestet without a formal break.

Let's stop a moment and consider this violation of convention. First of all, to perceive a violation one must be thoroughly schooled in that convention. For example, a gentleman who comes from a part of the world where people clap hands or rub noses when they meet would not think it strange if he saw your friend approach you and with a smile reach out his *left* hand to shake your *left* hand. If the foreign gentleman noticed it at all, it would seem only a minor infraction of a superficial rule of etiquette. Yet to you it would probably come as a weirdly disorienting surprise. You would say to yourself "What did he do that for? What's on his mind?" and you would try to find out from his words and gestures exactly what he did mean. This is just the type of reaction an experienced reader of poetry automatically makes when he encounters a variation like the one in lines 8 and 9 of "Sonnet 129." He doesn't even have to make a conscious note of it. He knows the sonnet form so well that he can immediately sense the variation as it happens and, as in the case of this sonnet, he can appreciate the appropriateness of having no logical break in a poem whose subject is the rushing impetuous illogicality of "lust in action."

John Milton considered himself a member of the Italian school of sonneteers. As a young man of twenty-two he tried his hand at writing sonnets not only in the Italian form (*a b b a, a b b a/ c d e c d e*), but in the Italian language. He later developed the sonnet structure which bears his name: a full-flowing, sonorous verse paragraph that, though it preserves the basic Italian rhyme scheme (except for a variation in the sestet), makes no thought break between the octave and the sestet. A good example of this solid but subtly modulated poetic utterance is his sonnet "On the Late Massacre in Piemont":

Avenge, O Lord, thy slaughtered saints, whose bones
  Lie scattered on the Alpine mountains cold;
  Even them who kept thy truth so pure of old,
  When all our fathers worshiped stocks and stones,
Forget not: in thy book record their groans
  Who were thy sheep, and in their ancient fold
  Slain by the bloody Piemontese, that rolled
  Mother with infant down the rocks. Their moans
The vales redoubled to the hills, and they
  To heaven. Their martyred blood and ashes sow
  O'er all the Italian fields, where still doth sway
The triple Tyrant; that from these may grow
  A hundredfold, who, having learnt thy way,
  Early may fly the Babylonian woe.

Perhaps inspired by the Biblical indignation of Milton's famous sonnet, Shelley composed his "England in 1819."

An old, mad, blind, despised, and dying king—
Princes, the dregs of their dull race, who flow
Through public scorn—mud from a muddy spring;
Rulers who neither see, nor feel, nor know,
But leechlike to their fainting country cling,
Till they drop, blind in blood, without a blow;
A people starved and stabbed in the untilled field—
An army, which liberticide and prey

Makes as a two-edged sword to all who wield;
Golden and sanguine laws which tempt and slay;
Religion Christless, Godless—a book sealed;
A Senate—Time's worst statute unrepealed—
Are graves, from which a glorious Phantom may
Burst, to illumine our tempestuous day.

Again, we find no break in thought in the expected place between the octave and the sestet (which do not even exist, as such, in this sonnet). The thought rushes on from the first line, through a series of grammatical subjects-in-search-of-predicates, down to line 13 where the predicate "are graves" completes the thought. And then out of this corrupt aggregate emerges the final image of a democratic world-revolution, a strange, calm apocalypse that takes us by surprise after the ruinous chaos of the first twelve lines.

On several occasions Wordsworth also violated the rules of the sonnet in order to achieve several small but startling effects. In his "The World Is Too Much with Us" (p. 64), he completes his octave perfectly and, as though unable to continue or transform his thought, sadly reiterates "It moves us not." Then, like Beethoven suddenly introducing a new, thunderous theme, he achieves that expected octave-sestet break: "Great God! I'd rather be/A pagan . . ." We expected it and it did not come. Then in the middle of the ninth line, when we do not expect it, it is suddenly upon us with a spondee, an oath, and an exclamation point.

Twentieth-century poets have increasingly regarded the sonnet as a quaint old museum piece. They have sometimes used it, not so much as a vehicle for feelings and ideas, but as a statement in itself—a statement of prim rigidity. E. E. Cummings, writing about "the Cambridge ladies who live in furnished souls," chose, also, to house them in a decorous sonnet. The next two sonnets, the first by Cummings and the second by W. H. Auden, both convey, partly by the poet's choice of form, a sense of conventionality and restriction.

next to of course god

"next to of course god america i
love you land of the pilgrims' and so forth oh
say can you see by the dawn's early my

country 'tis of centuries come and go
and are no more what of it we should worry
in every language even deafanddumb
thy sons acclaim your glorious name by gorry
by jingo by gee by gosh by gum
why talk of beauty what could be more beautiful than these heroic happy dead
who rushed like lions to the roaring slaughter
they did not stop to think they died instead
then shall the voice of liberty be mute?"

He spoke. And drank rapidly a glass of water

Our Bias

The hour-glass whispers to the lion's paw,
The clock-towers tell the gardens day and night,
How many errors Time has patience for,
How wrong they are in being always right.

Yet Time, however loud its chimes or deep,
However fast its falling torrent flows,
Has never put the lion off his leap
Nor shaken the assurance of the rose.

For they, it seems, care only for success:
While we choose words according to their sound
And judge a problem by its awkwardness;

And Time with us was always popular.
When have we not preferred some going round
To going straight to where we are?

In Cummings' sonnet, the rhythms are so conversational that at first reading most people fail to sense the traditional sequence of two rhymed quatrains, a formal break after the eighth line (not punctuated here, but syntactically present), and a conventional sestet. The rigid clichés of a political orator find a congenial setting within this highly restrictive form.

Auden's poem, however, has an even more restrictive form. It uses regular iambic pentameter rhythm (with only one variation). Its structure is highly logical: Time (or our man-made concept of routinized, scheduled time) preaches regularity to a world (the lion and rose) which does not suffer from human compulsiveness. This nonhuman world moves spontaneously toward what it seeks, while man talks about thinking about deciding about acting, and then, after all that, checks his watch to see if it is the right time to do it. In other words, we are fond of long, conventional, round-about ways of achieving very simple objectives. As though to accentuate his impatience with this process, Auden in the last line deliberately violates one established convention: he lops the last foot from his pentameter and goes "straight to where we are."

POEMS FOR COMPARISON

[A] *On His Blindness*

"They also serve who only stand and wait,"
  Said Patience to prevent my murmuring cries:
  "God needs nor man's complaisance nor his sighs—
  Nor his laborious tasks though they be great;
They bear his mild yolk best who bless their fate.
  Angels there are to sweep the sightless skies,
  Posting o'er land and sea in wondrous wise:
  These at God's bidding serve his kingly state."
But I still questioned how, my light being spent
  Ere half my days in this dark world and wide,
  I might yet use the talents of my mind,
To serve therewith my Maker and present
  My true account, lest Patience cruelly lied
  And God exacts day-labor from the blind.

[B] *On His Blindness*

When I consider how my light is spent,
  Ere half my days in this dark world and wide,
  And that one talent which is death to hide
  Lodged with me useless, though my soul more bent
To serve therewith my Maker, and present

My true account, lest He returning chide;
"Doth God exact day-labor, light denied?"
I fondly ask. But Patience, to prevent
That murmur, soon replies, "God doth not need
Either man's work or His own gifts. Who best
Bear His mild yoke, they serve Him best. His state
Is kingly: thousands at His bidding speed,
And post o'er land and ocean without rest;
They also serve who only stand and wait."

* * *

l. 8. *fondly:* foolishly.

[A] *A Sleeping City*

Two hours past midnight—how the city sleeps!
But how heaven marches! When I last lay down
No star I knew was in the azure deeps;
Blank was the vault as this vast silent town.
Look now! Look there! The obverse now upwhirled!
Bossy and spiked with fires from th' underworld,
With great Orion's mailèd arm and heel,
The Bull's horns tipped with suns, the hosts of steel
A serried stream, upon the mighty Way!
At what command? Whence is it all this sweeps?
Adown what drifting void, what black abyss?
Who knows? Sleep, then, not struggle, sting, and hiss!
Sleep close! sleep well! all Life that Nature steeps
And wakes but to remand to sleep, mold, growth, decay!

[B] *Lucifer in Starlight*

On a starred night Prince Lucifer uprose.
Tired of his dark dominion swung the fiend
Above the rolling ball in cloud part screened,
Where sinners hugged their spectre of repose.
Poor prey to his hot fit of pride were those.
And now upon his western wing he leaned,
Now his huge bulk o'er Afric's sands careened,

Now the black planet shadowed Arctic snows.
Soaring through wider zones that pricked his scars
With memory of the old revolt from Awe,
He reached the middle height, and at the stars,
Which are the brain of heaven, he looked, and sank.
Around the ancient track marched, rank on rank,
The army of unalterable law.

ADDITIONAL READINGS

Easter Wings

GEORGE HERBERT

Lord, who createdst man in wealth and store,
  Though foolishly he lost the same,
    Decaying more and more
      Till he became
        Most poor:

✠

        With thee
      O let me rise
    As larks, harmoniously,
  And sing this day thy victories:
Then shall the fall further the flight in me.

My tender age in sorrow did begin:
  And still with sicknesses and shame
    Thou didst so punish sin
      That I became
        Most thin.

✠

        With thee
      Let me combine,
    And feel this day thy victory;
  For, if I imp my wing on thine,
Affliction shall advance the flight in me.

Song

SIR JOHN SUCKLING

Why so pale and wan, fond lover?
  Prithee, why so pale?
Will, when looking well can't move her,
  Looking ill prevail?
  Prithee, why so pale?

Why so dull and mute, young sinner?
  Prithee, why so mute?
Will, when speaking well can't win her,
  Saying nothing do't?
  Prithee, why so mute?

Quit, quit, for shame; this will not move,
  This cannot take her.
If of herself she will not love,
  Nothing can make her:
  The devil take her!

Song

JOHN DONNE

Go and catch a falling star,
  Get with child a mandrake root,
Tell me where all past years are,
  Or who cleft the Devil's foot,
Teach me to hear mermaids singing,
  Or to keep off envy's stinging,
      And find
      What wind
Serves to advance an honest mind.

If thou be'st born to strange sights,
  Things invisible to see,
Ride ten thousand days and nights,
  Till age snow white hairs on thee,

Thou, when thou return'st, wilt tell me
  All strange wonders that befell thee,
        And swear
        Nowhere
Lives a woman true, and fair.

If thou find'st one, let me know;
  Such a pilgrimage were sweet.
Yet do not; I would not go,
  Though at next door we might meet.
Though she were true when you met her,
  And last till you write your letter,
        Yet she
        Will be
False, ere I come, to two or three.

The Canonization

JOHN DONNE

For God's sake hold your tongue, and let me love;
  Or chide my palsy, or my gout,
My five grey hairs, or ruined fortune flout;
  With wealth your state, your mind with arts improve,
    Take you a course, get you a place,
    Observe his Honour, or his Grace,
Or the king's real, or his stamped face
  Contemplate; what you will, approve,
  So you will let me love.

Alas, alas, who's injured by my love?
  What merchant's ships have my sighs drowned?
Who says my tears have overflowed his ground?
  When did my colds a forward spring remove?
    When did the heats which my veins fill
    Add one more to the plaguy bill?
Soldiers find wars, and lawyers find out still
  Litigious men, which quarrels move,
  Though she and I do love.

Call us what you will, we are made such by love;
  Call her one, me another fly,
We're tapers too, and at our own cost die,
  And we in us find the Eagle and the Dove.
    The Phoenix riddle hath more wit
    By us; we two being one, are it.
So, to one neutral thing both sexes fit.
  We die and rise the same, and prove
  Mysterious by this love.

We can die by it, if not live by love,
  And if unfit for tombs and hearse
Our legend be, it will be fit for verse;
  And if no piece of chronicle we prove,
    We'll build in sonnets pretty rooms;
    As well a well-wrought urn becomes
The greatest ashes, as half-acre tombs,
  And by these hymns all shall approve
  Us canonized for Love;

And thus invoke us: You whom reverend love
  Made one another's hermitage;
You, to whom love was peace, that now is rage;
  Who did the whole world's soul contract, and drove
    Into the glasses of your eyes
    (So made such mirrors, and such spies,
That they did all to you epitomize)
  Countries, towns, courts: beg from above
  A pattern of your love!

Ode on Solitude

ALEXANDER POPE

Happy the man whose wish and care
  A few paternal acres bound,
Content to breathe his native air,
                    In his own ground.

Whose herds with milk, whose fields with bread,
  Whose flocks supply him with attire,
Whose trees in summer yield him shade,
          In winter fire.

Blest, who can unconcernedly find
  Hours, days, and years slide soft away,
In health of body, peace of mind,
          Quiet by day,

Sound sleep by night; study and ease,
  Together mixed; sweet recreation;
And innocence, which most does please
          With meditation.

Thus let me live, unseen, unknown;
  Thus unlamented let me die;
Steal from the world, and not a stone
          Tell where I lie.

The Soul Selects Her Own Society

EMILY DICKINSON

The soul selects her own society,
Then shuts the door;
To her divine majority
Present no more.

Unmoved, she notes the chariots pausing
At her low gate;
Unmoved, an emperor be kneeling
Upon her mat.

I've known her from an ample nation
Choose one;
Then close the valves of her attention
Like stone.

The Beautiful Changes

RICHARD WILBUR

One wading a Fall meadow finds on all sides
The Queen Anne's Lace lying like lilies
On water; it glides
So from the walker, it turns
Dry grass to a lake, as the slightest shade of you
Valleys my mind in fabulous blue Lucernes.

The beautiful changes as a forest is changed
By a chameleon's tuning his skin to it;
As a mantis, arranged
On a green leaf, grows
Into it, makes the leaf leafier, and proves
Any greenness is deeper than anyone knows.

Your hands hold roses always in a way that says
They are not only yours; the beautiful changes
In such kind ways,
Wishing ever to sunder
Things and things' selves for a second finding, to lose
For a moment all that it touches back to wonder.

O Captain! My Captain!

WALT WHITMAN

O Captain! my Captain! our fearful trip is done,
The ship has weather'd every rack, the prize we sought is won,
The port is near, the bells I hear, the people all exulting,
While follow eyes the steady keel, the vessel grim and daring;
But O heart! heart! heart!
O the bleeding drops of red,
Where on the deck my Captain lies,
Fallen cold and dead.

O Captain! my Captain! rise up and hear the bells;
Rise up—for you the flag is flung—for you the bugle trills,

For you bouquets and ribbon'd wreaths—for you the shores
 a-crowding,
For you they call, the swaying mass, their eager faces turning;
Here Captain! dear father!
This arm beneath your head!
It is some dream that on the deck,
You've fallen cold and dead.

My Captain does not answer, his lips are pale and still,
My father does not feel my arm, he has no pulse nor will,
The ship is anchor'd safe and sound, its voyage closed and done,
From fearful trip the victor ship comes in with object won:
Exult O shores, and ring O bells!
But I with mournful tread,
Walk the deck my Captain lies,
Fallen cold and dead.

The Wild Old Wicked Man

WILLIAM BULTER YEATS

"Because I am mad about women
I am mad about the hills,"
Said that wild old wicked man
Who travels where God wills.
"Not to die on the straw at home,
Those hands to close these eyes,
That is all I ask, my dear,
From the old man in the skies,
Daybreak and a candle-end.

"Kind are all your words, my dear,
Do not the rest withhold.
Who can know the year, my dear,
When an old man's blood grows cold?
I have what no young man can have
Because he loves too much.
Words I have that can pierce the heart,
But what can he do but touch?"
Daybreak and a candle-end.

Then said she to that wild old man,
His stout stick under his hand,
"Love to give or to withhold
Is not at my command.
I gave it all to an older man:
That old man in the skies.
Hands that are busy with His beads
Can never close those eyes."
Daybreak and a candle-end.

"Go your ways, O go your ways,
I choose another mark,
Girls down on the seashore
Who understand the dark;
Bawdy talk for the fishermen;
A dance for the fisher-lads;
When dark hangs upon the water
They turn down their beds.
Daybreak and a candle-end.

"A young man in the dark am I,
But a wild old man in the light,
That can make a cat laugh, or
Can touch by mother wit
Things hid in their marrow-bones
From time long passed away,
Hid from all those warty lads
That by their bodies lay.
Daybreak and a candle-end.

"All men live in suffering,
I know as few can know,
Whether they take the upper road
Or stay content on the low,
Rower bent in his row-boat
Or weaver bent at his loom,
Horseman erect upon horseback
Or child hid in the womb.
Daybreak and a candle-end.

"That some stream of lightning
From the old man in the skies

Can burn out that suffering
No right-taught man denies.
But a coarse old man am I,
I choose the second-best,
I forget it all awhile
Upon a woman's breast."

Daybreak and a candle-end.

A Gentle Thought . . . .

DANTE ALGHIERI

A gentle thought there is will often start,
  Within my secret self, to speech of thee:
  Also of Love it speaks so tenderly
That much in me consents and takes its part.
"And what is this," the soul saith to the heart,
  "That cometh thus to comfort thee and me,
  And thence where it would dwell, thus potently
Can drive all other thoughts by its strange art?"
And the heart answers: "Be no more at strife
  'Twixt doubt and doubt: this is Love's messenger
    And speaketh but his words, from him received;
And all the strength it owns and all the life
  It draweth from the gentle eyes of her
    Who, looking on our grief, hath often grieved."

[Translated by D. G. ROSSETTI]

Surprised by Joy

WILLIAM WORDSWORTH

Surprised by joy—impatient as the Wind
I turned to share the transport—Oh! with whom
But thee, deep buried in the silent tomb,
That spot which no vicissitude can find?
Love, faithful love, recalled thee to my mind—
But how could I forget thee? Through what power,

Even for the least division of an hour,
Have I been so beguiled as to be blind
To my most grievous loss!—That thought's return
Was the worst pang that sorrow ever bore,
Save one, one only, when I stood forlorn,
Knowing my heart's best treasure was no more;
That neither present time, nor years unborn
Could to my sight that heavenly face restore.

God's Grandeur

Gerard Manley Hopkins

The world is charged with the grandeur of God.
  It will flame out, like shining from shook foil;
  It gathers to a greatness, like the ooze of oil
Crushed. Why do men then now not reck his rod?
Generations have trod, have trod, have trod;
  And all is seared with trade; bleared, smeared with toil;
  And wears man's smudge and shares man's smell: the soil
Is bare now, nor can foot feel, being shod.

And for all this, nature is never spent;
  There lives the dearest freshness deep down things;
And though the last lights off the black West went
  Oh, morning, at the brown brink eastward, springs—
Because the Holy Ghost over the bent
  World broods with warm breast and with ah! bright wings.

who's most afraid of death? thou art of him

E. E. Cummings

who's most afraid of death? thou
                                        art of him

utterly afraid, i love of thee
(beloved) this

                    and truly i would be
near when his scythe takes crisply the whim

of thy smoothness. and mark the fainting
murdered petals. with the caving stem.

But of all most would i be one of them

round the hurt heart which do so frailly cling . . . .)
i who am but imperfect in my fear

Or with thy mind against my mind, to hear
nearing our hearts' irrevocable play—
through the mysterious high futile day

an enormous stride
(and drawing thy mouth toward

my mouth, steer our lost bodies carefully downward)

[VII]

The Sense of Language

We have entered a universe that only answers to its own laws, supports itself, internally coheres, and has a new standard of truth. Information is true if it is accurate. A poem is true if it hangs together. Information points to something else. A poem points to nothing but itself. Information is relative. A poem is absolute.

E. M. Forster: *Anonymity: An Enquiry*

It is often said that man's most distinctive attribute is his ability to speak. He is the one animal who uses words to comprehend his world. It is with words that he mentally manipulates objects, situations, and events prior to acting. Again it is with words "after the fact" that he judges his own performance. Without words, thinking as we know it would be impossible.

Man's interaction with his world depends upon the efficiency of his external senses: he sees objects and listens to the sounds they make; when necessary he touches, tastes, and smells them; then he employs his senses of motion and balance to propel his body towards or away from them. But people, other people, are also part of his world. He may at times succeed in treating them merely as objects, but people have a way of eluding the net of the external senses. They are never really defined, nor even adequately described, by their color, shape, sound, smell, posture, and movements. No man can know them unless he knows what they *mean* and for this he must have an acute "sense of language." He uses his own words in his thinking process, but to understand other people he must learn to understand *their* use of words. To put it simply, he must listen to what they have to say.

Of course, in reading poetry, one form of verbal communication, we have been listening all along to people's words. The sense memories that a poem reactivates in us do not emerge from us spontaneously. They are coaxed out by the poet's words. Both poet and reader rely always and essentially upon that uniquely human sense—the internal sense of language.

READING BETWEEN THE LINES

Individual words, like images, can be very ambiguous if they are viewed in lonely isolation. The word "set," for example, is notorious for its multiple meanings. Most dictionaries ascribe to it well over sixty separate meanings. But if you read, "The surgeon *set* his collar bone and said that in four weeks he could return to work," or "It was a hard-fought *set,* but the defending amateur champion, relying on his powerful service, was finally victorious," you would know by means of the other words, the context, what the two "sets" signified.

The many meanings that the dictionary assigns to the word set are all separate **denotations.** Most words have only one denotation; some have one or two additional denotative meanings. Many denotations have, in addition to a single distinct meaning, the power to suggest further meanings. In the right context another meaning, a **connotation,** can radiate from the word. We are merely literate when we understand the denotations of words; we possess the sense of language when we also understand the connotations.

The word "saint" has one general denotative meaning: "a saint is a person designated by a church as one whose life was exceptionally holy and benevolent." Yet when Thomas Campion (1567–1620) writes,

Follow your saint, follow with accents sweet;
Haste you, sad notes, fall at her flying feet.
There, wrapped in cloud of sorrow, pity move,
And tell the ravisher of my soul I perish for her love.
But if she scorns my never-ceasing pain,
Then burst with sighing in her sight and ne'er return again,

the word has been connotatively extended to mean "the woman whom you love with the devotion of a religious man for a saint." When FitzGerald in the "Rubáiyát" says,

Why, all the Saints and Sages who discussed
Of the Two Worlds so wisely—they are thrust
  Like foolish Prophets forth; their Words to Scorn
Are scattered, and their Mouths are stopt with Dust,

his context suggests that a saint is a man who speculates on sacred subjects and on the nature of things unseen—and is terribly mistaken. And when Auden, discussing "The Unknown Citizen," declares that all official reports prove "That, in the modern sense of an old-fashioned word, he was a saint," we understand by the ironic context that the "modern sense" of the word is probably a person who is loyal, obedient, industrious, and in every other sense unexceptional.

The setting into which individual words are placed—the verbal **context**—determines both the denotation and the connotation of these words. By thus controlling the meanings of words, the verbal context contributes to the poem's overall mood, or **tone.**

Understanding people in everyday social encounters is a similar process. When a friend or acquaintance steps up to us and says something to us, we know presumably what the words mean (denotatively) but have to decide exactly what the speaker means by them (connotatively). That is, we have to decide how we are to take his statement: is he being sympathetic? sarcastic? humorous? bored? frightened? admiring? Fortunately, in our actual encounters with people we can usually rely on our knowledge of the social context—who the person speaking is; what his relationship is to the person addressed; what the immediate and antecedent circumstances are; and who else is present (or absent) at this encounter.

With this context in mind, we can usually succeed in correctly interpreting the speaker's tone of voice. For example, if a friend were sincerely enquiring about your health, he might emphasize the "are" in "How *are* you today?" and we might conclude that he was genuinely concerned. An important official, being officially considerate about the health of his office staff might ask them one by one: "How are *you* today," and thus communicate an attitude of casual and, perhaps, condescending concern. If he stressed the last word in addressing a secretary who on very busy days (like yesterday) always seemed to be conveniently "ill," his denotatively sympathetic question might actually convey a tone of irritation, or perhaps sarcasm—"How are you *today?*"

In poetry, this dramatic element is often called the **rhetorical context.** In reading poetry we not only weigh each word carefully, examining the denotative and connotative meanings of words within the verbal context, we also take stock of the whole human situation. Here, as in a spoken interchange between people, *someone* is telling *someone something.* In reading a poem for the first time we need answers to the following questions:

1. *Who is the speaker?* (the first person "I")
   a. The poet himself as an actual historical figure? (as in most meditative and lyric poems)
   b. The poet in the disguise of another character? (as in *dramatic monologues* such as Tennyson's "Ulysses"—a device known as a **persona** from the Latin name for a conventional mask used by actors in classical drama)
   c. A character in a monologue not identifiable as the poet, but representing a certain type of person? (as the envious, backbiting hypocrite in Browning's "Soliloquy of the Spanish Cloister" or the anonymous bureaucrat in "The Unknown Citizen")
2. *Who is his audience?* (the second person "you")
   a. Himself? Is he being "overheard" speaking or thinking to himself? (as in most meditations and short lyrics)
   b. A particular audience specified within the poem? (as in Tennyson's "Ulysses," Arnold's "Dover Beach," and Blake's "Tiger," and in all apostrophes, such as Donne's "Batter my heart, three-personed God")

c. The general reader? The "to whom it may concern" audience? (as in Wordsworth's "The World Is Too Much with Us" and in epitaphs and most narrative and philosophical poems)

3. *What is his main subject matter?* (the third person "he," "she," "it," or "they")
   a. Himself? (as in most meditations and lyrics)
   b. A thing or person present within the poem? (as in Williams' "The Red Wheelbarrow" and Keats' "La Belle Dame Sans Merci")
   c. The general condition of the world, the "way things are"? (as in Stevens' "Sunday Morning" and Auden's "Our Bias")

The verbal and rhetorical contexts are the most important means a poet has to lead his readers into the experience of his poem. As we will see in the next chapter, there is no way for a reader to know if he has read the poem precisely as the poet intended it to be read. He can only suppose that, because he knows what words mean and is fairly sensitive to social situations, his experience has been similar to that of the poet and to that of other trained readers. If he consistently follows the verbal context and understands the total rhetorical context, his reading experience and his subsequent interpretation will generally agree with those of other good readers. Yet his results may not be as fruitful if he disregards two other contexts, the **formal context** and the **historical context.**

As we have seen in the preceding chapters, the artistic form of a poem—its rhythm, sound, and stanzaic shape—may convey a considerable amount of its meaning. Often the form of a sonnet, a limerick, or a ballad is partly its meaning. No reader can safely ignore that possibility. **Formal context** also covers the area of formal **genres:** those literary patterns such as elegy, pastoral, comedy, tragedy, satire, ode, and hymn. These traditional patterns contain certain conventional features. A poet who chooses to work within such patterns expects his readers to be familiar enough with the prescribed features to appreciate how he handles them and what skillful variations he makes on them. When writing a pastoral he never expects his future readers to consider the fidelity of his shepherdess as an original touch. If he writes an elegy he may not, himself, be personally obsessed with mouldering bones and gravestones and autumnal sunsets.

The **historical context** of a poem can also be an important consideration. A poem, like any human production, is made at a particular point in time. For example, it might be helpful in some cases to understand the state of British foreign policy in 1818, or the ideas of Copernicus as they were discussed in 1623, or those of Freud and Einstein as they were understood in 1920. Poetry is never written in an intellectual vacuum. Historical context is an extremely relevant factor in poetry, for it conditions man's deepest reactions not only to "life," "death," and "love," but also to contemporary politics, religious theory, and scientific speculation. "I am a man," an ancient poet once wrote, "and nothing which is human is alien to me." The personal history of the poet may also be a part of the historical context. External events and his responses to them may become significant elements in the development of his poetry. Some poets have regarded their total poetic output as one lifelong work; others have developed throughout their careers certain themes and images that in individual poems may appear obscure or fragmentary. Such poets require that we become acquainted with *them* as historically evolving personalities and not simply with single isolated poems. It is true that we may satisfactorily read one poem by William Blake without having read, for example, both his *Songs of Innocence* and his *Songs of Experience,* but our experience will be much fuller if a single poem is read within the fuller context of his other works. Finally, an important factor of this historical context is the very language itself. Man's society changes, poets change, and so does language. If a seventeenth-century writer had the unlikely urge to say "I'm surprised to see how bravely arrogant the roosters are. Unable to fly aloft, they walk about in their crowded barnyards amid their bristling hens and enjoy a natural sort of life-style, unconcerned with the fact that they have been singled out for death," he might put it this way:

> I admire the virtuous stomach of those fowls
> that, unable to raise themselves sublime,
> expatiate frequent in their barnyards amid
> their horrid dames and enjoy a kindly con-
> versation, secure of their own devotion.

Few modern dictionaries would help us understand a poem that had been composed with such archaic—though quite standard seventeenth century—word meanings.

We have so far considered four separate contexts: verbal context, rhetorical context, formal context, and historical context. Since these four contexts all interact within every poem, we may say that, as a whole, they form the *total context* of a given poem. A sensitive awareness of this total context leads us to the *tone* of the poem, the implied attitude of the poet (and the reader) to himself, his audience, and his material. This attitude might be one of humor, bitter sarcasm, sympathy, condescension, anger, or suspicion. The poet has available to him whole spectrums of human emotions. Several tones may exist in a single poem. They may fluctuate, contradict one another, develop, or be ambivalent. Rigid consistency of tone should be no more required of a poem than of a person. For example, this sonnet by Michael Drayton (1563–1631):

Since there's no help, come let us kiss and part;
Nay, I have done, you get no more of me,
And I am glad, yea glad with all my heart
That thus so cleanly I myself can free;
Shake hands for ever, cancel all our vows,
And when we meet at any time again,
Be it not seen in either of our brows
That we one jot of former love retain.
Now at the last gasp of love's latest breath,
When, his pulse failing, passion speechless lies,
When faith is kneeling by his bed of death,
And innocence is closing up his eyes,
  Now if thou wouldst, when all have given him over,
  From death to life thou mightst him yet recover.

The first line suggests that some irrevocable event has cut short a close relationship between a man and a woman, and that the protagonist is bravely resigned. We notice immediately a dramatic element: the poet proposes a symbolic pantomime—that they "kiss and part." The last three lines of the first quatrain continue the pantomime. He says "Nay, I have done . . ." Why the urgency of this protest? Had her parting kiss been too long? Must he forcibly draw himself away? The second quatrain begins at a safer distance.

"Shake hands," the protagonist says, restraightening (we may imagine) his Elizabethan ruffles. As the octave draws to a close we realize that the tone of the first line has undergone some rather interesting changes. As we look back we see how poignantly solemn it began. Yet what an unseemly protestation of joy: "And I am glad, yea glad with all my heart . . ." By the beginning of the sestet we no longer find the protagonist's statements very convincing and, we suspect, neither does the young lady. Obviously he has to make up his mind: he must either surrender outright or propose peace terms to which she would quickly agree. He has tried several approaches already: poignant solemnity, bitter happiness, quiet resignation. Now comes the tragic approach. Their love (personified) is on "his," "love's," deathbed. Emblematic figurines of passion, faith, and innocence hover about "love." This pathetic scene is about to turn tearfully sentimental, when the protagonist abruptly contradicts his first line and playfully suggests that the young lady can still save the patient, a fact that we had already suspected for some time.

POEMS FOR COMPARISON

[A] *To the Virgins, to Make Much of Time*

Gather ye rose-buds while ye may,
    Dread Time is swiftly flying;
And this same flower that lives to-day,
    To-morrow will be dying.

Behold, ye virgins, how the sun
    Shines glorious in the morning,
But, ah, how soon his race is run—
    So let that be a warning.

That age is best which is the first,
    When youth and blood are warmer;
But being spent, the worse, and worst
    Times, still succeed the former.

Then be not coy, but use your time;
    Yield to a man's embraces,

For soon, when you outlive your prime,
  Dread Time will steal your graces.

[B] *To the Virgins, to Make Much of Time*

Gather ye rose-buds while ye may,
  Old Time is still a-flying;
And this same flower that smiles to-day,
  To-morrow will be dying.

The glorious lamp of heaven, the sun,
  The higher he's a-getting;
The sooner will his race be run,
  And nearer he's to setting.

That age is best which is the first,
  When youth and blood are warmer;
But being spent, the worse, and worst
  Times, still succeed the former.

Then be not coy, but use your time;
  And while ye may, go marry:
For having lost but once your prime,
  You may for ever tarry.

* * *

[A] *Infant Sorrow*

My mother groaned! my father wept.
Into the dangerous world I leapt:
Helpless, naked, piping loud:
Like a fiend hid in a cloud.

Struggling in my father's hands,
Striving against my swaddling bands,
Bound and weary I thought best
To sulk upon my mother's breast.

[B] *What Does Little Birdie Say*

What does little birdie say
In her nest at peep of day?
Let me fly, says little birdie,
Mother, let me fly away.
Birdie, rest a little longer,
Till the little wings are stronger.
So she rests a little longer,
Then she flies away.

What does little baby say,
In her bed at peep of day?
Baby says, like little birdie,
Let me rise and fly away.
Baby, sleep a little longer,
Till the little limbs are stronger.
If she sleeps a little longer,
Baby too shall fly away.

READING BEHIND THE LINES

Some poems live within a context of other poems. Though such a poem is usually readable without a knowledge of its literary setting, it generally makes more sense to a reader who knows its intended context—to cite one instance, the poetic style which it imitates. Stylistic imitation is an ancient literary art that often takes the form either of **homage** or **parody.**

In an homage, a poet shows his admiration of another poet by imitating him ("the sincerest form of flattery"). Ezra Pound, for example, wrote an "Homage to Propertius," the Latin elegist; Tennyson wrote one in homage of Vergil; and Swinburne did the same for Landor. This last case of literary reverence is surprising. Two more diverse styles could hardly be imagined: Swinburne's loosely organized, lushly orchestrated style and Landor's tightly disciplined style, intensely sensitive to the meanings of words. Yet, at the death of Landor in Florence ("the flower-town") in 1864, Swinburne wrote an homage which deliberately aimed at the classical compression of the older poet.

In Memory of Walter Savage Landor

Back to the flower-town, side by side,
  The bright months bring,
Newborn, the bridegroom and the bride,
  Freedom and spring.

The sweet land laughs from sea to sea,
  Filled full of sun;
All things come back to her, being free;
  All things but one.

In many a tender wheaten plot
  Flowers that were dead
Live, and old suns revive; but not
  That holier head.

By this white wandering waste of sea,
  Far north, I hear
One face shall never turn to me
  As once this year;

Shall never smile and turn and rest
  On mine as there,
Nor one most sacred hand be pressed
  Upon my hair.

I came as one whose thoughts half linger,
  Half run before;
The youngest to the oldest singer
  That England bore.

I found him whom I shall not find
  Till all grief end,
In holiest age our mightiest mind,
  Father and friend.

But thou, if anything endure,
  If hope there be
O spirit that man's life left pure,
  Man's death set free,

Not with disdain of days that were
  Look earthward now;
Let dreams revive the reverend hair,
  The imperial brow;

Come back in sleep, for in the life
  Where thou art not
We find none like thee. Time and strife
  And the world's lot

Move thee no more; but love at least
  And reverent heart
May move thee, royal and released,
  Soul, as thou art.

And thou, his Florence, to thy trust
  Receive and keep,
Keep safe his dedicated dust,
  His sacred sleep.

So shall thy lovers, come from far,
  Mix with thy name
As morning star with evening star
  His faultless fame.

Of course, we do not have to know Landor's style or even that he was a poet—he might just have been a revered old friend. But our familiarity with his poetry allows us to recognize how lovingly imitative Swinburne has been. Swinburne was not always so lovingly imitative. He regarded Tennyson as a sometimes pompous bore and composed a parody upon the poet laureate's "Higher Pantheism." In his poem Tennyson somewhat cryptically outlines a religious belief according to which God is not pantheistically identified with the natural universe, but is seen as merely using the world to illustrate His Will.

The sun, the moon, the stars, the seas, the hills and the plains—
Are not these, O Soul, the Vision of Him who reigns?

Is not the Vision He? though He be not that which He seems?
Dreams are true while they last, and do we not live in dreams?

Earth, these solid stars, this weight of body and limb,
Are they not sign and symbol of thy division from Him?

Dark is the world to thee: thyself art the reason why;
For is He not all but that which has power to feel "I am I"?

Glory about thee, without thee; and thou fulfillest thy doom,
Making Him broken gleams, and a stifled splendour and gloom.

Speak to Him, thou, for He hears, and Spirit with Spirit can meet—
Closer is He than breathing, and nearer than hands and feet.

God is law, say the wise; O Soul, and let us rejoice,
For if He thunder by law the thunder is yet His voice.

Law is God, say some: no God at all, says the fool;
For all we have power to see is a straight staff bent in a pool;

And the ear of man cannot hear, and the eye of man cannot see;
But if we could see and hear, this Vision—were it not He?

By exaggerating Tennyson's stance Swinburne is able to nudge paradox over the brink into absurdity and make the mystic's quest for cosmic meanings seem the stumblings of a dottering old man.

The Higher Pantheism in a Nutshell

One, who is not, we see: but one, whom we see not, is:
Surely this is not that: but that is assuredly this.

What, and wherefore, and whence? for under is over and under:
If thunder could be without lightning, lightning could be without thunder.

Doubt is faith in the main: but faith, on the whole, is doubt:
We cannot believe by proof: but could we believe without?

Why, and whither, and how? for barley and rye are not clover:
Neither are straight lines curves: yet over is under and over.

Two and two may be four: but four and four are not eight:
Fate and God may be twain: but God is the same thing as fate.

Ask a man what he thinks, and get from a man what he feels:
God, once caught in the fact, shows you a fair pair of heels.

Body and spirit are twins: God only knows which is which:
The soul squats down in the flesh, like a tinker drunk in a ditch.

More is the whole than a part: but half is more than the whole:
Clearly, the soul is the body: but is not the body the soul?

One and two are not one: but one and nothing is two:
Truth can hardly be false, if falsehood cannot be true.

Once the mastodon was: pterodactyls were common as cocks:
Then the mammoth was God: now is He a prize ox.

Parallels all things are: yet many of these are askew:
You are certainly I: but certainly I am not you.

Springs the rock from the plain, shoots the stream from the rock:
Cocks exist for the hen: but hens exist for the cock.

God, whom we see not, is: and God, who is not, we see:
Fiddle, we know, is diddle: and diddle, we take it, is dee.

Everyone knows Lewis Carroll's little nonsense verse, "The Crocodile":

How doth the little crocodile
  Improve his shining tail,
And pour the waters of the Nile
  On every shining scale!

How cheerfully he seems to grin,
  How neatly spreads his claws,
And welcomes little fishes in
  With gently smiling jaws!

But not everyone knows that this is a pointed parody of Isaac Watts' "How Doth the Little Busy Bee":

How doth the little busy bee
  Improve each shining hour,
And gather honey all the day
  From every opening flower!

How skillfully she builds her cell!
  How neat she spreads the wax!
And labors hard to store it well
  With the sweet food she makes.

In works of labor or of skill
  I would be busy too;
For Satan finds some mischief still
  For idle hands to do.

In books, or work, or healthful play,
  Let my first years be passed,
That I may give for every day
  Some good account at last.

Carroll's non-nonsensical point seems to be that it makes a great difference *how* one improves each shining hour. Idleness may be the "devil's workshop," but there is no special sanctity attached to busyness. After all, it may be the "work, or healthful play" of the cheerfully grinning crocodile. When we consider the virtues of busyness, it no doubt makes a great difference whether one is a crocodile or a "little fish."

In the twentieth century many poets have rediscovered a specialized form of imitation: **verbal allusion.** By inserting a word or phrase reminiscent of a particular work of another writer, a poet may demand that his reader read behind his lines and simultaneously think of the other work. Sometimes his poem is so constructed that it is meaningless unless the reader is aware of the verbal allusions and sensitively allows their meanings to interact with the words of the poem before him.

Examine the following poem by Robert Lowell:

Children of Light

Our fathers wrung their bread from stocks and stones
And fenced their gardens with the Redman's bones;
Embarking from the Nether Land of Holland,
Pilgrims unhouseled by Geneva's night,
They planted here the Serpent's seeds of light;
And here the pivoting searchlights probe to shock

The riotous glass houses built on rock,
And candles gutter by an empty altar,
And light is where the landless blood of Cain
Is burning, burning the unburied grain.

The historical context may give us some help with its meaning. If we know that Robert Lowell is a descendant of a very old and famous New England family, we can understand "Our fathers" to mean something more intimate and specific than the vague "pilgrim fathers" or "founding fathers." If we know that this poem was written during World War II, we can connect the "pivoting searchlights" with a night air raid drill. These and other references serve to develop two main ideas: American origins and American violence. The American fathers, the early British settlers, came by way of the Netherlands to North America where, the poet says, they planted "the Serpent's seeds" (a reference to a Greek myth in which a dragon's teeth are planted and armed warriors sprout up from the earth). Today (1944) in the land their forefathers took from the Indians, present-day Americans continue to live in a violent, sterile land, cursed by the crimes of their past.

It is a complex poem in which many historical elements interact. From Lowell's point of view, America was cursed from the beginning by two facts: it was discovered and colonized at the disastrous expense of its original settlers, the Indians; and it was settled by English Protestants "unhouseled" (deprived of the Catholic sacraments) by "Geneva's night" (by their own adherence to the austere and rigid beliefs of Calvinism—associated with Geneva). Lowell implies that their industrious Puritan beliefs have sown the "Serpent's seeds of light"—militaristic attitudes? satanic practices? extreme rationalism? In the last five lines the contemporary consequences are described: war, decline of religious faith (the "candles gutter by an empty altar"), and, in symbolic terms, the festering effects of murder and inhumanity (the "blood of Cain").

A reader with a sharp memory for poetic phrasing will discover even more verbal density in this poem. He will not "read into" these verses more than they contain; he will read between the lines to catch the connections between ideas and images. He will furthermore recognize in this poem an instance of verbal allusion and will read "behind" the lines, keeping in mind Milton's sonnet "On the Late Massacre in Piemont" (p. 207). The juxtaposition of meanings is interesting. No experienced reader has to set them forth in such a schematic way as below. In reading "Children of Light" he senses each comparison, each ironic twist, each ambiguous nuance as it appears in the poem. The following analysis is here only to demonstrate how potent this technique of verbal allusion can be.

The Poem at Hand: Lowell's "Children of Light"	**The Poem Alluded to by Lowell: Milton's "On the Late Massacre in Piemont"**
THE CRIME: the slaughter of American Indians by Protestant Christians who "fenced their gardens with the Redman's bones"	THE CRIME: the slaughter by Catholics of Protestant Christians whose "bones/Lie scattered on the Alpine mountains cold"
THE ANCESTRY OF THE POET: "Our fathers wrung their bread from stocks and stones"	THE ANCESTRY OF THE POET: "all our fathers worshipped stocks and stones"
THE VICTIMS: Indians murdered by faithful Christians, "Children of Light"	THE VICTIMS: faithful Christians, "who kept thy truth so pure of old"
THE AFTER EFFECTS: the sowing of the "Serpent's seeds," the harvest: the cold technology of war	THE AFTER EFFECTS: the sowing of "their martyred blood and ashes" from which will rise more Protestant converts

The historical ironies are underscored by the title, "Children of Light," a term used in the New Testament to refer to the chosen and purified worshipers of God. In Lowell's poem it is they who are the victimizers; they who, convinced that God was on their side, "fenced their gardens with the Redman's bones."

Imitation and verbal allusion refer us back to more or less specific poets and poems. By means of his choice of language, or **diction,** a poet can refer us back to past stages in the development of our language or can suggest the attitudes of certain groups or classes of English-speaking persons.

For example, Stevens' "Sunday Morning" (pp. 137–140) is uniformly elegant in its diction. Though twentieth century in sentiment, it is nineteenth or eighteenth century in its language. The one very deliberate exception occurs in the fourth stanza: there is no "golden underground, nor isle/ Melodious, where spirits gat them home . . ." "Gat," (archaic for "got") should register with the reader as a piece of medieval diction, as though excerpted from a legend of King Arthur or of the voyage of some miraculous English saint. Often a poet can suggest a whole set of attitudes associated with an historical period by using the diction of that period. Keats was fond of the language of Elizabethan England. Much of his poetry is flavored with it. But in his sonnet "On First Looking into Chapman's Homer," in which he describes his thrill in reading Chapman's 1611 translation of Homer, he makes special use of this diction: "goodly states," "in fealty," "his demesne" (feudal possession), "pure serene" (clear air).

Much have I traveled in the realms of gold,
   And many goodly states and kingdoms seen;
   Round many western islands have I been
Which bards in fealty to Apollo hold.
Oft of one wide expanse had I been told
   That deep-browed Homer ruled as his demesne;
   Yet did I never breathe its pure serene
Till I heard Chapman speak out loud and bold:
Then felt I like some watcher of the skies
   When a new planet swims into his ken;
Or like stout Cortez when with eagle eyes
   He stared at the Pacific—and all his men
Looked at each other with a wild surmise—
   Silent, upon a peak in Darien.

Besides historical cross-references, diction can also embody contemporary social attitudes. By using slang a poet can, in one context, insert an earthy tone of directness and, in another, a tone of crude anti-intellectualism. In a fairly formal context, a colloquial expression can convey a sense of ease and candor. Even the "new languages" of our technological world can sometimes be employed with devastating effects. Note the sociological jargon in Auden's "The Unknown Citizen" (p. 151): "The Greater Community" and "he was fully sensible to the advantages of the Instalment Plan."

In his use of words the poet is, at his best, only a little more expert than an excellent conversationalist. The poet has the advantage of possible revision. The conversationalist must choose his words and utter them extempore. But any fine conversationalist can imitate the wording, if not the intonation, of a distinctive speaker. He has such a love for language as a spoken art that he can be impressed or moved or amused by other peoples' styles of speech, and he can make those styles part of his own repertoire. He does not restrict his diction to the pallid language of radio announcers or tabloid editorials. If the social context calls for it, he can use the florid language of Elizabethan England or the cool elegance of the eighteenth century; he can speak in contemporary slang or in technical jargon. For him, as for the poet, language is a large pallet of many colors. We say of a good conversationalist: "You really have to pay attention and listen to every word he says." We must say the same of a good poet.

POEMS FOR COMPARISON

[A] *Father William*

"You are old, Father William," the young man said,
  "And your hair has become very white,
And yet you incessantly stand on your head—
  Do you think, at your age, it is right?"

"In my youth," Father William replied to his son,
  "I feared it might injure the brain;
But now that I'm perfectly sure I have none,
  Why, I do it again and again."

"You are old," said the youth, "as I mentioned before,
  And have grown uncommonly fat;
Yet you turned a back-somersault in at the door—
  Pray, what is the reason of that?"

"In my youth," said the sage, as he shook his gray locks,
  "I kept all my limbs very supple
By the use of this ointment—one shilling the box—
  Allow me to sell you a couple."

"You are old," said the youth, "and your jaws are too weak
  For anything tougher than suet;

Yet you finished the goose, with the bones and the beak;
  Pray, how did you manage to do it?"

"In my youth," said his father, "I took to the law,
  And argued each case with my wife;
And the muscular strength which it gave to my jaw
  Has lasted the rest of my life."

"You are old," said the youth, "one would hardly suppose
  That your eye was as steady as ever;
Yet you balanced an eel on the end of your nose—
  What made you so awfully clever?"

"I have answered three questions, and that is enough,"
  Said his father; "don't give yourself airs!
Do you think I can listen all day to such stuff?
  Be off, or I'll kick you downstairs!"

[B] *The Old Man's Comforts and How He Gained Them*

"You are old, Father William," the young man cried;
  "The few locks which are left you are gray;
You are hale, Father William,—a hearty old man:
  Now tell me the reason, I pray."

"In the days of my youth," Father William replied,
  "I remembered that youth would fly fast,
And abused not my health and my vigor at first,
  That I never might need them at last."

"You are old, Father William," the young man cried,
  "And pleasures with youth pass away;
And yet you lament not the days that are gone:
  Now tell me the reason, I pray."

"In the days of my youth," Father William replied,
  "I remembered that youth could not last;
I thought of the future, whatever I did,
  That I never might grieve for the past."

"You are old, Father William," the young man cried,
  "And life must be hastening away;

You are cheerful, and love to converse upon death:
  Now tell me the reason, I pray."

"I am cheerful, young man," Father William replied;
  "Let the cause thy attention engage;
In the days of my youth, I remembered my God,
  And He hath not forgotten my age."

* * *

[A] *Love Among the Ruins*

– 1 –

Where the quiet-colored end of evening smiles,
    Miles and miles
On the solitary pastures where our sheep
    Half-asleep
Tinkle homeward through the twilight, stray or stop
    As they crop—
Was the site once of a city great and gay
    (So they say),
Of our country's very capital, its prince
    Ages since
Held his court in, gathered councils, wielding far
    Peace or war.

– 2 –

Now—the country does not even boast a tree,
    As you see,
To distinguish slopes of verdure, certain rills
    From the hills
Intersect and give a name to (else they run
    Into one),
Where the domed and daring palace shot its spires
    Up like fires
O'er the hundred-gated circuit of a wall
    Bounding all,
Made of marble, men might march on nor be pressed,
    Twelve abreast.

– 3 –

And such plenty and perfection, see, of grass
    Never was!
Such a carpet as, this summertime, o'erspreads
    And embeds
Every vestige of the city, guessed alone,
    Stock or stone—
Where a multitude of men breathed joy and woe
    Long ago;
Lust of glory pricked their hearts up, dread of shame
    Struck them tame;
And that glory and that shame alike, the gold
    Bought and sold.

– 4 –

Now—the single little turret that remains
    On the plains,
By the caper overrooted, by the gourd
    Overscored,
While the patching houseleek's head of blossom winks
    Through the chinks—
Marks the basement whence a tower in ancient time
    Sprang sublime,
And a burning ring, all round, the chariots traced
    As they raced,
And the monarch and his minions and his dames
    Viewed the games.

– 5 –

And I know, while thus the quiet-colored eve
    Smiles to leave
To their folding, all our many-tinkling fleece
    In such peace,
And the slopes and rills in undistinguished gray
    Melt away—
That a girl with eager eyes and yellow hair
    Waits me there
In the turret whence the charioteers caught soul

For the goal,
When the king looked, where she looks now, breathless, dumb
Till I come.

– 6 –

But he looked upon the city, every side,
Far and wide,
All the mountains topped with temples, all the glades'
Colonnades,
All the causeys, bridges, aqueducts—and then,
All the men!
When I do come, she will speak not, she will stand,
Either hand
On my shoulder, give her eyes the first embrace
Of my face,
Ere we rush, ere we extinguish sight and speech
Each on each.

– 7 –

In one year they sent a million fighters forth
South and north,
And they built their gods a brazen pillar high
As the sky,
Yet reserved a thousand chariots in full force—
Gold, of course,
Oh heart! oh blood that freezes, blood that burns!
Earth's returns
For whole centuries of folly, noise, and sin!
Shut them in,
With their triumphs and their glories and the rest!
Love is best.

[B] *(ponder,darling,these busted statues*

(ponder,darling,these busted statues
of yon motheaten forum be aware
notice what hath remained
—the stone cringes
clinging to the stone, how obsolete

lips utter their extant smile . . . .
remark

a few deleted of texture
or meaning monuments and dolls

resist Them Greediest Paws of careful
time all of which is extremely
unimportant)whereas Life

matters if or

when the your- and my-
idle vertical worthless
self unite in a peculiarly
momentary

partnership(to instigate
constructive
            Horizontal
business . . . . even so, let us make haste
—consider well this ruined aqueduct

lady,
which used to lead something into somewhere)

ADDITIONAL READINGS

Brahma

RALPH WALDO EMERSON

If the red slayer think he slays,
  Or if the slain think he is slain,
They know not well the subtle ways
  I keep, and pass, and turn again.

Far or forgot to me is near;
  Shadow and sunlight are the same;
The vanished gods to me appear;
  And one to me are shame and fame.

They reckon ill who leave me out;
  When me they fly, I am the wings;
I am the doubter and the doubt,
  And I the hymn the Brahmin sings.

The strong gods pine for my abode,
  And pine in vain the sacred Seven,
But thou, meek lover of the good!
  Find me, and turn thy back on heaven.

Hamatreya

RALPH WALDO EMERSON

Bulkeley, Hunt, Willard, Hosmer, Meriam, Flint,
Possessed the land which rendered to their toil
Hay, corn, roots, hemp, flax, apples, wool and wood.
Each of these landlords walked amidst his farm,
Saying, " 'T is mine, my children's and my name's.
How sweet the west wind sounds in my own trees!
How graceful climb those shadows on my hill!
I fancy these pure waters and the flags
Know me, as does my dog: we sympathize;
And, I affirm, my actions smack of the soil."

Where are these men? Asleep beneath their grounds:
And strangers, fond as they, their furrows plough.
Earth laughs in flowers, to see her boastful boys
Earth-proud, proud of the earth which is not theirs;
Who steer the plough, but cannot steer their feet
Clear of the grave.
They added ridge to valley, brook to pond,
And sighed for all that bounded their domain;
"This suits me for a pasture; that's my park;
We must have clay, lime, gravel, granite-ledge,
And misty lowland, where to go for peat.
The land is well,—lies fairly to the south.
'T is good, when you have crossed the sea and back,
To find the sitfast acres where you left them."
Ah! the hot owner sees not Death, who adds

Him to his land, a lump of mold the more.
Hear what the Earth says:—

EARTH-SONG

"Mine and yours;
Mine, not yours.
Earth endures;
Stars abide—
Shine down in the old sea;
Old are the shores;
But where are old men?
I who have seen much,
Such have I never seen.

"The lawyer's deed
Ran sure,
In tail,
To them, and to their heirs
Who shall succeed,
Without fail,
Forevermore.

"Here is the land,
Shaggy with wood,
With its old valley,
Mound and flood.
But the heritors?—
Fled like the flood's foam.
The lawyer, and the laws,
And the kingdom,
Clean swept herefrom.

"They called me theirs,
Who so controlled me;
Yet every one
Wished to stay, and is gone.
How am I theirs,
If they cannot hold me,
But I hold them?"

When I heard the Earth-song,
I was no longer brave;
My avarice cooled
Like lust in the chill of the grave.

l. 39. *In tail:* in a specific limited (legal) sense.

My Last Duchess

ROBERT BROWNING

That's my last Duchess painted on the wall, 2
Looking as if she were alive. I call
That piece a wonder, now; Frà Pandolf's hands
Worked busily a day, and there she stands.
Will't please you sit and look at her? I said
"Frà Pandolf" by design, for never read
Strangers like you that pictured countenance,
The depth and passion of its earnest glance,
But to myself they turned (since none puts by
The curtain I have drawn for you, but I)
And seemed as they would ask me, if they durst,
How such a glance came there; so, not the first
Are you to turn and ask thus. Sir, 'twas not
Her husband's presence only, called that spot
Of joy into the Duchess' cheek; perhaps
Frà Pandolf chanced to say, "Her mantle laps
Over my lady's wrist too much," or "Paint
Must never hope to reproduce the faint
Half-flush that dies along her throat." Such stuff
Was courtesy, she thought, and cause enough
For calling up that spot of joy. She had
A heart—how shall I say?—too soon made glad,
Too easily impressed; she liked whate'er
She looked on, and her looks went everywhere.
Sir, 'twas all one! My favor at her breast,
The dropping of the daylight in the West,
The bough of cherries some officious fool
Broke in the orchard for her, the white mule

She rode with round the terrace—all and each
Would draw from her alike the approving speech,
Or blush, at least. She thanked men,—good! but thanked
Somehow—I know not how—as if she ranked
My gift of a nine-hundred-years-old name
With anybody's gift. Who'd stoop to blame
This sort of trifling? Even had you skill
In speech—(which I have not)—to make your will
Quite clear to such an one, and say, "Just this
Or that in you disgusts me; here you miss,
Or there exceed the mark"—and if she let
Herself be lessoned so, nor plainly set
Her wits to yours, forsooth, and made excuse,
—E'en then would be some stooping; and I choose
Never to stoop. Oh sir, she smiled, no doubt,
Whene'er I passed her; but who passed without
Much the same smile? This grew; I gave commands;
Then all smiles stopped together. There she stands
As if alive. Will't please you rise? We'll meet
The company below, then. I repeat,
The Count your master's known munificence
Is ample warrant that no just pretense
Of mine for dowry will be disallowed;
Though his fair daughter's self, as I avowed
At starting, is my object. Nay, we'll go
Together down, sir. Notice Neptune, though,
Taming a sea-horse, thought a rarity,
Which Claus of Innsbruck cast in bronze for me!

To His Coy Mistress

ANDREW MARVELL

Had we but world enough, and time,
This coyness, lady, were no crime.
We would sit down and think which way
To walk, and pass our long love's day.
Thou by the Indian Ganges' side—

Should'st rubies find; I by the tide
Of Humber would complain. I would
Love you ten years before the flood,
And you should, if you please, refuse
Till the conversion of the Jews.
My vegetable love should grow
Vaster than empires and more slow.
An hundred years should go to praise
Thine eyes, and on thy forehead gaze;
Two hundred to adore each breast,
But thirty thousand to the rest.
An age at least to every part,
And the last age should show your heart.
For, lady, you deserve this state,
Nor would I love at lower rate.
    But at my back I always hear
Time's wingèd chariot hurrying near;
And yonder all before us lie
Deserts of vast eternity.
Thy beauty shall no more be found,
Nor in thy marble vault shall sound
My echoing song; then worms shall try
That long preserved virginity,
And your quaint honor turn to dust,
And into ashes all my lust.
The grave's a fine and private place,
But none, I think, do there embrace.
    Now therefore, while the youthful hue
Sits on thy skin like morning dew,
And while thy willing soul transpires
At every pore with instant fires,
Now let us sport us while we may,
And now, like amorous birds of prey,
Rather at once our time devour,
Than languish in his slow-chapped power.
Let us roll all our strength and all
Our sweetness up into one ball,
And tear our pleasures with rough strife
Through the iron gates of life.

Thus, though we cannot make our sun
Stand still, yet we will make him run.

Naming of Parts

HENRY REED

Today we have naming of parts. Yesterday,
We had daily cleaning. And tomorrow morning,
We shall have what to do after firing. But today,
Today we have naming of parts. Japonica
Glistens like coral in all of the neighboring gardens,
And today we have naming of parts.

This is the lower sling swivel. And this
Is the upper sling swivel, whose use you will see,
When you are given your slings. And this is the piling swivel,
Which in your case you have not got. The branches
Hold in the gardens their silent, eloquent gestures,
Which in our case we have not got.

This is the safety-catch, which is always released
With an easy flick of the thumb. And please do not let me
See anyone using his finger. You can do it quite easy
If you have any strength in your thumb. The blossoms
Are fragile and motionless, never letting anyone see
Any of them using their finger.

And this you can see is the bolt. The purpose of this
Is to open the breech, as you see. We can slide it
Rapidly backwards and forwards: we call this
Easing the spring. And rapidly backwards and forwards
The early bees are assaulting and fumbling the flowers:
They call it easing the Spring.

They call it easing the Spring: it is perfectly easy
If you have any strength in your thumb: like the bolt,
And the breech, and the cocking-piece, and the point of balance,
Which in our case we have not got, and the almond-blossom
Silent in all of the gardens, the bees going backwards and forwards,
For today we have naming of parts.

Judging Distances

HENRY REED

Not only how far away, but the way that you say it
Is very important. Perhaps you may never get
The knack of judging a distance, but at least you know
How to report on a landscape: the central sector,
The right of arc and that, which we had last Tuesday,
  And at least you know

That maps are of time, not place, so far as the army
Happens to be concerned—the reason being,
Is one which need not delay us. Again, you know
There are three kinds of tree, three only, the fir and the poplar
And those which have bushy tops too; and lastly
  That things only seem to be things.

A barn is not called a barn, to put it more plainly,
Or a field in the distance, where sheep may be safely grazing.
You must never be over-sure. You must say, when reporting:
At five o'clock in the central sector is a dozen
Of what appear to be animals; whatever you do,
  Don't call the bleeders *sheep*.

I am sure that's quite clear; and suppose, for the sake of example,
The one at the end, asleep, endeavours to tell us
What he sees over there to the west, and how far away,
After first having come to attention. There to the west,
On the fields of summer the sun and the shadows bestow
  Vestments of purple and gold.

The still white dwellings are like a mirage in the heat,
And under the swaying elms a man and a woman
Lie gently together. Which is, perhaps, only to say
That there is a row of houses to the left of arc,
And that under some poplars a pair of what appear to be humans
  Appear to be loving.

Well that, for an answer, is what we might rightly call
Moderately satisfactory only, the reason being,
Is that two things have been omitted, and those are important.
The human beings, now: in what direction are they,
And how far away, would you say? And do not forget
  There may be dead ground in between.

There may be dead ground in between; and I may not have got
The knack of judging a distance; I will only venture
A guess that perhaps between me and the apparent lovers,
(Who, incidentally, appear by now to have finished,)
At seven o'clock from the houses, is roughly a distance
  Of about one year and a half.

Musée des Beaux Arts

W. H. AUDEN

About suffering they were never wrong,
The Old Masters: how well they understood
Its human position; how it takes place
While someone else is eating or opening a window or just walking
    dully along;
How, when the aged are reverently, passionately waiting
For the miraculous birth, there always must be
Children who did not specially want it to happen, skating
On a pond at the edge of the wood:
They never forgot
That even the dreadful martyrdom must run its course
Anyhow in a corner, some untidy spot
Where the dogs go on with their doggy life and the torturer's horse
Scratches its innocent behind on a tree.

In Brueghel's *Icarus,* for instance: how everything turns away
Quite leisurely from the disaster; the ploughman may
Have heard the splash, the forsaken cry,
But for him it was not an important failure; the sun shone
As it had to on the white legs disappearing into the green
Water; and the expensive delicate ship that must have seen

Something amazing, a boy falling out of the sky,
Had somewhere to get to and sailed calmly on.

from *Nephelidia*

ALGERNON CHARLES SWINBURNE

From the depth of the dreamy decline of the dawn through a notable nimbus of nebulous noonshine,
Pallid and pink as the palm of the flag-flower that flickers with fear of the flies as they float—
Are the looks of our lovers that lustrously lean from a marvel of mystic miraculous moonshine,
These that we feel in the blood of our blushes that thicken and threaten with throbs through the throat?
Thicken and thrill as a theatre thronged at appeal of an actor's appalled agitation,
Fainter with fear of the fires of the future than pale with the promise of pride in the past;
Flushed with the famishing fullness of fever that reddens with radiance of rathe recreation,
Gaunt as the ghastliest of glimpses that gleam through the gloom of the gloaming when ghosts go aghast?
Nay, for the nick of the tick of the time is a tremulous touch on the temples of terror,
Strained as the sinews yet strenuous with strife of the dead who is dumb as the dust-heaps of death:
Surely no soul is it, sweet as the spasm of erotic emotional exquisite error,
Bathed in the balms of beatified bliss, beatific itself by beatitude's breath.
Surely no spirit or sense of a soul that was soft to the spirit and soul of our senses
Sweetens the stress of suspiring suspicion that sobs in the semblance and sound of a sigh;
Only this oracle opens Olympian, in mystical moods and triangular tenses—
"Life is the lust of a lamp for the light that is dark till the dawn of the day that we die."

Elegy Written in a Country Churchyard

THOMAS GRAY

The curfew tolls the knell of parting day,
  The lowing herd wind slowly o'er the lea,
The plowman homeward plods his weary way,
  And leaves the world to darkness and to me.

Now fades the glimmering landscape on the sight,
  And all the air a solemn stillness holds,
Save where the beetle wheels his droning flight,
  And drowsy tinklings lull the distant folds;

Save that from yonder ivy-mantled tower
  The moping owl does to the moon complain
Of such, as wandering near her secret bower,
  Molest her ancient solitary reign.

Beneath those rugged elms, that yew-tree's shade,
  Where heaves the turf in many a mouldering heap,
Each in his narrow cell forever laid,
  The rude forefathers of the hamlet sleep.

The breezy call of incense-breathing morn,
  The swallow twittering from the straw-built shed,
The cock's shrill clarion, or the echoing horn,
  No more shall rouse them from their lowly bed.

For them no more the blazing hearth shall burn,
  Or busy housewife ply her evening care;
No children run to lisp their sire's return,
  Or climb his knees the envied kiss to share.

Oft did the harvest to their sickle yield,
  Their furrow oft the stubborn glebe has broke;
How jocund did they drive their team afield!
  How bowed the woods beneath their sturdy stroke!

Let not Ambition mock their useful toil,
  Their homely joys, and destiny obscure;

Nor Grandeur hear with a disdainful smile
  The short and simple annals of the poor.

The boast of heraldry, the pomp of power,
  And all that beauty, all that wealth e'er gave,
Awaits alike the inevitable hour.
  The paths of glory lead but to the grave.

Nor you, ye proud, impute to these the fault,
  If Memory o'er their tomb no trophies raise,
Where through the long-drawn aisle and fretted vault
  The pealing anthem swells the note of praise.

Can storied urn or animated bust
  Back to its mansion call the fleeting breath?
Can Honor's voice provoke the silent dust,
  Or Flattery soothe the dull cold ear of Death?

Perhaps in this neglected spot is laid
  Some heart once pregnant with celestial fire;
Hands that the rod of empire might have swayed,
  Or waked to ecstasy the living lyre.

But Knowledge to their eyes her ample page
  Rich with the spoils of time did ne'er unroll;
Chill Penury repressed their noble rage,
  And froze the genial current of the soul.

Full many a gem of purest ray serene,
  The dark unfathomed caves of ocean bear;
Full many a flower is born to blush unseen,
  And waste its sweetness on the desert air.

Some village Hampden, that with dauntless breast
  The little tyrant of his fields withstood;
Some mute inglorious Milton here may rest,
  Some Cromwell guiltless of his country's blood.

The applause of listening senates to command,
  The threats of pain and ruin to despise,
To scatter plenty o'er a smiling land,
  And read their history in a nation's eyes,

Their lot forbade; nor circumscribed alone
Their growing virtues, but their crimes confined;
Forbade to wade through slaughter to a throne,
And shut the gates of mercy on mankind,

The struggling pangs of conscious truth to hide,
To quench the blushes of ingenuous shame,
Or heap the shrine of Luxury and Pride
With incense kindled at the Muse's flame.

Far from the madding crowd's ignoble strife,
Their sober wishes never learned to stray;
Along the cool sequestered vale of life
They kept the noiseless tenor of their way.

Yet even these bones from insult to protect
Some frail memorial still erected nigh,
With uncouth rhymes and shapeless sculpture decked,
Implores the passing tribute of a sigh.

Their name, their years, spelt by the unlettered Muse,
The place of fame and elegy supply,
And many a holy text around she strews,
That teach the rustic moralist to die.

For who to dumb forgetfulness a prey,
This pleasing anxious being e'er resigned,
Left the warm precincts of the cheerful day,
Nor cast one longing lingering look behind?

On some fond breast the parting soul relies,
Some pious drops the closing eye requires;
E'en from the tomb the voice of Nature cries,
E'en in our ashes live their wonted fires.

For thee, who mindful of the unhonored dead
Dost in these lines their artless tale relate,
If chance, by lonely contemplation led,
Some kindred spirit shall inquire thy fate,

Haply some hoary-headed swain may say,
"Oft have we seen him at the peep of dawn

Brushing with hasty steps the dews away
  To meet the sun upon the upland lawn.

"There at the foot of yonder nodding beech
  That wreathes its old fantastic roots so high,
His listless length at noontide would he stretch,
  And pore upon the brook that babbles by.

"Hard by yon wood, now smiling as in scorn,
  Muttering his wayward fancies he would rove,
Now drooping, woeful wan, like one forlorn,
  Or crazed with care, or crossed in hopeless love.

"One morn I missed him on the customed hill,
  Along the heath and near his favorite tree;
Another came; nor yet beside the rill,
  Nor up the lawn, nor at the wood was he;

"The next with dirges due in sad array
  Slow through the church-way path we saw him borne.
Approach and read (for thou can'st read) the lay
  Graved on the stone beneath yon agéd thorn."

THE EPITAPH

Here rests his head upon the lap of earth
  A youth to Fortune and to Fame unknown.
Fair Science frowned not on his humble birth,
  And Melancholy marked him for her own.

Large was his bounty, and his soul sincere,
  Heaven did a recompense as largely send:
He gave to Misery all he had, a tear,
  He gained from Heaven ('twas all he wished) a friend.

No farther seek his merits to disclose,
  Or draw his frailties from their dread abode,
(There they alike in trembling hope repose)
  The bosom of his Father and his God.

Ode on the Death of a Favorite Cat Drowned in a Tub of Gold Fishes

THOMAS GRAY

'Twas on a lofty vase's side,
Where China's gayest art had dyed
  The azure flowers that blow;
Demurest of the tabby kind,
The pensive Selima reclined,
  Gazed on the lake below.

Her conscious tail her joy declared;
The fair round face, the snowy beard,
  The velvet of her paws,
Her coat, that with the tortoise vies,
Her ears of jet, and emerald eyes,
  She saw; and purred applause.

Still had she gazed; but 'midst the tide
Two angel forms were seen to glide,
  The genii of the stream:
Their scaly armor's Tyrian hue
Through richest purple to the view
  Betrayed a golden gleam.

The hapless nymph with wonder saw;
A whisker first and then a claw,
  With many an ardent wish,
She stretched in vain to reach the prize.
What female heart can gold despise?
  What cat's averse to fish?

Presumptuous maid! with looks intent
Again she stretched, again she bent,
  Nor knew the gulf between.
(Malignant Fate sat by, and smiled)
The slippery verge her feet beguiled,
  She tumbled headlong in.

Eight times emerging from the flood
She mewed to every watry god,
  Some speedy aid to send.
No dolphin came, no nereid stirred,
Nor cruel Tom nor Susan heard.
  A favorite has no friend!

From hence, ye beauties, undeceived,
Know, one false step is ne'er retrieved,
  And be with caution bold.
Not all that tempts your wandering eyes
And heedless hearts is lawful prize;
  Nor all that glisters, gold.

[VIII]

The Reader as Artist: The Work Ahead

> The lyf so short, the craft so long to lerne . . .
> CHAUCER: *The Parliament of Fowls*

Reading poetry is primarily a private affair—at least in our age. But, like most pleasurable forms of excitement, it can at times be a shared experience. Even the old conventional classroom situation can provide an interesting social milieu for reading poems, whether recited directly or read beforehand and then discussed. In this final chapter we will examine some of the practical problems that readers of poetry often encounter—problems which can be solved best in classroom discussions.

DISCUSSING POETRY

Readers' reactions to a given poem often vary widely, especially when the poem is read for the first time and is not presented as an "anthology-approved" classic. The following poem by William Blake was mimeographed and distributed to a group of college sophomores who were then asked to evaluate and interpret it.

Infant Sorrow

My mother groaned! my father wept.
Into the dangerous world I leapt:
Helpless, naked, piping loud:
Like a fiend hid in a cloud.

Struggling in my father's hands,
Striving against my swaddling bands,
Bound and weary I thought best
To sulk upon my mother's breast.

Two contrasting responses will illustrate how differently two persons may be affected by a poem.

RESPONSE 1. There is no tremendous depth in this poem. A child leaves his mother and father and takes a leap into the dangerous world. Because of the relative age of the child and because he had no important purpose in going into the world, the tone is rather light and humorous. The writer seems to have just written this poem to present an idea with no other strong connotations to be taken from the poem.

RESPONSE 2. The poet creates a mood of frantic, painful tension: the agonizing physical pain of the mother and the excruciating mental torture of the father; the hot, suffocating fear, anger, and feverish struggle of the child, and his eventual exhausted surrender. Time seems to move quickly. It is all over in a few explosive, intense moments.

The next two responses imply two preliminary approaches to the poem:

RESPONSE 3. The poem does not seem to have any hidden meanings. It just implies in a simple and direct manner the trauma of birth.

RESPONSE 4. The immediate reaction to this poem is that it deals with the birth of a child and the traumas of childbirth and infancy. The second stanza, however, suggests more. It suggests the development of interrelationships in the family: the father who had shown anguish at the birth of his child now possibly begins to feel ambivalent toward the child and show an anxiety regarding his position as father. We see also the child's instinctive reaction to this antagonism and, implicitly, the mother's protectiveness, which is also instinctive.

The third respondent is, of course, correct in saying there are no hidden meanings in the poem, if by "hidden" he means "ulterior." (A reader who read "ulterior" meanings into this poem might say, for example, that the poem seems to be about birth but is really about death or about the rise and fall of Czechoslovakian liberalism in 1968.) He is correct in stating that the poem is about the experience of birth, but fails to consider the depth and ambiguities of that "simple" scene. Neither does respondent 4 interpret the poem in terms other than those of birth. He feels that within those starkly delineated events more profound meanings are suggested. The next response provides a good example of the belief that for every poem there exists that secret "ulterior" key by which those otherwise inexplicable lines may be decoded:

Response 5. I feel that the poem represents, in a sense, the entire life cycle of a person from birth to death. A person struggles and strives, and after a long and weary trial he dies. Instead of sulking or finding comfort on his own mother's breast, he returns to Mother Nature's breast through burial. In another sense, this poem may be interpreted politically. The first stanza could signify the birth of a movement. "Hid in a cloud" suggests the mainstream of society. The "dangerous world," in this case, would be those who might actually threaten the movement. "Helpless" and "naked" indicate that the revolutionaries are not very strong and are in fact defenseless. On the other hand, they are "piping loud," intending to shout their myth and strive for support. The second stanza implies their struggle against the ideas or government in power, the "father" being the government. But in the end the father turns out to be stronger and the child ends up "bound and weary." The group is forced to disband and the individuals again join in the productive efforts of society ("sulk upon my mother's breast").

Some unsatisfactory readings occur simply through inattention to the text, for example:

Response 6. The first stanza concludes with the rather strange image of a "fiend hid in a cloud." Presumably this is a simile illustrating the fact that the baby is bundled up so completely that he is hidden from sight, but not from hearing, for his cries may be likened to the screams of a fiend.

That image is a troublesome one to interpret outside the context of Blake's other writings, but this interpretation is provably wrong. The baby is:

> Helpless, *naked,* piping loud:
> Like a fiend hid in a cloud.

Equally unsatisfactory and even more prevalent is the "let's-look-on-the-cheery-side-of-life" approach:

Response 7. This poem suggests how clean, fresh and alive with spirit, and ready to do all, the child is at birth. This birth is not just a physical event, but a mental awakening, a leaping into the world with fresh ideas ("piping loud") and no mental perversions. But then the fog ("cloud") lifts, the child is exposed to a struggle from which he tires easily, and, tired and frightened, seeks refuge and comfort. (I ask one question: is the "fiend" the devil? I dislike to believe that we are born with the devil lurking beneath such a thin and naïve covering.)

Rather than condemn the poem as a pessimistic, negative view of early infancy, this respondent has preferred to stretch the poem's connotations beyond the breaking point. The expression "I dislike to believe" is especially interesting. It is not an inability, but a disinclination to believe that there is anything demonic about an infant.

Actually, in a poem we *temporarily* accept the poet's entire world, and that includes his beliefs as well as his images and rhythms. This suspension of disbelief on our part in no way obliges us to make either Homer's Olympus, Dante's Inferno, or Blake's child psychology part of our permanent beliefs. Each poem may be regarded as a separate universe in which things function according to the unique rules of that universe. These rules sometimes resemble what we are used to in our external everyday world. But though they are often unfamiliar and strange, we must nevertheless assume their existence—as a scientist assumes the truth of a given hypothesis—in order to discover what general poetic conclusions may be drawn from them.

Another, perhaps subtler, type of misreading is a misreading of the rhetorical context:

RESPONSE 8. Quite obviously his birth is symbolic of his life to this point. The poet has fought relentlessly against the evils of the world, but has suddenly realized the futility of it all. Because he is tired and disillusioned, he has rejected the world and society and has withdrawn to sulk inside his mind, alone and unhappy.

RESPONSE 9. In the poem "Infant Sorrow," the poet attempts to give a first-person account of his birth. The effectiveness of the poem is somewhat limited by the inappropriate use of certain words and phrases. For example, "into the dangerous world I leapt" comes out sounding unintentionally humorous. The image "like a fiend hid in a cloud," though dramatic, isn't particularly accurate or, in this case, relevant. The poet seems to want to portray himself as a dislikable character and to show how he has been this way since his birth—which sounds rather maudlin.

Respondent 8, like 5, prefers to ignore the specific situation in favor of an ulterior meaning, but he also fails to consider the possibility that the author is allowing the baby to actually speak. And if the poet had identified himself with the baby, he might indeed deserve the dispraise of respondent 9.

At this point an important problem emerges: if the infant is not the poet (in the strict autobiographical sense), and if he cannot be regarded as a symbol of something else, why did the poet give him such unrealistic attributes? Why did he leap (almost consciously) into this world? Why is he fiendish? Why did he think it best to sulk upon his mother's breast? Finally, how can he speak if he is an infant? Or if he is old enough to write poetry, how can he remember his natal cogitations so precisely? Respondent 10 upholds the "no-poetic-nonsense" view:

RESPONSE 10. This poem is filled with inconsistencies. As an image of the period directly after childbirth it is very inaccurate. For example, the reactions of the child are here described as voluntary, whereas in reality they are all instinctual. It is unlikely that the father would hold his baby in his *hands* and not his arms. And it is implied that the child is immediately feeding at the breast —which seems rather a short time after birth.

Like respondent 7, he has denied the poet his most essential right, the right to state his own hypothetical premises. In this case the poet's premises are "let us assume (1) that this new born child has a certain degree of will, (2) that his reception into his new world is not to his liking, (3) that his father's one function is to restrain him, and (4) that, after considering the alternatives, he decides resentfully to accept comfort from his mother." Then comes the most important question: Does this combination of assumed reactions cast any light upon the inner conflicts of a small child? Is it one valid way in which to view a child? Does our experience in any way confirm the view that a small child leads a complex, if not necessarily a conflicted, emotional life?

The next two respondents permit the poet to set his own scene, to create his own temporary universe and give it his own hypothetical rules:

RESPONSE 11. The poet paints a bleak picture: the last stanza describes a scene of imprisonment where he is fighting in his father's hands, bound and weary. The crowning touch is that he "thought best/ To sulk upon my mother's breast." "Thought" is undoubtedly an exaggeration: he did not *plan* to do anything. Yet this use of "thought" makes the sense of entrapment more real because the child realizes that this is *all* he can do. "Sulk" is a very good word; it connotes unhappiness and it also resembles the more expected word "suck."

RESPONSE 12. I am struck by the speed and amount of movement early in the poem. It reads quickly, thus impressing one with the short duration of the action described. This feeling of rapidity and motion is aided by the words "leapt," "struggling," and "striving." The last two lines of the poem slow the action, both by means of the particular visual images and by the use of long vowel sounds. After this initial reaction, certain parts of the description of birth strike me—the anguished labor of both parents seems to be almost in opposition to the blind, nearly voluntary "leap" the child makes into a world full of dangers of which he is ignorant. Once having made this journey, the child is helpless, but he still makes vocal and muscular efforts against all that is binding: his clothes and his father. I am troubled by "Like a fiend hid in a cloud." I could perhaps come to see it as an expression of the fiend within the child, that is, the bad, or the anti-social. It is hidden but reveals itself through his anti-parental actions. To push this interpretation a little farther: we all seek freedom, often oblivious to the dangers that it may bring. The training within us, our "mother" and "father," our internalized social conscience, may seek to hold us back, but we still want to try freedom for ourselves. If our experiment fails, we return to nurse discontentedly at the breast of conventional so ciety.

POEMS FOR COMPARISON

[A] *London*

I wander thro' each charter'd street,
Near where the charter'd Thames does flow,
And mark in every face I meet
Marks of weakness, marks of woe.

In every cry of every Man,
In every Infant's cry of fear,
In every voice, in every ban,
The mind-forg'd manacles I hear.

How the Chimney-sweeper's cry
Every black'ning Church appalls;
And the hapless Soldier's sigh
Runs in blood down Palace walls.

But most thro' midnight streets I hear
How the youthful Harlot's curse
Blasts the new born Infant's tear,
And blights with plagues the Marriage hearse.

[B] *London*

Wending my way beside the busy shops
And by th' embankment where the old Thames flows,

I noted in the people whom I met
The grievous aspects of loose liberty.
I heard express'd in accents young and old
Pride, self-indulgence, and licentiousness:
The rude and ragged Chimney-sweeper's shouts
Disturbed the faithful worshippers of God;
The rebel Soldier at the flogging post
Denied his Trespass and reviled his King;
But most through midnight streets I heard the curse
That issu'd from old Whoredom's twisted lips,
A curse against all that is innocent—
Against chaste Marriage and pure Infancy!

The following are twelve responses that a group of college students made to the preceding exercise. Several are given in their entirety; several are only excerpted comments. On the basis of your own reading of the two "Londons" comment upon these responses.

Response 1. Dissatisfaction, unhappiness, and distress seem to be uppermost in the first author's mind. He reminds me of a man who wants power, prestige, and position and has gotten none of these. Struggling and depression also seem evident in this poem. It seems as if this author is degrading society as it realistically is. . . . The second poem is not as depressing as the first. The same incidents are discussed, but not in such a harsh or degrading fashion. Life does not seem as hopeless here as it seems in the first poem. I think this author has accepted the world in a more easygoing way than the first author. He is merely noting the scene as he sees it, whereas in the first case the author tends more to ridicule it.

Response 2. I prefer the first. The second poem tries to idealize institutions such as religion, the army, and marriage and puts the total blame on people. Since these institutions are man-made, they cannot be perfect either and to idealize them is to present them falsely.

Response 3. The first poem displays righteous indignation. One can almost imagine a minister reading it from his pulpit. The poem uses strong images to paint a picture of what it is reviling. The second poem seems to come from a man who isn't trying to impress someone else with what he feels, but simply to express what he feels. The tone is one of depression. The relative understatement of the scene underscores the emotion behind it—when one is deeply depressed, one does not use fiery language.

RESPONSE 4. I prefer version I of "London." I can sense the darkness, mysterious and murderous, up and down those chartered streets along the Thames. I can sense as well the deprivation, the hate, and the corruption that inhabit the dark, mysterious faces that wander along these streets. They are all in a state of misery. Considered as a whole, the poem is like a time bomb. Something must let all this out. I like the dark, tense imagery: cries, fear, blasts, sighs that run in blood. The second version features a more bland exposition of the theme, and therefore it lacks force. How could anyone "note" anything when confronted with such a dismal scene?

RESPONSE 5. The second poem is pedantic and lecturing in tone. It also employs more judgments than the first. The first does not say "this is evil," "this is nice." It is a description of the London of that time and thereby leaves more room for the reader to react without telling him what conclusions to draw.

RESPONSE 6. Although both poems are trying to say the same thing, I think I prefer the second one because its tone appears to be less gloomy than the first. In both poems the narrator has been hurt and is unhappy. Nothing looks good to this person. Nevertheless I like the second poem because the person speaking appears to have some faith in mankind. Note for example: "Disturbed the *faithful* worshippers of God." The "busy shops" give me an impression of people shopping during Christmas—a happy, cheerful time of the year.

RESPONSE 7. I would say that, technically, the first poem is better. But I did not *feel* it was better, because I simply do not agree with the poet's statement that life is a sordid, plague-ridden existence. The poet is explicitly speaking of life in London (or other cities), but I think his attitude can logically and easily be extended to include all life. He paints a grim picture of life, one which I do not find to be true.

RESPONSE 8. Somehow the second poem seems more real than the first. You can actually imagine someone walking along the busy shops and along the banks of the Thames. You can see this person observing the people the same as you do when you walk down Fifth Avenue and are not in any particular hurry. You walk along and watch the people, sometimes overhearing a conversation or parts of it. Often you will see men working, shouting orders back and forth, with church bells ringing in the background. I don't walk through the sections of town that are mentioned in the last line.

RESPONSE 9. The first poem has a negative outlook on London: it gives the impression that the men walk in fear, that all men are somewhat enslaved, and that they are really depressed. For some reason the first poem made me think of nighttime and darkness, while the second made me think of daylight and sunshine. This is probably because the second has a more positive attitude toward the people of London—they work busily, are faithful worshippers of God, and are free, and proud of it. But the first poem implies that they are not free and are in fear.

RESPONSE 10. The style of the first one bothers me, particularly in the first stanza where the repetition of such words as "charter'd" and "marks" gives the verse a monotonous tone. The first poem also sacrifices clarity for the sake of construction, and in some cases such as the third stanza, the images are decidedly obscure.

RESPONSE 11. I prefer the first poem. Its imagery seems to be far more vivid. The repetition of the word "charter'd" in the first two lines sets up the mood of the plotted, industrial, mechanized, and possibly inhuman city of London. Manacles are alluded to—perhaps manacles of sin, perhaps manacles of conformity. He does not say that appalling the church is wrong, nor that the soldier is "truant" or "traitorous" or "delinquent," but merely hapless, implying that the fault does not lie with him.

RESPONSE 12. The second poem is much more precise and vivid. For example, in the first poem the soldier's sigh runs in blood down palace walls. In the second poem the soldier is at a flogging post denying the charges against him and reviling his King. At the end of the two poems reference is made to a harlot cursing marriage and infancy. The first poem does not make any point of this. It merely states a fact. The impact of the meaning is hindered because it is a "youthful Harlot's curse." In the second poem, however, the statements come from "old Whoredom's twisted lips." The image immediately becomes vivid. Here it is not a person, but a state of degradation that curses innocence. Old and twisted lips implies that there is nothing innocent about the accuser. This second poem makes its point clear: pure innocence, as represented by infancy and marriage, is attacked by a state of degradation that is its exact opposite. One might also note that the author of the first poem used the term "hearse" with "marriage." The two seem to clash. Marriage suggests the beginning of life for the couple and for the children they may have, whereas the hearse suggests the end of a life.

THE LONG CRAFT

Few classroom circumstances are as difficult and as potentially frustrating for students and instructor alike as a classroom discussion on the meanings of a poem. The student feels entitled to his interpretation because he has arrived at it through his own unique imaginative process. His comments genuinely represent what the poem means to him. The instructor feels entitled to his interpretation because he has spent many years—college, graduate school, personal and professional studies—deeply involved in the study of literature, perhaps even in study of the poet now being discussed in class. Furthermore, he feels entitled to offer his as the one authoritative, or at least the most satisfactory, reading of the poem. The result is often an unresolved difference of opinion, sometimes a resentful deadlock of wills.

But poems are not all created by malicious riddlers. They are not labyrinths impenetrable to all but the few who possess some magic key. Most of the finest poems in English are accessible to any intelligent reader who understands and accepts the basic procedures of poetry. These procedures entail, first of all, what Coleridge called "that willing suspension of disbelief for the moment, which constitutes poetic faith." As we have pointed out, the reader must submit his consciousness—even his unconsciousness—to the suggestiveness of the poem. He should regard each poem as a small verbal universe that operates according to its own peculiar laws. It invites the reader on a journey of discovery, but, to quote once more from Coleridge, "the reader should be carried forward, not merely or chiefly by the mechanical impulse of curiosity, or by a restless desire to arrive at the final solution; but by the pleasurable activity of mind excited by the attractions of the journey itself." Secondly, he must read the entire poem; that is, he must not overemphasize one detail and totally ignore another. Our consciousness, psychologists tell us, is notoriously selective: we tend to block out some realities, while we fixate upon others. In our everyday life, this habit sometimes results in faulty conclusions; in reading poetry it always results in unsatisfactory interpretations.

The two basic procedures are, in other words, the active participation of the "total reader" and his active participation in the "total poem." These two ideals summarize the objectives of this book and together comprise that intense, totally absorbing "act of poetry" in which the artist-reader is trained, and trains himself, to perform.

But because the artistry of the poetry-reader is a slowly learned craft—a craft that takes many devoted years to master and a whole lifetime to expand and enhance—the apprentice reader should not become impatient with his own gradual progress. A semester's work can be extremely valuable, but at best it can only provide impetus and direction. The rest is up to us—a glib statement that everyone of us says and few of us act upon. There are, after all, two ways of regarding an area of study, as the following anecdote illustrates. A high school girl, one May afternoon, strolled into New York's Central Park to do some studying for her finals. She picked a quiet bench as far removed as possible from the softball game to the west and the bands of small indefatigable children to the east. At the far end of the bench sat a white-haired old man. His glasses kept slipping down his nose as he stared down at a book on his lap and made quick pencil-jottings on a pad. She had seen studious old men like that before, recent immigrants studying English in the adult classes in her high school. After half an hour the girl's curiosity got the better of her. She went over to the old man and said, "Pardon me, but you look like you're a student too." The old man stroked his large, white mustache with a nervous little gesture, smiled, and said, "Yes." "What are you studying?" she asked.

"Astronomy," said the slightly disheveled old man. "Oh," she said, "you'll like that. It's very interesting. Our class took that last year." She strolled back to her end of the bench, took a last look at her French verbs, and went home to dinner, never guessing that she had spoken that day with Albert Einstein.

In our consumer-oriented world we tend to regard all things as commodities. Some of us even believe that "every man has his price." We have a tendency to demand that a printed commodity, namely a book, make itself satisfactorily understandable to the purchaser. It should at least be worth the price we pay for it. Often after hearing about a book, we buy it, read it, and are only mildly absorbed in it. Afterwards, like the girl in the park, we can say, "Oh yes, I read that several years ago," and if our memory is good we can recall the main character's name and how the novel or poem ended. But perhaps we too seldom consider the possibility that *a particular poem may not have been written for us to read at that particular point in our life.*

Life *is* change. Those of us who are mentally and emotionally alive realize that next year we will understand ourselves and the world a little better, and that other men's accounts of their own insights will become just a little more intelligible to us. It is only the unfortunate person who has stopped developing, that demands that everything, immediately and on the spot, become clear to him. In his point of view what remains obscure has by that very fact proved its basic worthlessness.

We are all limited to our own frame of reference—that range of experience and conceptualization that we share with our ethnic or social group, our nation, and our generation. As we grow from childhood to adulthood, we watch our individual frame of reference expand and overlap those of others. (Of course, this process can be halted anywhere along the way. One can become a perfectly well-formed bigot even at the age of ten.) As we grow older and complete our formal education, it is true that a powerful tendency toward closed-mindedness sets in. Yet the reader of poetry, if he resists the premature senility of his postgraduate years, has an exciting revelation awaiting him: those monumental poets whom he read with distant respect in his college days are now gradually becoming his contemporaries. They "speak" to him more and more because, as each year passes, he has more and more within him with which to respond to them.

The reader of poetry whose mind and experience continue to expand has before him the fellowship of those others whose vision broadened steadily throughout their lifetime: men like Dante, Milton, Goethe, Blake, and Yeats. Such specimens of mankind do not really age. Their progress is through amplitudes into greater amplitudes.

ADDITIONAL READINGS

Lycidas

JOHN MILTON

In this Monody the Author bewails a learned Friend, unfortunately drowned in his passage from Chester on the Irish Seas, 1637; and, by occasion, foretells the ruin of our corrupted clergy, then in their height.

Yet once more, O ye laurels, and once more,
Ye myrtles brown, with ivy never sere,
I come to pluck your berries harsh and crude,
And with forced fingers rude
Shatter your leaves before the mellowing year.
Bitter constraint, and sad occasion dear,
Compels me to disturb your season due;
For Lycidas is dead, dead ere his prime,
Young Lycidas, and hath not left his peer.
Who would not sing for Lycidas? he knew
Himself to sing, and build the lofty rhyme.
He must not float upon his watery bier
Unwept, and welter to the parching wind,
Without the meed of some melodious tear.
  Begin then, sisters of the sacred well
That from beneath the seat of Jove doth spring,
Begin, and somewhat loudly sweep the string.

Hence with denial vain and coy excuse;
So may some gentle Muse
With lucky words favor my destined urn,
And as he passes, turn,
And bid fair peace be to my sable shroud.
For we were nursed upon the self-same hill,
Fed the same flock by fountain, shade, and rill.
   Together both, ere the high lawns appeared
Under the opening eye-lids of the morn,
We drove afield, and both together heard
What time the gray-fly winds her sultry horn,
Battening our flocks with the fresh dews of night,
Oft till the star that rose, at evening, bright
Toward heaven's descent had sloped his westering wheel.
Meanwhile the rural ditties were not mute,
Tempered to the oaten flute,
Rough satyrs danced, and fauns with cloven heel
From the glad sound would not be absent long;
And old Damoetas loved to hear our song.
   But O the heavy change, now thou art gone,
Now thou art gone, and never must return!
Thee, shepherd, thee the woods and desert caves,
With wild thyme and the gadding vine o'ergrown,
And all their echoes mourn.
The willows and the hazel copses green
Shall now no more be seen
Fanning their joyous leaves to thy soft lays.
As killing as the canker to the rose,
Or taint-worm to the weanling herds that graze,
Or frost to flowers, that their gay wardrobe wear
When first the white-thorn blows;
Such, Lycidas, thy loss to shepherd's ear.
   Where were ye, nymphs, when the remorseless deep
Closed o'er the head of your loved Lycidas?
For neither were ye playing on the steep
Where your old bards, the famous druids, lie,
Nor on the shaggy top of Mona high,
Nor yet where Deva spreads her wizard stream.
Ay me, I fondly dream!

Had ye been there—for what could that have done?
What could the Muse herself that Orpheus bore,
The Muse herself, for her enchanting son,
Whom universal nature did lament,
When by the rout that made the hideous roar
His gory visage down the stream was sent,
Down the swift Hebrus to the Lesbian shore?
  Alas! what boots it with uncessant care
To tend the homely, slighted, shepherd's trade,
And strictly meditate the thankless Muse?
Were it not better done, as others use,
To sport with Amaryllis in the shade,
Or with the tangles of Neaera's hair?
Fame is the spur that the clear spirit doth raise
(That last infirmity of noble mind)
To scorn delights, and live laborious days;
But the fair guerdon when we hope to find,
And think to burst out into sudden blaze,
Comes the blind Fury with the abhorrèd shears
And slits the thin-spun life. "But not the praise,"
Phoebus replied, and touched my trembling ears:
"Fame is no plant that grows on mortal soil,
Nor in the glistering foil
Set off to the world, nor in broad rumor lies,
But lives and spreads aloft by those pure eyes
And perfect witness of all-judging Jove;
As he pronounces lastly on each deed,
Of so much fame in heaven expect thy meed."
  O fountain Arethuse, and thou honored flood,
Smooth-sliding Mincius, crowned with vocal reeds,
That strain I heard was of a higher mood.
But now my oat proceeds,
And listens to the herald of the sea
That came in Neptune's plea.
He asked the waves, and asked the felon winds,
What hard mishap hath doomed this gentle swain?
And questioned every gust of rugged wings
That blows from off each beakèd promontory:
They knew not of his story,

And sage Hippotades their answer brings,
That not a blast was from his dungeon strayed;
The air was calm, and on the level brine
Sleek Panopè with all her sisters played.
It was that fatal and perfidious bark,
Built in the eclipse, and rigged with curses dark,
That sunk so low that sacred head of thine.
  Next Camus, reverend sire, went footing slow,
His mantle hairy, and his bonnet sedge,
Inwrought with figures dim, and on the edge
Like to that sanguine flower inscribed with woe.
"Ah, who hath reft," quoth he, "my dearest pledge?"
Last came, and last did go,
The Pilot of the Galilean lake;
Two massy keys he bore of metals twain
(The golden opes, the iron shuts amain).
He shook his mitred locks, and stern bespake:
"How well could I have spared for thee, young swain,
Enow of such as for their bellies' sake
Creep and intrude and climb into the fold!
Of other care they little reckoning make
Than how to scramble at the shearers' feast,
And shove away the worthy bidden guest.
Blind mouths! that scarce themselves know how to hold
A sheep-hook, or have learned aught else the least
That to the faithful herdman's art belongs!
What recks it them? What need they? They are sped;
And when they list, their lean and flashy songs
Grate on their scrannel pipes of wretched straw;
The hungry sheep look up, and are not fed,
But, swol'n with wind and the rank mist they draw,
Rot inwardly, and foul contagion spread;
Besides what the grim wolf with privy paw
Daily devours apace, and nothing said;
But that two-handed engine at the door
Stands ready to smite once, and smite no more."
  Return, Alpheus; the dread voice is past
That shrunk thy streams; return, Sicilian Muse,
And call the vales, and bid them hither cast

Their bells and flowerets of a thousand hues.
Ye valleys low, where the mild whispers use
Of shades and wanton winds and gushing brooks,
On whose fresh lap the swart star sparely looks,
Throw hither all your quaint enameled eyes
That on the green turf suck the honeyed showers,
And purple all the ground with vernal flowers.
Bring the rathe primrose that forsaken dies,
The tufted crow-toe, and pale jessamine,
The white pink, and the pansy freaked with jet,
The glowing violet,
The musk-rose, and the well-attired woodbine,
With cowslips wan that hang the pensive head,
And every flower that sad embroidery wears.
Bid amaranthus all his beauty shed,
And daffadillies fill their cups with tears,
To strew the laureate hearse where Lycid lies.
For so to interpose a little ease,
Let our frail thoughts dally with false surmise;
Ay me! whilst thee the shores and sounding seas
Wash far away, where'er thy bones are hurled,
Whether beyond the stormy Hebrides,
Where thou perhaps under the whelming tide
Visit'st the bottom of the monstrous world;
Or whether thou, to our moist vows denied,
Sleep'st by the fable of Bellerus old,
Where the great Vision of the guarded mount
Looks toward Namancos and Bayona's hold;
Look homeward, Angel, now, and melt with ruth;
And, O ye dolphins, waft the hapless youth.
   Weep no more, woeful shepherds, weep no more,
For Lycidas, your sorrow, is not dead,
Sunk though he be beneath the watery floor;
So sinks the day-star in the ocean bed,
And yet anon repairs his drooping head,
And tricks his beams, and with new-spangled ore
Flames in the forehead of the morning sky:
So Lycidas sunk low, but mounted high,
Through the dear might of Him that walked the waves,

Where, other groves and other streams along,
With nectar pure his oozy locks he laves,
And hears the unexpressive nuptial song
In the blest kingdoms meek of joy and love.
There entertain him all the saints above,
In solemn troops and sweet societies
That sing, and singing in their glory move,
And wipe the tears for ever from his eyes.
Now, Lycidas, the shepherds weep no more;
Henceforth thou art the genius of the shore,
In thy large recompense, and shalt be good
To all that wander in that perilous flood.
  Thus sang the uncouth swain to the oaks and rills,
While the still morn went out with sandals gray;
He touched the tender stops of various quills,
With eager thought warbling his Doric lay.
And now the sun had stretched out all the hills,
And now was dropped into the western bay;
At last he rose, and twitched his mantle blue:
Tomorrow to fresh woods, and pastures new.

The Rime of the Ancient Mariner

SAMUEL TAYLOR COLERIDGE

Part i

An ancient Mariner meeteth three Gallants bidden to a wedding-feast, and detaineth one.

It is an ancient Mariner,
And he stoppeth one of three.
"By thy long grey beard and glittering eye,
Now wherefore stopp'st thou me?

The Bridegroom's doors are opened wide,
And I am next of kin;
The guests are met, the feast is set:
May'st hear the merry din."

He holds him with his skinny hand,
"There was a ship," quoth he.
"Hold off! unhand me, grey-beard loon!"
Eftsoons his hand dropt he.

The Wedding-Guest is spell-bound by the eye of the old sea-faring man, and constrained to hear his tale.

He holds him with his glittering eye—
The Wedding-Guest stood still,
And listens like a three years' child:
The Mariner hath his will.

The Wedding-Guest sat on a stone:
He cannot choose but hear;
And thus spake on that ancient man,
The bright-eyed Mariner.

"The ship was cheered, the harbor cleared,
Merrily did we drop
Below the kirk, below the hill,
Below the lighthouse top.

The Mariner tells how the ship sailed southward with a good wind and fair weather, till it reached the Line.

The Sun came up upon the left,
Out of the sea came he!
And he shone bright, and on the right
Went down into the sea.

Higher and higher every day,
Till over the mast at noon—"
The Wedding-Guest here beat his breast,
For he heard the loud bassoon.

The Wedding-Guest heareth the bridal music; but the Mariner continueth his tale.

The bride hath paced into the hall,
Red as a rose is she;
Nodding their heads before her goes
The merry minstrelsy.

The Wedding-Guest he beat his breast,
Yet he cannot choose but hear;
And thus spake on that ancient man,
The bright-eyed Mariner.

The ship driven by a storm toward the south pole.

"And now the STORM-BLAST came, and he
Was tyrannous and strong:
He struck with his o'ertaking wings,
And chased us south along.

With sloping masts and dipping prow,
As who pursued with yell and blow

Still treads the shadow of his foe,
And forward bends his head,
The ship drove fast, loud roared the blast,
And southward aye we fled.

And now there came both mist and snow,
And it grew wondrous cold:
And ice, mast-high, came floating by,
As green as emerald.

The land of ice, and of fearful sounds where no living thing was to be seen.

And through the drifts the snowy clifts
Did send a dismal sheen:
Nor shapes of men nor beasts we ken—
The ice was all between.

The ice was here, the ice was there,
The ice was all around:
It cracked and growled, and roared and howled,
Like noises in a swound!

Till a great sea-bird, called the Albatross, came through the snow-fog, and was received with great joy and hospitality.

At length did cross an Albatross,
Through the fog it came;
As if it had been a Christian soul,
We hailed it in God's name.

It ate the food it ne'er had eat,
And round and round it flew.
The ice did split with a thunder-fit;
The helmsman steered us through!

And lo! the Albatross proveth a bird of good omen, and followeth the ship as it returned northward through fog and floating ice.

And a good south wind sprung up behind;
The Albatross did follow,
And every day, for food or play,
Came to the mariners' hollo!

In mist or cloud, on mast or shroud,
It perched for vespers nine;
Whiles all the night, through fog-smoke white,
Glimmered the white Moon-shine."

The ancient Mariner inhospitably killeth the pious bird of good omen.

"God save thee, ancient Mariner!
From the fiends, that plague thee thus!—
Why look'st thou so?"—"With my cross-bow
I shot the ALBATROSS."

Part ii

"The Sun now rose upon the right:
Out of the sea came he,
Still hid in mist, and on the left
Went down into the sea.

And the good south wind still blew behind,
But no sweet bird did follow,
Nor any day for food or play
Came to the mariners' hollo!

His shipmates cry out against the ancient Mariner, for killing the bird of good luck.

And I had done a hellish thing,
And it would work'em woe:
For all averred, I had killed the bird
That made the breeze to blow.
Ah wretch! said they, the bird to slay,
That made the breeze to blow!

But when the fog cleared off, they justify the same, and thus make themselves accomplices in the crime.

Nor dim nor red, like God's own head,
The glorious Sun uprist:
Then all averred, I had killed the bird
That brought the fog and mist.
'Twas right, said they, such birds to slay,
That bring the fog and mist.

The fair breeze continues; the ship enters the Pacific Ocean, and sails northward, even till it reaches the Line.

The fair breeze blew, the white foam flew,
The furrow followed free;
We were the first that ever burst
Into that silent sea.

The ship hath been suddenly becalmed.

Down dropped the breeze, the sails dropped down,
'Twas sad as sad could be;
And we did speak only to break
The silence of the sea!

All in a hot and copper sky
The bloody Sun, at noon,
Right up above the mast did stand,
No bigger than the Moon.

Day after day, day after day,
We stuck, nor breath nor motion;

As idle as a painted ship
Upon a painted ocean.

And the Albatross begins to be avenged.

Water, water, every where,
And all the boards did shrink;
Water, water, every where,
Nor any drop to drink.

The very deep did rot: O Christ!
That ever this should be!
Yea, slimy things did crawl with legs
Upon the slimy sea.

A Spirit had followed them; one of the invisible inhabitants of this planet, neither departed souls nor angels; concerning whom the learned Jew, Josephus, and the Platonic Constantinopolitan, Michael Psellus, may be consulted. They are very numerous, and there is no climate or element without one or more.

About, about, in reel and rout
The death-fires danced at night;
The water, like a witch's oils,
Burned green, and blue and white.

And some in dreams assuréd were
Of the Spirit that plagued us so;
Nine fathom deep he had followed us
From the land of mist and snow.

And every tongue, through utter drought,
Was withered at the root;
We could not speak, no more than if
We had been choked with soot.

The shipmates, in their sore distress, would fain throw the whole guilt on the ancient Mariner: in sign whereof they hang the dead sea-bird round his neck.

Ah! well a-day! what evil looks
Had I from old and young!
Instead of the cross, the Albatross
About my neck was hung."

Part iii

"There passed a weary time. Each throat
Was parched, and glazed each eye.
A weary time! a weary time!
How glazed each weary eye,
When looking westward, I beheld
A something in the sky.

The ancient Mariner beholdeth a sign in the element afar off.

At first it seemed a little speck,
And then it seemed a mist;

It moved and moved, and took at last
A certain shape, I wist.

A speck, a mist, a shape, I wist!
And still it neared and neared:
As if it dodged a water-sprite,
It plunged and tacked and veered.

At its nearer approach, it seemeth him to be a ship; and at a dear ransom he freeth his speech from the bonds of thirst.

With throats unslaked, with black lips baked,
We could nor laugh nor wail;
Through utter drought all dumb we stood!
I bit my arm, I sucked the blood,
And cried, A sail! a sail!

A flash of joy;

With throats unslaked, with black lips baked,
Agape they heard me call:
Gramercy! they for joy did grin,
And all at once their breath drew in,
As they were drinking all.

And horror follows. For can it be a ship that comes onward without wind or tide?

See! see! (I cried) she tacks no more!
Hither to work us weal;
Without a breeze, without a tide,
She steadies with upright keel!

The western wave was all a-flame.
The day was well nigh done!
Almost upon the western wave
Rested the broad bright Sun;
When that strange shape drove suddenly
Betwixt us and the Sun.

It seemeth him but the skeleton of a ship.

And straight the Sun was flecked with bars,
(Heaven's Mother send us grace!)
As if through a dungeon-grate he peered
With broad and burning face.

And its ribs are seen as bars on the face of the setting Sun.

Alas! (thought I, and my heart beat loud)
How fast she nears and nears!
Are those *her* sails that glance in the Sun,
Like restless gossamers?

The Spectre-Woman and her Deathmate, and no other on board the skeleton ship.

Are those *her* ribs through which the Sun
Did peer, as through a grate?
And is that Woman all her crew?
Is that a DEATH? and are there two?
Is DEATH that woman's mate?

Like vessel, like crew! Death and Life-in-Death have diced for the ship's crew, and she (the latter) winneth the ancient Mariner.

Her lips were red, *her* looks were free,
Her locks were yellow as gold:
Her skin was as white as leprosy,
The Night-mare LIFE-IN-DEATH was she,
Who thicks man's blood with cold.

The naked hulk alongside came,
And the twain were casting dice;
'The game is done! I've won! I've won!'
Quoth she, and whistles thrice.

No twilight within the courts of the Sun.

The Sun's rim dips; the stars rush out:
At one stride comes the dark;
With far-heard whisper, o'er the sea,
Off shot the spectre-bark.

At the rising of the Moon,

We listened and looked sideways up!
Fear at my heart, as at a cup,
My life-blood seemed to sip!
The stars were dim, and thick the night,
The steersman's face by his lamp gleamed white;
From the sails the dew did drip—
Till clomb above the eastern bar
The hornéd Moon, with one bright star
Within the nether tip.

One after another,

One after one, by the star-dogged Moon,
Too quick for groan or sigh,
Each turned his face with a ghastly pang,
And cursed me with his eye.

His shipmates drop down dead.

Four times fifty living men,
(And I heard nor sigh nor groan)
With heavy thump, a lifeless lump,
They dropped down one by one.

But Life-in-Death begins her work on the ancient Mariner.

The souls did from their bodies fly,—
They fled to bliss or woe!
And every soul, it passed me by,
Like the whizz of my cross-bow!"

Part iv

The Wedding-Guest feareth that a Spirit is talking to him;

"I fear thee, ancient Mariner!
I fear thy skinny hand!
And thou art long, and lank, and brown,
As is the ribbed sea-sand.

I fear thee and thy glittering eye,
And thy skinny hand, so brown."—

But the ancient Mariner assureth him of his bodily life, and proceedeth to relate his horrible penance.

"Fear not, fear not, thou Wedding-Guest!
This body dropt not down.

Alone, alone, all, all alone,
Alone on a wide wide sea!
And never a saint took pity on
My soul in agony.

He despiseth the creatures of the calm,

The many men, so beautiful!
And they all dead did lie:
And a thousand thousand slimy things
Lived on; and so did I.

And envieth that they should live, and so many lie dead.

I looked upon the rotting sea,
And drew my eyes away;
I looked upon the rotting deck,
And there the dead men lay.

I looked to heaven, and tried to pray;
But or ever a prayer had gushed,
A wicked whisper came, and made
My heart as dry as dust.

I closed my lids, and kept them close,
And the balls like pulses beat;
For the sky and the sea, and the sea and the sky
Lay like a load on my weary eye,
And the dead were at my feet.

But the curse liveth for him in the eye of the dead men.

The cold sweat melted from their limbs,
Nor rot nor reek did they:
The look with which they looked on me
Had never passed away.

An orphan's curse would drag to hell
A spirit from on high;
But oh! more horrible than that
Is the curse in a dead man's eye!
Seven days, seven nights, I saw that curse,
And yet I could not die.

In his loneliness and fixedness he yearneth towards the journeying Moon, and the stars that still sojourn, yet still move onward; and every where the blue sky belongs to them, and is their appointed rest, and their native country and their own natural homes, which they enter unannounced, as lords that are certainly expected and yet there is a silent joy at their arrival.

The moving Moon went up the sky,
And no where did abide:
Softly she was going up,
And a star or two beside—

Her beams bemocked the sultry main,
Like April hoar-frost spread;
But where the ship's huge shadow lay,
The charméd water burnt alway
A still and awful red.

By the light of the Moon he beholdeth God's creatures of the great calm.

Beyond the shadow of the ship,
I watched the water-snakes:
They moved in tracks of shining white,
And when they reared, the elfish light
Fell off in hoary flakes.

Within the shadow of the ship
I watched their rich attire:
Blue, glossy green, and velvet black,
They coiled and swam; and every track
Was a flash of golden fire.

Their beauty and their happiness.

O happy living things! no tongue
Their beauty might declare:
A spring of love gushed from my heart,

He blesseth them in his heart.

And I blessed them unaware:
Sure my kind saint took pity on me,
And I blessed them unaware.

The spell begins to break.

The self-same moment I could pray;
And from my neck so free
The Albatross fell off, and sank
Like lead into the sea."

Part v

"Oh sleep! it is a gentle thing,
Beloved from pole to pole!
To Mary Queen the praise be given!
She sent the gentle sleep from Heaven,
That slid into my soul.

By grace of the holy Mother, the ancient Mariner is refreshed with rain.

The silly buckets on the deck,
That had so long remained,
I dreamt that they were filled with dew;
And when I awoke, it rained.

My lips were wet, my throat was cold,
My garments all were dank;
Sure I had drunken in my dreams,
And still my body drank.

I moved, and could not feel my limbs:
I was so light—almost
I thought that I had died in sleep,
And was a blessèd ghost.

He heareth sounds and seeth strange sights and commotions in the sky and the element.

And soon I heard a roaring wind:
It did not come anear;
But with its sound it shook the sails,
That were so thin and sere.

The upper air burst into life!
And a hundred fire-flags sheen,
To and fro they were hurried about!
And to and fro, and in and out,
The wan stars danced between.

And the coming wind did roar more loud,
And the sails did sigh like sedge;
And the rain poured down from one black cloud;
The Moon was at its edge.

The thick black cloud was cleft, and still
The Moon was at its side:
Like waters shot from some high crag,
The lightning fell with never a jag,
A river steep and wide.

The bodies of the ship's crew are inspired and the ship moves on;

The loud wind never reached the ship,
Yet now the ship moved on!
Beneath the lightning and the Moon
The dead men gave a groan.

They groaned, they stirred, they all uprose,
Nor spake, nor moved their eyes;
It had been strange, even in a dream,
To have seen those dead men rise.

The helmsman steered, the ship moved on;
Yet never a breeze up-blew;
The mariners all 'gan work the ropes,
Where they were wont to do;
They raised their limbs like lifeless tools—
We were a ghastly crew.

The body of my brother's son
Stood by me, knee to knee:
The body and I pulled at one rope,
But he said nought to me."

But not by the souls of the men, nor by dæmons, of earth or middle air, but by a blessed troop of angelic spirits, sent down by the invocation of the guardian saint.

"I fear thee, ancient Mariner!"
"Be calm, thou Wedding-Guest!
'Twas not those souls that fled in pain,
Which to their corses came again,
But a troop of spirits blest:

For when it dawned—they dropped their arms,
And clustered round the mast;
Sweet sounds rose slowly through their mouths,
And from their bodies passed.

Around, around, flew each sweet sound,
Then darted to the Sun;
Slowly the sounds came back again,
Now mixed, now one by one.

Sometimes a-dropping from the sky
I heard the sky-lark sing;
Sometimes all little birds that are,
How they seemed to fill the sea and air
With their sweet jargoning!

And now 'twas like all instruments,
Now like a lonely flute;
And now it is an angel's song,
That makes the heavens be mute.

It ceased; yet still the sails made on
A pleasant noise till noon,
A noise like of a hidden brook
In the leafy month of June,
That to the sleeping woods all night
Singeth a quiet tune.

Till noon we quietly sailed on,
Yet never a breeze did breathe:
Slowly and smoothly went the ship,
Moved onward from beneath.

The lonesome Spirit from the south-pole carries on the ship as far as the Line, in obedience to the angelic troop, but still requireth vengeance.

Under the keel nine fathom deep,
From the land of mist and snow,
The spirit slid: and it was he
That made the ship to go.
The sails at noon left off their tune,
And the ship stood still also.

The Sun, right up above the mast,
Had fixed her to the ocean:
But in a minute she 'gan stir,
With a short uneasy motion—
Backwards and forwards half her length
With a short uneasy motion.

Then like a pawing horse let go,
She made a sudden bound:
It flung the blood into my head,
And I fell down in a swound.

The Polar Spirit's fellow-dæmons, the invisible inhabitants of the element, take part in his wrong; and two of them relate, one to the other, that penance long and heavy for the ancient Mariner hath been accorded to the Polar Spirit, who returneth southward.

How long in that same fit I lay,
I have not to declare;
But ere my living life returned,
I heard and in my soul discerned
Two voices in the air.

'Is it he?' quoth one, 'Is this the man?
By him who died on cross,
With his cruel bow he laid full low
The harmless Albatross.

The spirit who bideth by himself
In the land of mist and snow,
He loved the bird that loved the man
Who shot him with his bow.'

The other was a softer voice,
As soft as honey-dew:
Quoth he, 'The man hath penance done,
And penance more will do.' "

Part vi

FIRST VOICE

" 'But tell me, tell me! speak again,
Thy soft response renewing—
What makes that ship drive on so fast?
What is the ocean doing?'

SECOND VOICE

'Still as a slave before his lord,
The ocean hath no blast;
His great bright eye most silently
Up to the Moon is cast—

If he may know which way to go;
For she guides him smooth or grim.
See, brother, see! how graciously
She looketh down on him.'

FIRST VOICE

The Mariner hath been cast into a trance; for the angelic power causeth the vessel to drive northward faster than human life could endure.

'But why drives on that ship so fast,
Without or wave or wind?'

SECOND VOICE

'The air is cut away before,
And closes from behind.

Fly, brother, fly! more high, more high!
Or we shall be belated:
For slow and slow that ship will go,
When the Mariner's trance is abated.'

The supernatural motion is retarded; the Mariner awakes, and his penance begins anew.

I woke, and we were sailing on
As in a gentle weather:
'Twas night, calm night, the moon was high;
The dead men stood together.

All stood together on the deck,
For a charnel-dungeon fitter:
All fixed on me their stony eyes,
That in the Moon did glitter.

The pang, the curse, with which they died,
Had never passed away:
I could not draw my eyes from theirs,
Nor turn them up to pray.

The curse is finally expiated.

And now this spell was snapped: once more
I view the ocean green,
And looked far forth, yet little saw
Of what had else been seen—

Like one, that on a lonesome road
Doth walk in fear and dread,
And having once turned round walks on,
And turns no more his head;
Because he knows, a frightful fiend
Doth close behind him tread.

But soon there breathed a wind on me,
Nor sound nor motion made:
Its path was not upon the sea,
In ripple or in shade.

It raised my hair, it fanned my cheek
Like a meadow-gale of spring—
It mingled strangely with my fears,
Yet it felt like a welcoming.

Swiftly, swiftly flew the ship,
Yet she sailed softly too:
Sweetly, sweetly blew the breeze—
On me alone it blew.

And the ancient Mariner beholdeth his native country.

Oh! dream of joy! is this indeed
The light-house top I see?
Is this the hill? is this the kirk?
Is this mine own countree?

We drifted o'er the harbor-bar,
And I with sobs did pray—
O let me be awake, my God!
Or let me sleep alway.

The harbor-bay was clear as glass,
So smoothly it was strewn!
And on the bay the moonlight lay,
And the shadow of the Moon.

The rock shone bright, the kirk no less,
That stands above the rock:
The moonlight steeped in silentness
The steady weathercock.

The angelic spirits leave the dead bodies,

And the bay was white with silent light,
Till rising from the same,
Full many shapes, that shadows were,
In crimson colors came.

And appear in their own forms of light.

A little distance from the prow
Those crimson shadows were:
I turned my eyes upon the deck—
Oh, Christ! what saw I there!

Each corse lay flat, lifeless and flat,
And, by the holy rood!

A man all light, a seraph-man,
On every corse there stood.

This seraph-band, each waved his hand:
It was a heavenly sight!
They stood as signals to the land,
Each one a lovely light;

This seraph-band, each waved his hand,
No voice did they impart—
No voice; but oh! the silence sank
Like music on my heart.

But soon I heard the dash of oars,
I heard the Pilot's cheer;
My head was turned perforce away
And I saw a boat appear.

The Pilot and the Pilot's boy,
I heard them coming fast:
Dear Lord in Heaven! it was a joy
The dead men could not blast.

I saw a third—I heard his voice:
It is the Hermit good!
He singeth loud his godly hymns
That he makes in the wood.
He'll shrieve my soul, he'll wash away
The Albatross's blood."

Part vii

The Hermit of the Wood,

"This Hermit good lives in that wood
Which slopes down to the sea.
How loudly his sweet voice he rears!
He loves to talk with mariners
That come from a far countree.

He kneels at morn, and noon, and eve—
He hath a cushion plump:
It is the moss that wholly hides
The rotted old oak-stump.

The skiff-boat neared: I heard them talk,
'Why, this is strange, I trow!
Where are those lights so many and fair,
That signal made but now?'

Approacheth the ship with wonder.

'Strange, by my faith!' the Hermit said—
'And they answered not our cheer!
The planks looked warped! and see those sails,
How thin they are and sere!
I never saw aught like to them,
Unless perchance it were

Brown skeletons of leaves that lag
My forest-brook along;
When the ivy-tod is heavy with snow,
And the owlet whoops to the wolf below,
That eats the she-wolf's young.'

'Dear Lord! it hath a fiendish look—
(The Pilot made reply)
I am a-feared'—'Push on, push on!'
Said the Hermit cheerily.

The boat came closer to the ship,
But I nor spake nor stirred;
The boat came close beneath the ship,
And straight a sound was heard.

The ship suddenly sinketh.

Under the water it rumbled on,
Still louder and more dread:
It reached the ship, it split the bay;
The ship went down like lead.

The ancient Mariner is saved in the Pilot's boat.

Stunned by that loud and dreadful sound,
Which sky and ocean smote,
Like one that hath been seven days drowned
My body lay afloat;
But swift as dreams, myself I found
Within the Pilot's boat.

Upon the whirl, where sank the ship,
The boat spun round and round;

And all was still, save that the hill
Was telling of the sound.

I moved my lips—the Pilot shrieked
And fell down in a fit;
The holy Hermit raised his eyes,
And prayed where he did sit.

I took the oars: the Pilot's boy,
Who now doth crazy go,
Laughed loud and long, and all the while
His eyes went to and fro.
'Ha! ha!' quoth he, 'full plain I see,
The Devil knows how to row.'

And now, all in my own countree,
I stood on the firm land!
The Hermit stepped forth from the boat,
And scarcely he could stand.

The ancient Mariner earnestly entreateth the Hermit to shrieve him; and the penance of life falls on him.

O shrieve me, shrieve me, holy man!
The Hermit crossed his brow.
'Say quick,' quoth he, 'I bid thee say—
What manner of man art thou?'

Forthwith this frame of mine was wrenched
With a woful agony,
Which forced me to begin my tale;
And then it left me free.

And ever and anon through out his future life an agony constraineth him to travel from land to land;

Since then, at an uncertain hour,
That agony returns:
And till my ghastly tale is told,
This heart within me burns.

I pass, like night, from land to land;
I have strange power of speech;
That moment that his face I see,
I know the man that must hear me:
To him my tale I teach.

What loud uproar bursts from that door!
The wedding-guests are there:

But in the garden-bower the bride
And bride-maids singing are:
And hark the little vesper bell,
Which biddeth me to prayer!

O Wedding-Guest! this soul hath been
Alone on a wide wide sea:
So lonely 'twas, that God himself
Scarce seeméd there to be.

O sweeter than the marriage-feast,
'Tis sweeter far to me,
To walk together to the kirk
With a goodly company!—

To walk together to the kirk,
And all together pray,
While each to his great Father bends,
Old men, and babes, and loving friends
And youths and maidens gay!

And to teach, by his own example, love and reverence to all things that God made and loveth.

Farewell, farewell! but this I tell
To thee, thou Wedding-Guest!
He prayeth well, who loveth well
Both man and bird and beast.

He prayeth best, who loveth best
All things both great and small;
For the dear God who loveth us,
He made and loveth all."

The Mariner, whose eye is bright,
Whose beard with age is hoar,
Is gone: and now the Wedding-Guest
Turned from the bridegroom's door.

He went like one that hath been stunned,
And is of sense forlorn:
A sadder and a wiser man,
He rose the morrow morn.

When Lilacs Last in the Dooryard Bloomed

WALT WHITMAN

– 1 –

When lilacs last in the dooryard bloomed,
And the great star early drooped in the western sky in the night,
I mourned, and yet shall mourn with ever-returning spring.

Ever-returning spring, trinity sure to me you bring,
Lilac blooming perennial and drooping star in the west,
And thought of him I love.

– 2 –

O powerful western fallen star!
O shades of night—O moody, tearful night!
O great star disappeared—O the black murk that hides the star!
O cruel hands that hold me powerless—O helpless soul of me!
O harsh surrounding cloud that will not free my soul.

– 3 –

In the dooryard fronting an old farm-house near the white-washed palings,
Stands the lilac-bush tall-growing with heart-shaped leaves of rich green,
With many a pointed blossom rising delicate, with the perfume strong I love,
With every leaf a miracle—and from this bush in the dooryard,
With delicate-colored blossoms and heart-shaped leaves of rich green,
A sprig with its flower I break.

– 4 –

In the swamp in secluded recesses,
A shy and hidden bird is warbling a song.
Solitary the thrush,
The hermit withdrawn to himself, avoiding the settlements,
Sings by himself a song.

Song of the bleeding throat,
Death's outlet song of life, (for well dear brother I know,
If thou wast not granted to sing thou would'st surely die.)

– 5 –

Over the breast of the spring, the land, amid cities,
Amid lanes and through old woods, where lately the violets peeped from the ground, spotting the gray debris,
Amid the grass in the fields each side of the lanes, passing the endless grass,
Passing the yellow-speared wheat, every grain from its shroud in the dark-brown fields uprisen,
Passing the apple-tree blows of white and pink in the orchards,
Carrying a corpse to where it shall rest in the grave,
Night and day journeys a coffin.

– 6 –

Coffin that passes through lanes and streets,
Through day and night with the great cloud darkening the land,
With the pomp of the inlooped flags with the cities draped in black,
With the show of the States themselves as of crape-veiled women standing,
With processions long and winding and the flambeaus of the night,
With the countless torches lit, with the silent sea of faces and the unbared heads,
With the waiting depot, the arriving coffin, and the sombre faces,
With dirges through the night, with the thousand voices rising strong and solemn,
With all the mournful voices of the dirges poured around the coffin,
The dim-lit churches and the shuddering organs—where amid these you journey,
With the tolling bells' perpetual clang,
Here, coffin that slowly passes,
I give you my sprig of lilac.

– 7 –

(Nor for you, for one alone,
Blossoms and branches green to coffins all I bring,
For fresh as the morning, thus would I chant a song for you
O sane and sacred death.

All over bouquets of roses,
O death, I cover you over with roses and early lilies,
But mostly and now the lilac that blooms the first,
Copious I break, I break the sprigs from the bushes,
With loaded arms I come, pouring for you,
For you and the coffins all of you O death.)

– 8 –

O western orb sailing the heaven,
Now I know what you must have meant as a month since I
walked,
As I walked in silence the transparent shadowy night,
As I saw you had something to tell as you bent to me night after
night,
As you drooped from the sky low down as if to my side, (while
the other stars all looked on,)
As we wandered together the solemn night, (for something I
know not what kept me from sleep,)
As the night advanced, and I saw on the rim of the west how full
you were of woe,
As I stood on the rising ground in the breeze in the cool
transparent night,
As I watched where you passed and was lost in the netherward
black of the night,
As my soul in its trouble dissatisfied sank, as where you sad orb,
Concluded, dropt in the night, and was gone.

– 9 –

Sing on there in the swamp,
O singer bashful and tender, I hear your notes, I hear your call,
I hear, I come presently, I understand you,
But a moment I linger, for the lustrous star has detained me,
The star my departing comrade holds and detains me.

– 10 –

O how shall I warble myself for the dead one there I loved?
And how shall I deck my song for the large sweet soul that has gone?
And what shall my perfume be for the grave of him I love?

Sea-winds blown from east and west,
Blown from the Eastern sea and blown from the Western sea, till there on the prairies meeting,
These and with these and the breath of my chant,
I'll perfume the grave of him I love.

– 11 –

O what shall I hang on the chamber walls?
And what shall the pictures be that I hang on the walls,
To adorn the burial-house of him I love?

Pictures of growing spring and farms and homes,
With the Fourth-month eve at sundown, and the gray smoke lucid and bright,
With floods of the yellow gold of the gorgeous, indolent, sinking sun, burning, expanding the air,
With the fresh sweet herbage under foot, and the pale green leaves of the trees prolific,
In the distance the flowing glaze, the breast of the river, with a wind-dapple here and there,
With ranging hills on the banks, with many a line against the sky, and shadows,
And the city at hand with dwellings so dense, and stacks of chimneys,
And all the scenes of life and the workshops, and the workmen homeward returning.

– 12 –

Lo, body and soul—this land,
My own Manhattan with spires, and the sparkling and hurrying tides, and the ships,
The varied and ample land, the South and the North in the light, Ohio's shores and flashing Missouri,

And ever the far-spreading prairies covered with grass and corn.
Lo, the most excellent sun so calm and haughty,
The violet and purple morn with just-felt breezes,
The gentle soft-born measureless light,
The miracle spreading bathing all, the fulfilled noon,
The coming eve delicious, the welcome night and the stars,
Over my cities shining all, enveloping man and land.

– 13 –

Sing on, sing on you gray-brown bird,
Sing from your swamps, the recesses, pour your chant from the bushes,
Limitless out of the dusk, out of the cedars and pines.

Sing on dearest brother, warble your reedy song,
Loud human song, with voice of uttermost woe.

O liquid and free and tender!
O wild and loose to my soul—O wondrous singer!
You only I hear—yet the star holds me, (but will soon depart,)
Yet the lilac with mastering odor holds me.

– 14 –

Now while I sat in the day and looked forth,
In the close of the day with its light and the fields of spring, and the farmers preparing their crops,
In the large unconscious scenery of my land with its lakes and forests,
In the heavenly aerial beauty, (after the perturbed winds and the storms,)
Under the arching heavens of the afternoon swift passing, and the voices of children and women,
The many-moving sea-tides, and I saw the ships how they sailed,
And the summer approaching with richness, and the fields all busy with labor,
And the infinite separate houses, how they all went on, each with its meals and minutia of daily usages,
And the streets how their throbbings throbbed, and the cities pent—lo, then and there,

Falling upon them all and among them all, enveloping me with the rest,
Appeared the cloud, appeared the long black trail,
And I knew death, its thought, and the sacred knowledge of death.

Then with the knowledge of death as walking one side of me,
And the thought of death close-walking the other side of me,
And I in the middle as with companions, and as holding the hands of companions,
I fled forth to the hiding receiving night that talks not,
Down to the shores of the water, the path by the swamp in the dimness,
To the solemn shadowy cedars and ghostly pines so still.

And the singer so shy to the rest received me,
The gray-brown bird I know received us comrades three,
And he sang the carol of death, and a verse for him I love.

From deep secluded recesses,
From the fragrant cedars and the ghostly pines so still,
Came the carol of the bird.

And the charm of the carol rapt me,
As I held as if by their hands my comrades in the night,
And the voice of my spirit tallied the song of the bird.

Come lovely and soothing death,
Undulate round the world, serenely arriving, arriving,
In the day, in the night, to all, to each,
Sooner or later delicate death.

Praised be the fathomless universe,
For life and joy, and for objects and knowledge curious,
And for love, sweet love—but praise! praise! praise!
For the sure-enwinding arms of cool-enfolding death.

Dark mother always gliding near with soft feet,
Have none chanted for thee a chant of fullest welcome?
Then I chant it for thee, I glorify thee above all,
I bring thee a song that when thou must indeed come, come unfalteringly.

Approach strong deliveress,
When it is so, when thou hast taken them I joyously sing the dead,
Lost in the loving floating ocean of thee,
Laved in the flood of thy bliss O death.

From me to thee glad serenades,
Dances for thee I propose saluting thee, adornments and feastings for thee,
And the sights of the open landscape and the high-spread sky are fitting,
And life and the fields, and the huge and thoughtful night.
The night in silence under many a star,
The ocean shore and the husky whispering wave whose voice I know,
And the soul turning to thee O vast and well-veiled death,
And the body gratefully nestling close to thee.

Over the tree-tops I float thee a song,
Over the rising and sinking waves, over the myriad fields and the prairies wide,
Over the dense-packed cities all and the teeming wharves and ways,
I float this carol with joy, with joy to thee O death.

– 15 –

To the tally of my soul,
Loud and strong kept up the gray-brown bird,
With pure deliberate notes spreading filling the night.

Loud in the pines and cedars dim,
Clear in the freshness moist and the swamp-perfume,
And I with my comrades there in the night.

While my sight that was bound in my eyes unclosed,
As to long panoramas of visions.

And I saw askant the armies,
I saw as in noiseless dreams hundreds of battle-flags,
Borne through the smoke of the battles and pierced with missiles I saw them,
And carried hither and yon through the smoke, and torn and bloody,
And at last but a few shreds left on the staffs, (and all in silence,)
And the staffs all splintered and broken.

I saw battle-corpses, myriads of them,
And the white skeletons of young men, I saw them,
I saw the debris and debris of all the slain soldiers of the war,
But I saw they were not as was thought,
They themselves were fully at rest, they suffered not,
The living remained and suffered, the mother suffered,
And the wife and the child and the musing comrade suffered
And the armies that remained suffered.

– 16 –

Passing the visions, passing the night,
Passing, unloosing the hold of my comrades' hands,
Passing the song of the hermit bird and the tallying song of my soul,
Victorious song, death's outlet song, yet varying ever-altering song,
As low and wailing, yet clear the notes, rising and falling, flooding the night,
Sadly sinking and fainting, as warning and warning, and yet again bursting with joy,
Covering the earth and filling the spread of the heaven,
As that powerful psalm in the night I heard from recesses,
Passing, I leave thee lilac with heart-shaped leaves,
I leave thee there in the door-yard, blooming, returning with spring.

I cease from my song for thee,
From my gaze on thee in the west, fronting the west, communing with thee,
O comrade lustrous with silver face in the night.

Yet each to keep and all, retrievements out of the night,
The song, the wondrous chant of the gray-brown bird,
And the tallying chant, the echo aroused in my soul,
With the lustrous and drooping star with the countenance full of woe,
With the holders holding my hand nearing the call of the bird,
Comrades mine and I in the midst, and their memory ever to keep, for the dead I loved so well,

For the sweetest, wisest soul of all my days and lands—and this
for his dear sake,
Lilac and star and bird twined with the chant of my soul,
There in the fragrant pines and the cedars dusk and dim.

The Love Song of J. Alfred Prufrock

T. S. Eliot

S'io credesse che mia risposta fosse
A persona che mai tornasse al mondo,
Questa fiamma staria senza piu scosse.
Ma per ciò che giammai di questo fondo
Non tornò vivo alcun, s'i'odo il vero,
Senza tema d'infamia ti rispondo.

Let us go then, you and I,
When the evening is spread out against the sky
Like a patient etherised upon a table;
Let us go, through certain half-deserted streets,
The muttering retreats
Of restless nights in one-night cheap hotels
And sawdust restaurants with oyster-shells:
Streets that follow like a tedious argument
Of insidious intent
To lead you to an overwhelming question . . .
Oh, do not ask, "What is it?"
Let us go and make our visit.

In the room the women come and go
Talking of Michelangelo.

The yellow fog that rubs its back upon the window-panes,
The yellow smoke that rubs its muzzle on the window-panes
Licked its tongue into the corners of the evening,
Lingered upon the pools that stand in drains,
Let fall upon its back the soot that falls from chimneys,
Slipped by the terrace, made a sudden leap,
And seeing that it was a soft October night,
Curled once about the house, and fell asleep.

And indeed there will be time
For the yellow smoke that slides along the street,
Rubbing its back upon the window-panes;
There will be time, there will be time
To prepare a face to meet the faces that you meet;
There will be time to murder and create,
And time for all the works and days of hands
That lift and drop a question on your plate;
Time for you and time for me,
And time yet for a hundred indecisions,
And for a hundred visions and revisions,
Before the taking of a toast and tea.

In the room the women come and go
Talking of Michelangelo.

And indeed there will be time
To wonder, "Do I dare?" and, "Do I dare?"
Time to turn back and descend the stair,
With a bald spot in the middle of my hair—
(They will say: "How his hair is growing thin!")
My morning coat, my collar mounting firmly to the chin,
My necktie rich and modest, but asserted by a simple pin—
(They will say: "But how his arms and legs are thin!")
Do I dare
Disturb the universe?
In a minute there is time
For decisions and revisions which a minute will reverse.

For I have known them all already, known them all:
Have known the evenings, mornings, afternoons,
I have measured out my life with coffee spoons;
I know the voices dying with a dying fall
Beneath the music from a farther room.
  So how should I presume?

And I have known the eyes already, known them all—
The eyes that fix you in a formulated phrase,
And when I am formulated, sprawling on a pin,
When I am pinned and wriggling on the wall,

Then how should I begin
To spit out all the butt-ends of my days and ways?
  And how should I presume?

And I have known the arms already, known them all—
Arms that are braceleted and white and bare
(But in the lamplight, downed with light brown hair!)
Is it perfume from a dress
That makes me so digress?
Arms that lie along a table, or wrap about a shawl.
  And should I then presume?
  And how should I begin?

Shall I say, I have gone at dusk through narrow streets
And watched the smoke that rises from the pipes
Of lonely men in shirt-sleeves, leaning out of windows? . . .

I should have been a pair of ragged claws
Scuttling across the floors of silent seas.

And the afternoon, the evening, sleeps so peacefully!
Smoothed by long fingers,
Asleep . . . tired . . . or it malingers,
Stretched on the floor, here beside you and me.
Should I, after tea and cakes and ices,
Have the strength to force the moment to its crisis?
But though I have wept and fasted, wept and prayed,
Though I have seen my head (grown slightly bald) brought in
    upon a platter,
I am no prophet—and here's no great matter;
I have seen the moment of my greatness flicker,
And I have seen the eternal Footman hold my coat, and snicker,
And in short, I was afraid.

And would it have been worth it, after all,
After the cups, the marmalade, the tea,
Among the porcelain, among some talk of you and me,
Would it have been worth while,
To have bitten off the matter with a smile,
To have squeezed the universe into a ball

To roll it toward some overwhelming question,
To say: "I am Lazarus, come from the dead,
Come back to tell you all, I shall tell you all"—
If one, settling a pillow by her head,
  Should say: "That is not what I meant at all;
  That is not it, at all."

And would it have been worth it, after all,
Would it have been worth while,
After the sunsets and the dooryards and the sprinkled streets,
After the novels, after the teacups, after the skirts that trail along the floor—
And this, and so much more?—
It is impossible to say just what I mean!
But as if a magic lantern threw the nerves in patterns on a screen:
Would it have been worth while
If one, settling a pillow or throwing off a shawl,
And turning toward the window, should say:
  "That is not it at all,
  That is not what I meant, at all."

No! I am not Prince Hamlet, nor was meant to be;
Am an attendant lord, one that will do
To swell a progress, start a scene or two,
Advise the prince; no doubt, an easy tool,
Deferential, glad to be of use,
Politic, cautious, and meticulous;
Full of high sentence, but a bit obtuse;
At times, indeed, almost ridiculous—
Almost, at times, the Fool.

I grow old . . . I grow old . . .
I shall wear the bottoms of my trousers rolled.

Shall I part my hair behind? Do I dare to eat a peach?
I shall wear white flannel trousers, and walk upon the beach.
I have heard the mermaids singing, each to each.

I do not think that they will sing to me.

I have seen them riding seaward on the waves
Combing the white hair of the waves blown back
When the wind blows the water white and black.

We have lingered in the chambers of the sea
By sea-girls wreathed with seaweed red and brown
Till human voices wake us, and we drown.

Index of Authors, Titles, and Terms